MAKING MORAL JUDGMENTS

This fascinating new book examines diversity in moral judgments, drawing on recent work in social, personality, and evolutionary psychology, reviewing the factors that influence the moral judgments people make.

Why do reasonable people so often disagree when drawing distinctions between what is morally right and wrong? Even when individuals agree in their moral pronouncements, they may employ different standards, different comparative processes, or entirely disparate criteria in their judgments. Examining the sources of this variety, the author expertly explores morality using ethics position theory, alongside other theoretical perspectives in moral psychology, and shows how it can relate to contemporary social issues from abortion to premarital sex to human rights. Also featuring a chapter on applied contexts, using the theory of ethics positions to gain insights into the moral choices and actions of individuals, groups, and organizations in educational, research, political, medical, and business settings, the book offers answers that apply across individuals, communities, and cultures.

Investigating the relationship between people's personal moral philosophies and their ethical thoughts, emotions, and actions, this is fascinating reading for students and academics from psychology and philosophy and anyone interested in morality and ethics.

Donelson R. Forsyth is a social and personality psychologist who studies groups, leadership, ethical thought, and the psychological bases of teaching and learning. He is a professor at the University of Richmond, US, where he holds the Colonel Leo K. and Gaylee Thorsness Endowed Chair in Ethical Leadership. He has authored or edited ten books (including *Group Dynamics*, now in its seventh edition) and over 140 chapters and articles on ethics, groups, and related topics. He was recognized as the Outstanding Group Psychologist by the American Psychological Association in 1996, and received the State of Virginia Outstanding Faculty Award in 2002.

This book, and the research that it summarizes, would not have been possible if not for the support provided to the Jepson School of Leadership Studies and the University of Richmond by Barbara and Thomas Matthews. The Matthews endowed the Colonel Leo K. and Gaylee Thorsness Chair in Ethical Leadership, to honor the civic work and the moral principles of Colonel Thorsness and his wife, Gaylee. Colonel Thorsness received the Medal of Honor for his actions in the Vietnam War "for conspicuous gallantry and intrepidity in action at the risk of his life above and beyond the call of duty." He was the most ethically honorable man I have ever met. By way of expressing my deep gratitude, I am dedicating this book to Barbara and Thomas Matthews, Leo and Gaylee Thorsness, and their families.

CONTENTS

ACKNOWLEDGMENTS

Why do reasonable people so often disagree when drawing distinctions between what is morally right and wrong? Some people, but not others, oppose the death penalty. Some believe that any action that benefits them personally is allowable, whereas others base their moral appraisals on a more egalitarian code of ethics. There are those that strive each day to help others, but there are others who consider time spent in service to others to be time wasted. Why do the citizens of some nations embrace one set of moral beliefs and vilify the standards and practices common elsewhere in the world?

This book examines the sources of this diversity in moral judgments, drawing on recent work in social, personality, and evolutionary psychology. But none of the insights it offers would have been possible if not for the work of the many researchers who have diligently investigated moral judgment, in general, and individual differences in moral positions, specifically. People like Rick Berger, Joanne Ciulla, Karl Kelley, Mike McDaniel, Judy Nye, Ray Pope, Bill Scott, and Betsy Singh. All deserve my thanks, although none should be held accountable for the portions of the book that are ill considered or misguided; they did all they could to prevent me from making mistakes along the way.

Four of my colleagues deserve special thanks. Barry Schlenker used his intellect, insight, and research prowess to launch our initial investigations into individual differences in moral outlook. Bob Giacalone encouraged me to consider the implications of my largely theoretical work for business contexts—a shift that dramatically increased the theory's scope. Terry Price shared his vast knowledge of moral philosophy with me. He identified and corrected the many mistakes I made when I waded into the realm of moral philosophy. Ernest O'Boyle collaborated with me on many of the studies described in the pages of this book, and he is the reason these projects were so successful. Since his intellect is matched by his scientific drive, he is a continual source of ideas, insights, and inspiration. When in this book I write that "we examined this process" or "we discovered that," the "we" is usually me and Ernest. Without his support, initiative, and quantitative skills, this book could not have been written.

I wish to also thank Ravi Iyer and Jonathan Haidt, the coordinators of Your-Morals.org, for including the Ethics Position Questionnaire (EPQ) on the site and for sharing the data (de-identified) they collected with me. The Your-Morals.org research group includes Peter Ditto, Jesse Graham, Jonathan Haidt, Ravi Iyer, Sena Koleva, Matt Motyl, Gary Sherman, and Sean Wojcik. There are those, too, who helped me deal with the process of turning the words in my computer files into a finished book. They include Cassie Price, Susan Taylor, and Dean Sandra Peart in the Jepson School of Leadership at the University of Richmond, and Eleanor Reedy and the editorial and production team at Taylor and Francis. Their support was essential at each step along the way from the book's initial conception to the final printed product. Last, but of course not least, I wish to thank my ever-supportive wife Claire, who so often helps me think through my ill-formed ideas and half-baked insights. Writing this particular book was, after all, her idea.

Donelson R. Forsyth
Montebello, Virginia

1

JUDGING MORALITY

The elementary forces in ethics are probably as plural as those of physics are. The various ideals have no common character apart from the fact that they are ideals.
—William James (1897/1979, p. 153)

Moral judgments are the most significant social inferences people make about others and themselves. Those who are judged to be immoral are not just thought to be mistaken or misguided, but unacceptable in a fundamental way: corrupt, untrustworthy, malevolent, and possibly even evil. Moral philosophers' detailed conceptual analyses of the nature of these judgments, along with psychologists' more recent empirical studies, suggest that moral judgments are reserved for particularly offensive actions: those that cause harm to others and are inconsistent with standards that, in the given social setting, demarcate the morally good and the morally bad. Yet, despite the critical importance of morality for maintaining stable interpersonal relationships in human societies, disagreement over what is moral and what is immoral is as likely as complete moral consensus. Many factors contribute to this diversity, but among them are differences in each person's ethics position: Their personal moral philosophy regarding actions that cause others harm (idealism) and their stance with regard to the universality of moral standards (relativism).

* * *

What will the seven-and-a-half billion people on the planet Earth do today? Some will work, toil at their tasks. Some will relax, vacationing with family and friends. Some will sleep the day away, others will exercise diligently, and some will study, cook dinner, or join with others in shared pursuits. But some will do things that differ from these routine, day-to-day activities. Some will save others' lives. Some will donate their time to worthy causes. Some will spend another day working to make their community a better place. And then there are the others. The others who commit actions that are socially untoward: From the bigot who insults someone in a despised outgroup, the philandering husband who cheats on his wife of 20 years, the accountant who looks the other way when the boss asks him to obscure the company's losses, to the thief, the rapist, the molester, and the murderer. On any given day, people will do things that are judged as commendable: good, fair, just, and moral. But they will also do things that earn them moral condemnation: they and their actions will be considered bad, unfair, unjust, and wrong.

These moral judgments, like other types of valuations, range along a continuum from positive to negative. But unlike judgments of a person's social skills, coordination, conscientiousness, and so on, moral judgments are perceptually and interpersonally persistent and their effects are far-reaching. They are not merely momentary inclinations or personal preferences but socially significant inferences that determine our understanding of ourselves, other people, and our most significant interactions and relationships. Since those who act in ways that others consider to be immoral are often met with negative sanctions, people must be able to predict how others are going to evaluate the things they do if they wish to avoid such sanctions. A pattern of conflict-free interaction implies that we are able to restrict our behaviors so that they do not conflict too greatly with society's conception of morality, and that those around us are similarly so self-regulated. Moral judgments also make the future seem more predictable, as we expect that those who act ethically today can be trusted to act that way tomorrow. A case could be made that moral judgments are the most significant social inferences people formulate about others and about themselves.

This book examines the making of moral judgments, but with a focus on one puzzling aspect of these judgments: their diversity. Philosophers have been examining matters of morality for thousands of years, yet they continue to disagree when discussing what makes something morally right rather than wrong. Socrates believed that morality and wisdom are so closely associated that virtuous action flows effortlessly from knowledge, but Aristotle demurred by suggesting virtue is manifested in one's actions. Hume made the case that morality is more a matter of emotion and sentiment than reason and rationality but Bentham considered morality to be a question of utility: Does the action promote or interfere with happiness? Kant, in contrast to all, believed that intentions separated out the good and bad, for good will matters absolutely, whereas good effects count for nothing when it comes to morality (MacIntyre, 2003).

These divergences in moral conceptions are not unique to philosophers. Humans have a tendency to drift toward conformity and agreement, yet any two people's moral appraisals of the very same act in clearly defined circumstances can spin off into different directions. Certainly, some actions receive nearly universal commendation and condemnation—altruistic, self-sacrificing acts, for example, or actions that are done to intentionally harm innocents—but this consensus is lost when the discussion turns to less clear-cut issues. The person who dismisses a small harm done to achieve greater good runs afoul of the person who condemns anyone who causes suffering. Some are certain that lies that serve a positive purpose—white lies—are ethically allowed, but others say any and all lies are immoral. For every person who publicly announces a moral claim about some contemporary social issue, such as abortion, gay marriage, and universal health care, is another person who takes an opposing view. Even when individuals agree in their moral pronouncements, they may employ different standards, different comparative processes, or entirely disparate criteria in their judgments. Given that moral judgments significantly influence our perceptions of one another, our choices in morally charged situations, and the interpersonal processes that sustain adaptive, healthy social relationships, this diversity in moral thought is puzzling.

This book reviews the factors that influence the moral judgments people make, with a particular emphasis on the impact of individual differences in ethical ideologies people adopt on their inferences about morality. This chapter introduces that analysis by first examining the defining features of moral judgments and their implications: What distinguishes such judgments from the many other inferences about people's traits, tendencies, strengths, and weaknesses? And what psychological and interpersonal purposes do these judgments serve?

Moral Inferences

We are all psychologists of a sort, for whenever we encounter other people we set to work deciphering them. We do not passively observe those around us, but instead actively scrutinize others' actions, drawing inferences about their dispositional tendencies, their preferences and attitudes, and their intentions and designs. When we meet other people we intuitively gather the data we need to make these inferences: We appraise their appearance, their gestures, their words, and their actions. As Heider (1958, p. 2) stated in his classic work, *The Psychology of Interpersonal Relations*: "the ordinary person has a great and profound understanding of himself and of other people which, though unformulated and only vaguely conceived, enables him to interact with others in more or less adaptive ways."

Many of these inferences about other people pertain to their basic traits, skills, competencies, moods, interests, and values. But some go deeper; they speak not to surface level, transitory attributes of the individual, but something more basic, more fundamental. Listening to a friend explain how she impressed her boss at work by misleading him about the quality of her work product, we may conclude she is clever, resourceful, and successful, but that she is also a person who cannot be trusted to always tell the truth. When we hear about a firefighter who intervened to save a child stranded in a burning building we may admire his courage and dedication, but also perceptually promote him into a select group of those we admire for their distinctive moral pureness: the morally advanced exemplars. When we see parents spank their misbehaving child at the mall we not only draw inferences about their parenting skills and their control of their tempers, but we may also question their ethics; is it ever justified to physically harm a defenseless minor who you are charged to nurture and protect?

These construals are more than detached descriptions of individuals' qualities and the actions they performed. They are *moral judgments*: evaluative appraisals of the goodness, rightness, and propriety of individuals and their actions. These judgments are not just evaluative, but profoundly evaluative. An immoral person is not just objectionable or unsavory, but wicked or evil, and a person judged to be moral is not just nice or fun to be with, but saintly or virtuous. Moral judgments also tend to be more definitive than opinions, preferences, or other more circumspect inferences—people are generally quite confident when they express their conclusions about morality—even though these judgments are often systematically biased ones. Morality is, more often than not, in the eye of the beholder.

Moral Judgments Are Profoundly Evaluative

To be considered inept, good natured, inconsiderate, wise, or lazy is one thing, but these perceptual inferences pale in their social and psychological impact in comparison to judgments of ethicality. Moral judgments are not tepid, wishy-washy appraisals, but strongly valenced pronouncements of worth and approval or condemnation and disapproval. Words associated with morality are uniquely evaluative, as Anderson (1968) discovered in his analysis of 555 words that people use to describe other people. When he asked 100 people to rate the words on a scale from "least favorable or desirable" to "most favorable or desirable," words pertaining to morality tended to cluster at the extremes. Such qualities as mature, warm, earnest, kind, friendly, happy, and clean were rated positively, but significantly lower that words that signaled morality: *sincere, honest, loyal, truthful, honorable*, and *trustworthy*. Conversely, negative, socially objectionable qualities, including self-conceit, hard-hearted, prejudiced, irresponsible, unpleasant, impolite, and crude were rated very negatively, but not as negatively as the words on the list that signaled immorality: *insincere, unkind, untrustworthy, deceitful, dishonorable, malicious, untruthful, dishonest, phony*, and *liar*. Anderson also asked respondents to rate each word for "meaningfulness." Positive, negative, and relatively neutral words (e.g., cautious, innocent, inoffensive, nonchalant, self-contented) were rated as similar in meaningfulness. Words indicating morality and immorality, in contrast, were rated as significantly more meaningful compared to the more neutral words. Variance in the ratings of the words was also significantly less for moral and immoral attributes, relative to negative and neutral qualities.[1]

Morally good and bad actions may garner more extreme appraisals because they are relatively unusual and so they violate people's expectations. As expectancy-theory suggests, characteristics or actions that perceivers' consider to be highly unusual generate, in most cases, a more extreme evaluation (Skowronski & Carlston, 1989). Although moral behaviors such as honesty, self-sacrifice, and compassion are socially desired qualities, they are more rarely observed than more common qualities such as friendliness, self-indulgence, and impatience. Those who are unfailingly truthful or act to help others violate base rates, and so their salient and unexpected acts trigger a more extreme (and positive) evaluation. In contrast, actions that are roundly condemned if identified are, fortunately, also rarer than more quotidian types of activities. These negative but unexpected qualities thus trigger an extreme evaluation, albeit one that is negative rather than positive (Mende-Siedlecki, Baron, & Todorov, 2013).

Moral Judgments Are Inferences

The word *judgment* is usually applied to people's appraisals of morality, suggesting that these construals are different in some way from other types of interpersonal inferences and appraisals. In everyday talk people do not say they estimate, perceive, take in, or appreciate another person's moral goodness or badness: They *judge* that person's morality. Calling these psychological assessments judgments suggests that they have more in common with a magistrate's objective ruling or decree rather than a person's idiosyncratic opinion or preference. Moral judgments, more so than other inferences, are thought to be transpersonal; it makes no matter who the individuals involved are, the judgment should apply across persons. Moreover, as judgments rather than opinions or estimates, they are often considered to be more matters of fact rather than matters of personal preference. As Smith (2011), in his analysis of the relationship between dehumanization and collective aggression explains, "When a person sincerely judges that an act is morally wrong, this entails that they want to avoid it, and that they believe everyone else should avoid it, too" (p. 219).

As with a judge's decision, individuals often express their moral judgments with a relatively high degree of definitiveness. Those who dislike the color beige likely recognize that this preference is a matter of taste. But those who consider an action such as abortion, cheating, or stealing to be morally wrong are less likely to feel these pronouncements are a matter of opinion (Skitka, 2010). As the philosopher Frank Chapman Sharp (1898, p. 201) writes: "From the uniformity and immediacy of the moral judgment follows directly its certainty, the sense of necessity, untroubled by a single doubt."

The word *judgment* also suggests that people's inferences about morality are based on their rational review of all available evidence. Moral philosophers such as Socrates, Kant, and Bentham argued over most aspects of morality, but they generally agreed that people make moral judgments through rational reflection. Socrates, for example, reduced moral "virtues to knowledge and did away with the non-rational part of the soul, feelings, and character" (Irwin, 1995, p. 9). Kant concluded: "The pre-eminent good which we call moral can therefore consist in nothing else than the conception of law in itself, which certainly is only possible in a rational being" (1788/2014). And Bentham's felicific calculus requires considerable cognitive bookkeeping, for one must carefully estimate the nature of the pain and pleasure an action will likely produce (e.g., intensity, duration, purity) and then "take the balance; which, if on the side of pleasure, will give the general good tendency of the act, if on the side of pain, the general evil tendency" (Bentham, 1789/1948, p. 31).

Many psychologists, too, assume moral judgments are guided by the same basic psychological processes that determine decision making in general. Dewey (1922, p. 207), in his analysis of character and conduct, maintained that "the moral is to develop conscientiousness, ability to judge the significance of what we are doing and to use that judgment in directing what we do . . . by fostering those impulses and habits which experience has shown to make us sensitive, generous, imaginative, impartial in perceiving the tendency of our inchoate dawning activities." Kohlberg (1958), too, underscored the cognitive foundations of morality when he proposed that "moral action is oriented to or preceded by a value judgment. . . . this distinction does not mean that moral action is motivated by pure reason as Kant thought, but the need to see moral action as determined by reason seems to spring from the experience of moral judgments as motivating" (pp. 8–9). Turiel and his colleagues, in their studies of developmental changes in moral judgment, concluded that older children "form distinct, organized systems of thought" which subsequently guide the processing of information about moral and conventional actions: "features of events are processed and interpreted by individuals from the perspective of their own domain-differentiated judgment" (Turiel, Hildebrandt, Wainryb, & Saltzstein, 1991, pp. 5–7). He concludes "the substantive aspects of morality" are "connected with judgment, thought, and reflections" (Turiel, 2018, p. 9).

But moral judgments are not entirely rational conclusions reached through dispassionate review of all the available information. People, when making decisions, sometimes rely on simplifying cognitive heuristics that can cause them to reach erroneous conclusions, and evidence indicates that moral judgments are not immune to the biasing effects of these heuristics (e.g., Sunstein, 2005). Moral judgments are also influenced, to a degree, by the same types of biases that influence other inferences, such as primacy effects, framing, and hindsight. Imagine, for example, people learn about a person's intentions either before or after they are told that the person acted in ways that caused harmed to others. The sequencing of the information should not influence judgments, but it does: The impact of information about intentions is greater when presented after, rather than before, the description of the harm that was done (Leloup, Meert, & Samson, 2018). People's moral judgments are also influenced by how an action is described or how a moral choice is framed. For example, individuals respond differently when asked to consider a difficult moral choice, such as treating 100 patients with an experimental drug that will save some patients, but kill others due to the treatment's severe side effects. Individuals will tend to approve the use of the drug if told "it will save the lives of 80 patients," but reject the use of the drug if it will "kill 20 patients" (Sinnott-Armstrong, 2008). The hindsight bias also distorts people's moral inferences, for once we know if an action resulted in some negative consequences, we judge the action as less moral—even though the negative outcomes were not intended or foreseeable (Fleischhut, Meder, & Gigerenzer, 2017).

Moral judgments, like other inferences about people and the things they do, are also often sustained as much by emotion as they are by the dispassionate review of all available information. Haidt's (2001) social intuitionist model of moral judgment, for example, suggests that a quick, emotional intuition or "gut feeling" often guides people's moral judgments, and that these emotional reactions may prompt them to make moral decisions that are not entirely consistent with reason. Only after the judgment is made does cognition's role become activated as a post hoc justification tool.

Our judgments of our own morality are no less biased than our judgments of others. People are more positive when they compare their personal qualities and accomplishments to others' qualities and accomplishments, and this self-serving bias applies equally to moral qualities. Most people believe that they are more moral than other people, and they judge themselves more leniently if they should ever stray from the proper moral path (Dunning, 2016). In a demonstration of this tendency, we arranged for college students to complete various tests of social and intellectual skills in groups of two. Unbeknown to the participants, one of the group members was part of the research team, and during the testing phase he cheated and, in nearly all cases, convinced the participant to cheat as well. At the end of the session, participants completed a survey asking them to identify the factors that caused them to cheat. Compared to the responses of neutral observers who watched a recording of the cheating, individuals who cheated claimed their actions were unusual for them personally but also ones that anyone would have performed in those circumstances. They claimed they were morally good people, who had been pressured into acting badly (Forsyth, Pope, & McMillan, 1985; Forsyth & Scott, 1984).

Moral Judgments Are Influential

Moral judgments are dispositional inferences, so calling a person a liar or a hero is very different than calling that same person inept or foolish. Moral judgments identify a stable, highly personal characteristic of a person—their morality—as the cause of their behaviors. Because moral judgments locate the cause of action within the person rather than in the press of circumstance, this inference will likely have an enduring influence on perceivers' cognitive construals. If people we know seem socially reserved or awkward, we might tentatively conclude they are introverts who are uncomfortable in socially demanding circumstances. But if we discover they have lied to us, and we saddle them with the label of liar, their truthfulness will be questioned retrospectively and prospectively. Those judged to be moral or immoral are seen in a unique psychological light that, once cast, is rarely dimmed.

Moral judgments, then, define individuals and actions at a level more fundamental than all other perceptual pronouncements. Philosophically, moral concerns are said to override all other reasons for selecting and justifying action. An action might be expedient, healthy, lawful, or pleasurable, but if it is judged to be morally wrong, then many normative philosophers would likely argue against engaging in the action. As Hare (1981, p. 56) explains: "To treat a principle as overriding, then, is to let it always override other principles when they conflict with it and, in the same way, let it override all other prescriptions, including non-universalizable ones." Psychologically, moral judgments also override other inferences when perceivers are forming impressions of other people and their actions. Individuals characterized as boastful, dull, and irritating will likely be viewed negatively by others, but this negative impression can shift to a positive one should they exhibit features associated with morality (e.g., truthfulness, ethicality) or engage in morally commendable actions. Similarly, those with any number of positive qualities, such as reliability, warmth, and good manners, may be judged quite negatively should they act in morally suspect ways or display qualities that suggest they are not ethical (Birnbaum, 1972). Like the central traits identified by Asch (1946) in his studies of impression formation, moral judgments about an individual have a relatively larger impact on people's overall conception of a person than other perceptual information (Landy & Uhlmann, 2018). In consequence, "moral character information powerfully determines the overall impression we form of another person with whom we have or expect to have an important or meaningful relationship" (Goodwin, Piazza, & Rozin, 2014, p. 163).

Evidence of immorality is particularly influential. Birnbaum and his colleagues, in their studies of the way perceivers combine information to form impressions of other people, discovered that a single morally reprehensible act is sufficient to garner a negative impression, even if that information is combined with more positive, complimentary information about a person. Birnbaum confirmed that a person who performed such good deeds as talking a friend out of suicide, preventing a forcible rape, or rescuing a family from a burning building was rated very positively, but not if the person had also behaved immorally on one or more occasions (e.g., by torturing prisoners of war during an interrogation or selling food known to be contaminated). Even as many as nine highly positive moral actions were not sufficient to undo the negative effects of an immoral action (Riskey & Birnbaum, 1974). From Ezekiel (3:20): "when a righteous person turns from their righteousness and does evil . . . the righteous things that person did will not be remembered" (see, too, Chakroff, Russell, Piazza, & Young, 2017; Klein & O'Brien, 2016; Meindl, Johnson, & Graham, 2016).

Morality's perceptual reach is not limited to only perceptions of other people: Appraisals of morality also substantially influence our conception of ourselves. Aquino & Reed (2002) suggest that most people's self-conceptions are organized, at least in part, around moral qualities and characteristics. Morality is considered by most people to be one of their key personal attributes, and so their appraisals of their own morality influences their self-definition, self-esteem, and their actions across a wide range of contexts. For example, their satisfaction with themselves increases when their moral judgments of themselves are positive, but declines when they judge themselves to have acted in morally suspect ways. When individuals fail a test, lose a game, or burn the evening meal their self-esteem drops, but should they act in an immoral way—and they cannot justify the action psychologically—their self-appraisals decline more precipitously. In contrast, those who believe they have acted in a moral, rather than immoral way, express heightened levels of happiness and a sense of purpose (Hofmann, Wisneski, Brandt, & Skitka, 2014). The moral self is viewed as so fundamental to identity that people believed they would be the same person if, after a brain injury, they retained moral qualities but lost their distinctive personality traits, such as creativity, sense of humor, and assertiveness (Strohminger & Nichols, 2014).[2]

Moral Scrutiny

Humans, as a species, may be wise—Homo sapiens—but they could have easily been classified as Homo criticus—the animal that evaluates, criticizes, and judges. But only some of these judgments are moral ones. Someone who is rude, lacks good table manners, dresses badly, or roots for a team we dislike may be judged negatively, just as the person who is polite, engaging, well dressed, and roots for our favorite team may be viewed positively. But people reserve their moral approval and condemnation for only certain people and certain kinds of action (Jones, 1991).

Although the line between moral judgments and other types of evaluative pronouncements is often an uncertain one, philosophical and psychological investigations have consistently identified two necessary conditions for creating a shift from judgment to *moral* judgment: the degree of harm or benefit produced by the action and the consistency of the action with standards that define what is considered moral (Butterfield, Treviño, & Weaver; 2000; Reynolds, 2008).

Harm

The U.S. Department of Justice once surveyed over 60,000 citizens, asking them to evaluate the severity of actions ranging from vagrancy to murder. The respondents, quite reasonably, rated actions that caused harm to other people or to their property most negatively. Planting "a bomb in a public building" that explodes and kills 20 people, murder, and rape (e.g., "a person stabs a victim to death"), or setting "fire to a building causing $100,000 worth of damage" were all viewed as very negative actions that were deserving of prosecution and punishment. But when asked to judge such victimless crimes as public intoxication, loitering, truancy, trespassing, and vagrancy they were more lenient. The majority of the respondents did not consider these actions to be sufficiently aberrant to warrant punishment, for they caused no harm (Wolfgang, Figlio, Tracy, & Singer, 1985, pp. vi–vii).

Harm is central to most philosophical analyses of morality. The Hippocratic corpus dating to the fourth century BCE enjoined physicians to heal the sick as best they could, but first of all: Do no harm to others (*primum non nocere*). Both Hinduism and Buddhism embrace the principle of *ahimsa*, which roughly translates into "cause no harm or injury to another." One of the leading schools of thought in the philosophy of ethics, consequentialism, also suggests that morality fundamentally depends on the amount of harm that results from an action. Bentham's (1834, pp. 169–170) concept of utilitarianism, for example, is one such approach to ethics, for it argues that what is good and right will be the action that maximizes the greatest good, but also minimizes harm. The virtue of beneficence, as described by Frankena (1973), requires that a person should not inflict harm on others, should prevent evil or harm to others, and should, when possible, act to remove evil and promote good. John Stuart Mill (1859/2011), in his essay *On Liberty*, proposed a morality based on the harm principle: "The only purpose for which power can be rightfully exercised over any member of a civilized community, against his will, is to prevent harm to others." Even Adam Smith (1759/2016), whose analyses of economic transactions assume individuals strive to maximize their personal gains and minimize their losses, recognized that these tendencies operate in tandem with another natural force: concern for the welfare of others.

Studies in moral psychology further affirm the significance of harm in triggering a shift from general evaluation and appraisal to moral valuation and judgment (May & Pauli, 2002). Gray and his colleagues, for example, suggest that moral cognition is guided by a harm-based template that organizes people's thinking about what is right and what is wrong (Gray, Young, & Waytz, 2012). When they asked people to write down actions that are morally wrong, their lists were filled with extremely harmful actions: murder, adultery, child abuse. When asked to categorize these actions, the respondents described some as unfair and others as gross, but the majority (68%) used the same word to describe them: harmful (Gray & Schein, 2016; Schein & Gray, 2018).

We, too, confirmed the significance of harmful consequences in instigating moral review by asking participants to evaluate individuals whose actions produced consequences that ranged from the extremely beneficial to the extremely harmful. Their judgments, as consequentialists would predict, tracked the quality of consequences closely. A person who delayed others so they missed an appointment, caused a child to miss a meal, or broke someone's fishing rod was not judged as immoral, but a person whose actions caused significant harm—death, psychological damage, disfigurement, or permanent physical injury—was. Conversely, acting to produce mildly positive consequences for others, such as giving someone a small gift, weeding an elderly woman's garden, or giving a young boy a free dinner, did not generate any moral approbation, but rescuing a person from a fire or from drowning, searching for and finding a child lost in the wilderness, and giving a needy family $20,000 did (Forsyth, 1978).[3]

Harm's unique influence on people's moral judgments was further confirmed in studies of the neurological bases of moral judgment. Investigators who tracked respondents' neurological responses when making moral judgments found specific areas of the brain (dorsolateral prefrontal cortex) were more active when people were asked to evaluate actions that caused substantial harm, and that activity in those sites was associated with more negative moral judgments (Schaich Borg, Hynes, Van Horn, Grafton, & Sinnott-Armstrong, 2006). Evidence also suggests that people's sensitivity to harmful outcomes is mediated, in part, by certain neurotransmitters (i.e., serotonin); when levels of serotonin are elevated, people are even more likely to condemn actions that result in harm (Crockett, Clark, Hauser, & Robbins, 2010).

Moral Standards

Some actions result in no discernable consequences, either positive or negative, and yet they still elicit moral condemnation. Sexual preferences, dietary predilections, religious practices—even thoughts and feelings which are never openly expressed—may be considered immoral despite the utter lack of any harm resulting from these actions (Alicke, 2012). This tendency to identify some actions, and the individuals who perform them, independently of the consequences they yield, results from a second process that can instigate a moral scrutiny: conformity to rules, standards, and principles that explicitly define criteria for moral approval and reproach. All human societies identify certain actions as ones that are prohibited as morally wrong, and those individuals who violate these social rules are likely to find themselves facing moral censure (Brown, 1991). Although the content of these social standards (or rules, principles, maxims, or norms) varies across cultures, the process itself is universal: Individuals who act in ways that are inconsistent with prescriptive moral standards are considered to be less than moral than those who act in ways that are consistent with moral standards.

A standard, according to Higgins (1990, p. 302), is "a criterion or rule established by experience, desires, or authority for the measure of quantity and extent, or quality and value." Such standards have three basic features. First, they share a similar structure, which is of the general form: "Actions of type X are morally bad (or good) and should not (or should) be done." Thus, these rules consist of both an evaluative component (e.g., lying to others is bad or telling the truth is good) and a prescriptive/proscriptive component (e.g., one should not lie or one should tell the truth). Unlike descriptive norms—expectations about what people typically do in any given situation—moral norms are injunctive: they describe what people should do (prescriptive norms) and what they should not do (proscriptive norms). Violating a descriptive norm pertaining to some commonly accepted standard for interpersonal behavior—such as smiling back when someone smiles at you—may be considered unusual, but violations of moral norms are considered wrong (Janoff-Bulman & Carnes, 2013).

Second, these rules tend to be integrated in a coherent moral framework. For example, the rules endorsed by any specific person may be derived from an overarching religious or philosophical perspective. Rather than a checklist of things that one should or should not do, they are hierarchically organized mandates for action.

Third, these rules are socially shared rather than wholly private and personal. Moral standards are commonly accepted by all or nearly all members of one's social group, and so they are transpersonal (Ellemers, 2017). In some instances, these moral norms are made explicit in codes of ethics, and they may also provide the basis of legal statutes that identify unlawful actions and the sanctions that will be imposed should these standards be violated. But the lists of what is considered immoral and what is considered illegal are not necessarily identical—some actions which are legal may be viewed as morally wrong whereas some illegal acts may be viewed, in some situations, as morally commendable (Berkowitz & Walker, 1967).

Just as perceivers' sensitivity to the harm and benefit is consistent with consequentialist moral philosophies, so their attentiveness to the consistency between actions and moral rules is consistent with the second major school of thought in moral philosophy: deontology. Deontologists reject consideration of consequences as a basis for moral evaluation and rely, instead, on universal moral rules to which no exceptions can be made. For example, the philosopher Immanuel Kant (1873/1973), generally regarded as the foremost proponent of the deontological position, maintained that "all practical principles of justice must contain strict truths . . . since exceptions destroy the universality, on account of which alone they bear the name principles" (p. 258). Kant argued that the universal maxim "always keep your promises" was a command of reason that should be acted on irrespective of the consequences. To support his position, Kant explained that if people acted on the opposite universal maxim (i.e., only keep your promises when it is to your advantage), that principle would be negated. Promises, for example, are not actually promises if one permits exceptions.

Psychologists who study moral judgment have also confirmed that many people are, at least in part, intuitive deontologists who respond negatively to actions that violate moral standards (e.g., Holyoak & Powell, 2016). For example, if people are asked to judge a doctor who sought to undo a greater harm—the death of five patients—by deliberately sacrificing a single patient, most people objected to this violation of the moral rule "thou shalt not kill" and a physician's duty to heal rather than harm. Most, too, later rejected the very idea of consequentialism, preferring instead to base their judgments on moral standards (Horne, Powell, & Hummel, 2015). When researchers have directly manipulated the consistency of actions with moral norms and the consequences that follow, they find that normative choices are viewed more positively than those that yield positive results (e.g., Gawronski, Armstrong, Conway, Friesdorf, & Hütter, 2017). We also confirmed this tendency when we asked people to evaluate individuals who violated basic moral principles—they lied, stole, broke promises, or failed to do their duty—and those who acted in ways that were consistent with moral rules—they were truthful, resisted taking what did not belong to them, kept their promises, and did their duty. Rule breakers were consistently rated as less moral, even when the action yielded positive consequences (Forsyth, 1978).

Moral Divergence

Even though humans live in an astonishing variety of habitats and ethnographic configurations, all share one fundamental feature: People the world over live with others rather than in isolation. Homo sapiens are capable of surviving alone, but few do, for the need to join with others is stronger than the desire to remain free of interpersonal entanglements (Baumeister & Leary, 1995).

Our serious sociality requires we achieve a level of sustained, cooperative interdependence far beyond that of more detached, nonsocial species. If you are not entirely self-sufficient and so depend on others for food, shelter, protection from harm, as well as your overall happiness and well-being, you will likely prosper if your relationships with others are cooperative ones—marked by mutual trust, low levels of conflict, sharing of resources, and united defense against threats. Social species therefore benefit from biological and cultural mechanisms that sustain positive, cooperative relationships among its members, and morality is one such mechanism: It shines an approving light on those who are trustworthy, cooperative, fair, and loyal, and singles out for rebuke those who are dishonest, belligerent, unjust, and selfish (Curry, Chesters, & Van Lissa, 2019).

If morality is a psychological and interpersonal process that promotes cooperation and minimizes conflict, it likely functions more effectively when all or nearly all members of society agree when defining the difference between what is ethically good and what is ethically condemned. Social conventions, including morality, derive much of their influence simply from their widespread acceptance, for other people provide social proof of the validity of a position or choice (Cialdini, 2009). Those who veer from the accepted course of action raise doubts about the legitimacy of social prescriptions, and so those who challenge the status quo are pressured to amend their actions. When people learn that their associates consider an action to be morally acceptable, they tend to conform to the others' opinion (Kundu & Cummins, 2013).

Yet, diversity in moral beliefs is hardly an unusual state of affairs. Consider, for example, the findings from a Gallup Poll of over one thousand adults in the U.S. When asked if it was morally acceptable or morally wrong to have a baby outside of marriage, 32% declared that to be morally wrong, whereas 65% stated it was morally acceptable. And what about the use of the death penalty to punish those who commit horrendous crimes? Many felt that such capital punishment was morally justified (67%), but many others considered the death penalty to be immoral. Similar levels of disagreement held for most moral issues, including cloning, abortion, stem cell research, gay or lesbian relations, and medical testing on animals. People agreed, for the most part, on only two issues: 88% condemned extramarital affairs and 94% considered birth control to be morally acceptable (Gallup Organization, May, 2018). Such variance is paradoxical, given morality's effectiveness in promoting stable interpersonal relations depends, in part, on the extent to which moral standards are clearly defined by the status quo.

Ethics Position Theory

Some of the variance in people's moral judgments is caused by the same thing that causes most disagreements: A reasonable, informed, knowledgeable person has encountered an unreasonable, uninformed, ignorant person, and the two therefore cannot reach consensus. But even the capacity to reason well does not guarantee agreement when it comes to morality, and researchers have traced the source of these variations to a number of stable dispositional differences across people. For example, developmental psychologist Lawrence Kohlberg (1983) suggested that the cognitive changes that occur as people learn more about ethical choices prompts shifts from simpler, punishment-oriented thinking to more principled thought. Identity theory suggests that for some people, morality sustains their sense of self: the goals they select, their ideals, and their everyday actions (e.g., Aquino & Kay, 2018). Neuroscientists trace morality, and variations in the judgments people make when faced with moral temptation, to the intricate circuitry, neurotransmitters, and structures of the human brain (e.g., Yoder & Decety, 2018). Personality theorists, such as Lee and Ashton (2012), believe that ethicality ranks alongside introversion, contentiousness, and stability as one of the cornerstones of personality, and individuals will differ in their moral actions and judgments depending on their modesty, greediness, and concern for fairness. Dahlsgaard, Peterson, and Seligman (2005) further extend this dispositional approach by proposing that people vary in virtuousness, with the result that those with a larger share of human strengths will respond differently than those whose moral character is weaker. And there is always psychoanalytic theory, which argues that morality is substantially influenced by early life experiences and psychological forces that are often unrecognized, and so differences in morality are the inevitable result of varied psychosocial development and deep-seated psychological tensions (Freud, 1920).

The research reviewed in this book also seeks to explain individual differences in moral judgments, but it traces these differences back to variations in people's intuitive, personal moral philosophies (Forsyth, 1980, 1992). This perspective, ethics position theory, assumes that philosophers are not the only ones who have thought seriously about moral issues. For their entire lives people have confronted and considered issues of right and wrong, and so have developed their own perspective on these issues. Although these beliefs about morality are often implicit, unstated, or unintegrated, they nonetheless influence their moral judgments, emotions, and actions.

Individuals' personal philosophies about ethics will likely contain a number of unique, idiosyncratic elements produced by their personal experiences when confronting and resolving moral issues, but the theory assumes two nomothetic regularities appear consistently across most people's moral values and beliefs. First, most people agree that morality requires acting in ways that minimize harming or injuring others, but people are not equal in their sensitivity to harm and its various psychological, physical, and economic forms. Some, the idealists among us, are more attentive to the welfare of others, whereas others believe that even the best intentioned actions may nonetheless cause harm and hardship. Second, not everyone believes that moral absolutes should serve as guides to action and judgment. Relativistic individuals are skeptical about the possibility of formulating universal moral standards, and so they eschew moral rules or principles when deciding between what is right and what is wrong. Other people, in contrast, rely on rules, standards, or principles to define morality. They believe that moral standards, such as "Tell the truth to others" and "Do unto others as you would have them do unto you," provide an unambiguous benchmark for judging and guiding actions.

These two dimensions of difference regarding harm and moral standards parallel the distinction between moral theories in philosophy that are based on the consequences of actions (consequentialism) and those that underscore the relationship between principles and morality (deontological models). These dimensions are also consistent with psychological analyses of morality, which have similarly suggested that some individual's respond more to the consistency of actions with fundamental principles of justice and fairness, whereas others are primarily concerned with minimizing harm (e.g., Gilligan, 1982; Haan, 1978). The theory has also been examined in a series of empirical investigations of moral cognition, emotion, and action, and the results of these investigations are reviewed in subsequent chapters of this book.

Empirical Tests of the Theory

Any psychological theory of moral judgment, to adequately deal with the many factors which may affect judgments, must take into account aspects of the perceiver, the circumstances which surround the act, the nature of the act, the relationship between the perceiver and the individual who is being appraised, and so on. Although a formidable task, ethics position theory provides a means of organizing these multifarious causes and consequences of moral judgment in a coherent conceptual framework.

Chapter 2, "Ethics Position Theory," describes the origins of this theoretical perspective and its consistency with previous moral theory in philosophy and related theories pertaining to the psychology of moral judgment. This chapter also describes the steps taken to develop a method of measuring individual differences in personal moral philosophies—the Ethics Position Questionnaire (EPQ)—and four perspectives on morality: situationism, subjectivism, exceptionism, and absolutism.

Chapter 3, "Measured Morality," explores the relationship between individual moral positions and four theories that have dominated the psychological study of morality for the last 50 years: Kohlberg's (1983) theory of cognitive moral development, Gilligan's (1982) ethic of caring, Schwartz's (1992) social values theory, and Haidt's (2012) moral foundations theory. Both Kohlberg's theory and ethics position theory consider people to be natural moral philosophers, for they both assume individuals' life experiences have taught them to discriminate between what is right and wrong, and each person has developed the criteria that they rely on to make that distinction. Gilligan's ethic of caring contrasts moralities that are based on justice and those based on caring, whereas Schwartz's theory identifies universally recognized differences in people's values. Haidt's moral foundation theory counterbalance this emphasis on ratiocination by adding intuition and feelings into the mix. Taken in combination, these five theories provide a fuller explanation for morality than any one taken separately.

Chapter 4, "Individuals Differ," provides an extended description of the four types of people who differ in idealism and relativism—the situationists, the absolutists, the exceptionists, and the subjectivists—by considering their demographic characteristics (e.g., age, sex, religiosity), their personal characteristics (e.g., personality traits, values, empathy), and their "darker" qualities (e.g., Machiavellianism, authoritarianism). Are situationists, for example, likely to be younger or older? Who is more religious, in general: those who are highly idealistic, or those who are relativistic? Reviewing the relationship between the Ethics Position Questionnaire (EPQ) and related individual characteristics provides evidence of the scale's concurrent, predictive, and discriminant validity.

Chapter 5, "Moral Thought," examines the factors that influence moral judgments, including consequences, intentionality, and the consistency of the action with moral standards. It begins by first examining the relationship between idealism, relativism, and moral beliefs and reactions to various moral indiscretions, such as cheating, lying, and so on. It then considers the results of experimental studies of moral judgment processes based on methods drawn from cognitive psychology, and concludes by considering the impact of intentionality on moral judgments.

Chapter 6, "Moral Behaviors and Emotions," asks if differences in ethics positions predict who will act in morally commendable ways, and who will not. In general, the empirical evidence based on self-reports of moral tendencies indicates that idealism is associated with resistance to moral temptation, whereas relativism predicts willingness to act in ways that run counter to traditional moral standards. However, studies that have examined how people actually act in morally turbulent situations do not conform to their relatively rosy prognostications. The evidence pertaining to emotional reactions following moral missteps is more consistent: Idealistic individuals who are not relativistic tend to display higher levels of guilt if they do act in ways that are inconsistent with moral standards. The chapter concludes by considering the implications of these findings for individuals' overall well-being and happiness.

Chapter 7, "The Geography of Ethics," examines a potentially contentious issue in the study of morality: Do the findings regarding morality reported in studies of individuals living in one country and at one time generalize to individuals elsewhere in the world? As continuing globalization brings people from different cultures together in shared enterprises, they often find that they do not see eye-to-eye in their moral appraisals. All would agree that international relations are shaped, in part, by ethics, but what is considered moral differs to some extent from one culture to another. This chapter reviews the findings of studies of individual differences in ethics positions in thirty different countries, and integrates the findings with two prominent theories of cross-cultural differences: Hofstede's (1980) theory of cultural dimensions and Inglehart's (1997) dimensions of world values.

Chapter 8, "Ethics in Context," uses the theory of ethics positions to gain insights into the moral choices and actions of individuals, groups, and organizations in business, leadership, educational, and research contexts. The review of this work is selective, but provides examples of the practical implications of ethics position theory.

Caveats

This book is a work in psychology rather than philosophy. It strives to explain the processes by which people make judgments about right and wrong and the personal and interpersonal causes and consequences of such judgments. To achieve this goal, it draws on multiple sources, including philosophers' theories of knowledge, ethics, and judgment. But it is fundamentally a scientific, rather than a philosophical, analysis.

The Psychology of Morality

Social interaction necessarily involves ethical considerations. Situations frequently arise in which a person must make a choice between available alternatives which vary in their perceived moral quality. Once the choice is made, those knowledgeable of the person and the choice may form a judgment of the morality of such a person who would make such a choice in such a situation. The philosophical study of ethics addresses the issues which underlie these various judgments. Moral philosophers recognize that individuals do, should, and must make moral judgments, and in examining morality ask the same kinds of questions psychologists ask, such as "What are the meanings of ethical terms like good, bad, right, and wrong?"; "Do good actions share some common characteristics which determine the application of this label—a set of characteristics which do not apply to bad actions?"; and "What are the reasons which support the assumption that the possession of these characteristics makes a thing good rather than bad?" Philosophers' analyses of ethics, however, tend to be normative as well as descriptive. They not only strive to describe the foundational elements of moral judgments and action, they extend that analysis to draw conclusions about how individuals should be morally evaluated, and how individuals ought to act in moral contexts.

A psychological analysis, on the other hand, performs only a descriptive function by proposing and testing theoretical formulations of how individuals make moral judgments. Psychologists, using accepted methods of theory development and research, develop conceptual models that explain moral thought, action, and emotion, and then test the adequacy of their explanations by collecting data that will support or contradict predictions derived from the theory. They may, through research, identify the key factors that influence moral judgment, but they would not use their findings to make inferences about how individuals should make moral judgments. They avoid committing the naturalistic fallacy, which warns against concluding how people ought to act given how they naturally act. As Kelley, a social psychologist, said of his insightful analysis of moral judgments as cognitive appraisals of achievement and reality, "I find no basis in this analysis for saying what is morally good or bad, or what people should regard as morally good or bad" (Kelley, 1971, p. 293).

Stating that science is descriptive while moral philosophy is prescriptive is to oversimplify, however. Philosophical analyses of morality are, to some extent, constrained by the limits of human understanding, and those limits are determined through research. As Flanagan, a moral philosopher, argues in his principle of minimal psychological realism, philosophers must "make sure when constructing a moral theory or projecting a moral ideal that the character, decision processing, and behaviors are possible, or are perceived to be possible, for creatures like us" (Flanagan, 1991, p. 32).

Scientific evidence can also, in some cases, inform the ethicist's conclusions about a morally fraught issue. For example, a political policy may be adopted based on an ethical ideal, such as each citizen's right to life, liberty, and the pursuit of happiness. When such principles are accepted as the basis for action, scientific procedures become useful in determining if the means proposed to achieve these ideals are viable, the short- and long-term implications of implementing certain programs or actions designed to fulfill the standards expressed in the moral principle, and the psychological, political, sociological, and economic reactions which may accompany the implementation of the programs. Scientific evidence may more directly influence ethical discussions by providing an indication of the validity of factual assumptions that underpin moral positions on issues. The death penalty, for example, may be justified as moral by citing its utility as a deterrent to violent crime. If this reason is the only justification for this penalty and if, through scientific analysis, it can be demonstrated that in all likelihood the penalty does not function as a deterrent, then the scientific results should have an impact on the moral evaluation of the practice. A scientific analysis thus becomes relevant if it can provide evidence that the action being considered will lead to the morally evaluated consequences.

Philosophical analyses also provide insights which may be utilized in constructing a psychological theory of moral judgment processes. Aristotle's analyses of morality were as much psychological theories as they were philosophical arguments defining right and wrong, for he argued that morality is the result of habit formation and self-perception processes. Intuitionist analyses of ethical concepts suggest that terms like *good* are indefinable since they are simple qualities of reality that are directly perceived. As a psychological proposition, whether or not this is the case is a question which is open to empirical examination (Cohen & Ahn, 2016). Many of the philosophers of the Scottish Enlightenment proposed that morality is grounded fundamentally in the human capacity to understand and sympathize with the plight of others, and studies in psychology offer evidence that supports their claim (Decety & Cowell, 2014). Ethics position theory provides a final example of the interplay between philosophy and psychology. Philosophers have examined the factors that influence moral judgments for centuries, and their analyses likely provide valuable insight into the psychological processes that sustain such judgments. Philosophers adopt varying positions with regards to ethics, including deontology and consequentialism. Might not these moral positions correspond to those adopted by people trying to resolve questions of right and wrong in their everyday lives?

Ethics or Morality?

Is the study of people's tendency to appraise the quality of an action or individual along the continuum from bad to good an investigation of ethics or morality? Ethics, to some, focuses on the analysis of moral processes, and so describes how people go about making distinctions between what is good and what is bad. Morality, in contrast, pertains to the results of that process, and includes normative pronouncements of wrong and right. Others have suggested that morality is a more basic, and more personal, evaluation of the rightness or wrongness of an act, whereas ethics are complex decisional processes that reflect moral leanings, but also consider broader social considerations. Individuals, they suggest, have a moral code, but businesses, organizations, and institutions have codes of ethics. Yet, others suggest just the opposite. Foucault (1990), for example, considered morality to be a codified prescriptive system defined by such authorities as the church or family, whereas ethics are those processes that create the alignment of individual actions and the moral code.

Many philosophers and social scientists, however, use the terms interchangeably. Etymologically, the root of the word *moral* is the Latin word *mōrālis*: Cicero's translation of the Greek word *ethos*, which meant habits, customs, and mores. A course or book examining moral philosophy or moral psychology will cover the same material as a course on ethical philosophy or psychology. Dictionaries, too, tend to use one term to define the other. The *Oxford English Dictionary*, for example, defines the word *moral* as "of or relating to the distinction between right and wrong, or good and evil, in relation to the actions, desires, or character of responsible human beings; ethical" (Moral, 2018). That dictionary defines *ethics* as "of or relating to moral principles" (Ethics, 2018). Given the lack of consistency in distinguishing these two terms, this analysis will use them interchangeably, with no distinction implied.

Notes

1. Participants in Anderson's study rated items on a scale from 0 to 6, with 0 indicating "least favorable or desirable" and 6 indicating "most favorable or desirable" (1968, p. 272). We classified a subset of the items into five categories: moral (e.g., honest, honorable), immoral (e.g., untrustworthy, dishonest), positive (e.g., warm, kind, interesting), negative (e.g., self-conceited, unpleasant), and neutral (e.g., cautious, shrewd, nonchalant). Our analysis indicated the moral items were rated as the most positive and the immoral items as the most negative; $F(4, 47) = 2771.88$, $p < 0.01$; the means were, respectively, 5.45, 0.52, 5.16, 1.04, and 3.25. The moral and immoral items were also rated as more meaningful, relative to the neutral items; $F(4, 47) = 2.54$, $p = 0.05$. Variance in the ratings was also more pronounced for the neutral items, relative to the moral and immoral items; $F(4, 47) = 18.54$, $p < 0.05$.

2. Morality is not an influential component of all people's self-conception. Individuals who have elevated levels of psychopathy, for example, are less likely to define themselves as moral actors, particularly in comparison to individuals whose self-definitions emphasize moral qualities such as caring, compassion, fairness, generosity, and honesty (Glenn, Koleva, Iyer, Graham, & Ditto, 2010).
3. Some individuals are sensitive to particular types of harm; environmentalists, for example, may be sensitive to harm done to the natural world and some vegetarians believe that animals should be not be killed and eaten. But, in general, it is harm to other people that is most likely to trigger a moral judgment across most people and, in particular, intentional harm done to those who are members of our own group, such as family, tribe, community, region, or nation.

2

ETHICS POSITION THEORY

> Whatever exists at all exists in some quantity. To know it thoroughly involves knowing its quantity as well as its quality.
>
> —Edward L. Thorndike (1918, p. 16)

Ethics position theory assumes that philosophers are not the only ones who think seriously about morality. In their everyday lives people confront and consider issues of right and wrong, and so have developed their own intuitive moral philosophies. Although these beliefs about morality likely contain any number of unique, idiosyncratic elements, for most people two moral concerns are tantamount: apprehension that the action caused or may cause harm to others (idealism) and the compatibility of the action with moral standards (relativism). The theory originated in psychological studies of people's judgments of the ethics of research, but is consistent with philosophers' distinctions between an ethics based on moral principles (deontology) and one that emphasizes the consequences that may result from an action (consequentialism). The Ethics Position Questionnaire (EPQ), which measures respondents' degree of idealism and moral relativism, can be used to classify individuals into one of four different moral positions: exceptionism, subjectivism, absolutism, and situationism.

* * *

In 1898 the moral philosopher Frank Chapman Sharp published his paper "An Objective Study of Some Moral Judgments" in *The American Journal of Psychology*. In that paper he argued that the morally right action was that single action that all people would choose over alternatives if they were fully informed of the circumstances, were consistent in their values, and impartial when weighing evidence. But Sharp was also something of a psychologist. Eschewing the methods typical of philosophy—the logical analysis of ideas and alternative perspectives—he instead took an empirical approach. He developed a series of moral dilemmas and asked the students in his classes at the University of Wisconsin to identify the right and wrong choice among alternatives. This procedure is now commonplace, but Sharp's approach was far from orthodox at the time (Sharp, 1950). He even included an early version of a moral problem that would eventually become one of the most famous cases in the analysis of moral thought: the Trolley Car dilemma. His version stated, "In a small western village a switchman was just about to turn the switch for an approaching express train when he saw his little son, his only child, playing upon the track. The choice had to be made between the life of the babe and the lives of the passengers. What ought he to have done?" (Sharp, 1898, p. 202).

Sharp discovered that people's judgments were substantially determined by the two critical elements examined in Chapter 1 that instigate moral appraisal: the consequences that the actions caused and the consistency of the act with rules that define duty, responsibility, and justice. But Sharp complained that his research was hindered by the lack of agreement among his students concerning what was moral and what was not. Even when people with apparently similar characteristics were making judgments about the same person or action, they still managed to sometimes reach opposite conclusions. He had predicted that all human minds, if fully informed, would agree on what is right and what is wrong, but his findings did not support his prediction.

Sharp (1898) entertained the notion that the lack of consensus that typifies moral deliberations indicates that people, including moral philosophers, are incompetent, careless, or both incompetent and careless, but he preferred an alternative explanation: "that there exist different types of moral judgment, which are represented with varying degrees of completeness in different persons" (p. 198). People facing a decision about morality base this decision on their personal beliefs about ethics, and disagreements concerning morality must necessarily surface when personal ethical systems are different.

Psychologists since Sharp worked to explain this divergence in moral judgment. Developmental psychologists identified how people's moral judgments become more sophisticated as they age. Cognitive psychologists related moral judgment and decision making back to differences in how perceivers access and process information, in general, and about morality, in particular. Personality researchers identified a number of factors that influence moral judgments, including dispositional differences in such morally relevant traits as psychopathy, Machiavellianism, and narcissism. Ethics position theory, in its extension of that work, suggested that variations in moral judgments derive, in part, from variations in people's sensitivity to the two factors that prompt perceivers to question the ethics of an action or individual—harmful consequences and the consistency of an action with moral standards. This chapter examines that assumption, and also discusses the development of the Ethics Position Questionnaire (EPQ), which is an inventory that can be used to measure these differences.

Sources of Variation in Moral Judgments

Ethics position theory suggests that some of the distinctions made by moral philosophers are also made by laypersons when they are formulating moral judgments. Just as Kant (1788/2014) maintained that the moral person must always act in ways that are consistent with fundamental moral principles, might not perceivers, too, react negatively when judging actions that are inconsistent with moral standards? Similarly, just as Bentham (1789/1948) suggested that the most morally proper actions yield positive consequences that outweigh the negative, might not perceivers consider the outcomes generated by actions when making moral judgments? Does this idea—that perceivers adopt divergent personal moral philosophies—explain why reasonable people sometimes disagree when discussing matters of morality?

Origins

In the 1960s, social psychologist Stanley Milgram carried out a series of scientifically instructive but ethically controversial studies of obedience to authority. His studies used the same basic paradigm: Adults who thought they were volunteering to take part in a study of learning were ordered to administer increasingly powerful electric shocks to another person. They were led to believe that this person was a volunteer, like themselves, who had the bad luck to be assigned to the role of the learner in the study; in actuality, the learner was part of the research staff and received no shocks at all. The goal was to test the limits of authority: Would people obey, even if it meant hurting someone? Contrary to expectations, most obeyed, but few did so willingly. About ten percent of the people Milgram studied were so upset by the procedure that they seemed to be on the verge of a psychological breakdown (Milgram, 1963, 1965).

Milgram's studies did more than illuminate the interpersonal processes that determine the social power of authorities and people's inability to resist that influence. His work sparked a debate over the ethics of research with human participants. Baumrind (1964), for example, argued that Milgram violated fundamental principles of morality when he deceived his participants and caused them to experience stress and discomfort. She pointed out that lying and deceiving are not tolerated by people in everyday social situations, and that researchers have no right to put themselves above the fundamental moral injunction, "Thou shalt not lie." Milgram, and the American Psychological Association (APA), disagreed. The *Ethical Principles in the Conduct of Research with Human Participants* promulgated by the APA at that time asserted that "The general ethical question always is whether there is a negative effect upon the dignity and welfare of the participants that the importance of the research does not warrant. . . . The nearest that the principles in this document come to an immutable 'thou shalt' or 'thou shalt not' is in the insistence that the human participants emerge from their research experience unharmed—or at least that the risks are minimal, understood by the participants, and accepted as reasonable" (APA, 1973, p. 11).

Intrigued by these varying reactions to Milgram's research, we decided to study the factors that influence people's ethical reactions to Milgram's research methods (Schlenker & Forsyth, 1977). We recruited volunteers who were unfamiliar with Milgram's work and asked them to read a description of his study and its results before judging the morality of the study and the researcher who designed and implemented it. The participants, we discovered, were more likely to condemn the study as unethical if they believed that the study was harmful, that it threatened participants' well-being, and that the experimenter should have foreseen the harm he may have caused. But they also rated the study as more moral if they felt the study was scientifically valid, that it yielded information about obedience that was not previously known, and that the researcher exercised care in designing the project.[1]

We also found, however, considerable variation in people's judgments. Some roundly condemned Milgram and his studies, others gave him their full moral support, and still others resisted the idea that the research raised any morally significant questions. So, we pursued these variations in a second study by asking participants to not only evaluate Milgram's study, but to also describe their attitudes, values, and beliefs related to the ethics of scientific research. The items they answered ran the gamut from ones concerned with the feasibility of universal ethical codes to ones concerned with deception, harm to research participants, and the ability of science to solve the world's problems: "If a researcher can foresee any type of harm, no matter how small, physical or psychological, he or she should not conduct the study," "Scientific concerns sometimes justify potential harm to participants," "It is possible to develop rigid codes of ethics that can be applied without exception to all psychological research," and so on (Schlenker & Forsyth, 1977, p. 383).

This attempt to link people's position on philosophical issues related to morality and their moral judgments was largely exploratory; we were unsure that this idea had any merit, or if people's responses to a simple survey would yield sufficient information about their moral outlook. But, when we examined their responses using exploratory factor analysis (EFA), we identified two basic themes underlying participants' responses. One theme, which we labeled idealism-pragmatism, pertained to the benefits and costs of research. Individuals who were relatively idealistic insisted that no harm, however small, was permissible in research, that people's welfare was crucial, and that it was of primary importance that a project might advance science. Individuals who were pragmatic, in contrast, felt that some degree of harm was permissible and that it was not of primary importance for a scientific advance to follow from research. The second theme, which we labelled rule-universality, included items that pertained to principles that serve as guides for moral choices. Some of these items stressed the need to comply with moral rules that defined the difference between right and wrong. Other items in the cluster opposed universal moral principles; these negatively worded items expressed skepticism about the possibility of developing universal principles.

These findings were encouraging, for they suggested that despite the many ways in which people differ in their moral thinking, certain consistent differences could be identified and assessed. These differences, in addition to being measurable, also explained some of the variation seen in people's moral judgments, for individuals who were more idealistic were more concerned with protecting the participants from foreseeable harm, but those who were more pragmatic stressed scientific contribution in their moral assessments. The findings, however, were quite preliminary. Our measure of these differences was relatively untested.

Idealism and Relativism

Our initial foray into the assessment of differences in individual's beliefs about morality focused specifically on their evaluations of research that yielded scientific advances, but in so doing violated certain moral principles and caused harm to those who took part in the research. The findings were promising, so we extended our analysis to moral issues, in general. For example, the question "If a researcher can foresee any type of harm, no matter how small, physical or psychological, he or she should not conduct the study" was reworded to read "One should never psychologically or physically harm another person." Similarly, "Rigidly codifying an ethical position that prevents certain types of research could stand in the way of scientific advancement and prevent the accumulation of knowledge" became "Rigidly codifying an ethical position that prevents certain types of actions could stand in the way of better human relations and adjustment" (Forsyth, 1980).

We also added items that paraphrased ideas expressed by prominent philosophers of ethics in relatively simple form. Deontology generated such items as "The essence of moral behavior lies in doing one's duty" and "If one makes certain to always try to 'do one's duty,' then he or she can be certain that they will always be acting morally." Items based on utilitarianism stressed consequences, such as "Conduct should be judged as good or bad depending upon the consequences it produces" and "The positive or negative consequences of an action are the only considerations that are important to moral judgment; whether or not the action violates some abstract moral principles is irrelevant." Other items were consistent with relativism (e.g., "What is ethical varies from one situation and society to another"), intuitionism (e.g., "It is impossible to resolve moral issues through either reason or evidence"), skepticism (e.g., "Others actions should not be judged"), egoism (e.g., "Personal concerns sometimes justify potential harm to others"), humanitarianism (e.g., "The dignity and welfare of people should be the most important concern in any society"), and non-maleficence (e.g., "A person should make certain that their actions never intentionally harm another, even to a small degree").

We asked a group of volunteers to indicate their agreement with this set of 55 items, and then used EFA to distill them down to a small number of dimensions that would best summarize their responses. Those analyses again revealed two core clusters. One cluster comprised nearly all the items that included admonitions to do no harm to others, such as "never intentionally harm another," and "risks to another should never be tolerated." It also included several statements that were idealistic in tone; they were visionary, optimistic, and quite possibly impractical. For example, "it is never necessary to sacrifice the welfare of others," the "dignity and welfare of people should be the most important concern in any society," and "moral actions are those which closely match ideals of the most 'perfect' action." We labeled this set of beliefs *idealism*, and assumed people who endorse these beliefs would react negatively to actions that cause harm to others. We also assumed that individuals who did not strongly endorse such beliefs—the moral realists—would not be so quick to judge an action as immoral if it caused others to be harmed.

The second set comprised beliefs that addressed the value of relying on moral rules or codes of ethics when making moral judgments. Although we included items that were consistent with both principled morality (e.g., "There are some ethical principles that are so important that no exceptions should ever be made to them" and "It is possible to develop codes of ethics that can be applied to nearly all situations") as well as statements that favored a more relativistic stance (e.g., "There are no ethical principles that are so important that they should be a part of any code of ethics" and "Moral standards are simply personal rules that indicate how a person should behave, and are not to be applied in making judgments of others"), the relativistic items clustered together more consistently than the items that favored reliance on principles. We therefore labeled this set of beliefs *relativism*, and assumed individuals who agree with such items would not necessarily condemn an action as immoral simply because it violated a commonly accepted moral principle. We also assumed that individuals who disagreed with the statements in the relativism cluster would respond negatively when evaluating actions that ran counter to traditionally accepted moral guidelines, such as "Thou shalt not lie" and "Do unto others as you would have them do unto you."

These two dimensions did not capture every nuance of each person's meta-ethical beliefs: A substantial portion of variance in people's personal moral beliefs was left unaccounted for by these two factors. But our confidence in the significance of these two factors was buttressed by their consistency with distinctions made by philosophers in their analysis of the morality, as well as the work of developmental and personality psychologists (Boyce & Jensen, 1978; Waterman, 1988). First, as noted in Chapter 1, consequentialist philosophers have traditionally argued that what matters the most when distinguishing right from wrong are the outcomes that result from the action: to decide if an action is a moral one the perceiver must calculate the pains and pleasures that resulted from the action (Bentham, 1789/1948). The items that coalesced to form the idealism cluster were consistent with consequentialism, in general, but not traditional utilitarianism. They stressed not causing harm, but statements that explicitly suggested that positive outcomes could compensate for negative outcomes did not correlate with these more idealistic beliefs. For example, this informal statement of utilitarianism, "An action which will produce some bad consequences is moral provided it produces some good consequences which obviously outweigh the bad," was not frequently endorsed by individuals who endorsed the other idealism items. Moreover, statements that explicitly rejected balancing the good with the bad were included in the idealism cluster (e.g., "Deciding whether or not to perform an act by balancing the positive consequences of the act against the negative consequences of the act is immoral" and "The existence of potential harm to others is always wrong, irrespective of the benefits to be gained"). Thus, the idealism items converged on a theme of avoiding harm; they did not include items that require acting in ways that generate positive outcomes (benevolence) or items that suggested positive consequences can make up for negative consequences in a cost/benefit calculus (utilitarianism).[2]

Second, the items in the relativism cluster also corresponded to one of the most discussed issues in moral philosophy: ethical skepticism. People are more likely to question the morality of an action when it runs counter to well-received moral rules, but this principled orientation is not universally supported in philosophical analyses of ethics. Some philosophies, such as deontology, offer compelling arguments for relying on absolute standards when formulating judgments. They suggest some actions are inherently moral or immoral, irrespective of the background contextual factors. Philosophical relativists, in contrast, have far less faith in the value of principles serving as the foundation of morality. Skeptics value uncertainty, and so doubt the validity of truth claims in any domain, including morality. Moral relativists note that the empirically documented variations in moral practices across cultures, ethnicities, religions, nationalities, time, and so on are inconsistent with a deontological perspective on ethics: Universal moral principles cannot exist since morality is inevitably embedded in a given context. And, at the extreme, ethical nihilists deny the existence of morality altogether, and in so doing argue that principles that define what is right or wrong are not just arbitrary, but fictive.

The idea that moral judgments are substantially influenced by both the consequences of an action and the consistency of the action with moral principles—the two themes that emerged in our exploratory analysis of individuals' moral beliefs—also resonates with psychological theory and research examining moral thought, emotion, and action. Piaget (1932), for example, in his studies of moral development found that younger children tend to base their moral judgments on the consequences of an action, but older children weight moral principles more when judging themselves and others. Hogan (1973) and Kurtines (1986), distinguish between an "ethics of personal conscience" which is inner-focused and an "ethics of responsibility" which stresses societal regulatory standards that define duties. Kohlberg (1963, 1983), as noted in Chapter 3 in more detail, concentrates on differences in principled thought, but he also notes that most moral dilemmas occur when "acts of obedience to legal-social rules or to commands of authority conflict with the human needs of welfare of other individuals" (1963, p. 12). Indeed, Kohlberg and his colleagues, recognizing the importance of variations in relativism, revised the Moral Judgment Interview they used to measure moral development to not only classify individuals as to stage of development but also degree of relativism within a particular stage (Candee & Kohlberg, 1987).

Measuring Ethics Positions

Our initial findings suggested that some of the marked variation in people's moral judgments could be explained by taking into account their intuitive beliefs about morality and that these beliefs may vary in two basic ways—concern for the consequences of the action (idealism) and the consistency of the action with moral standards (relativism). Encouraged by these findings, we embarked on an admittedly optimistic attempt to develop a measure that could be used to index these two aspects of individuals' moral philosophies. We reviewed the initial items we used in the preliminary index and revised the wording as necessary to clarify their meaning. We then administered the items to new sets of volunteers, each time revising the items in response to participants' questions and after examining each item's relationship to the two underlying concepts. After the sixth iteration we settled on a final set of 20 items, 10 for idealism and 10 for relativism, and named the survey the *Ethics Position Questionnaire*, or EPQ.

The EPQ

The Ethics Position Questionnaire (EPQ) measures individual differences in idealism and relativism. To complete the EPQ, respondents indicate their degree of agreement or disagreement with a series of 20 statements, using a Likert-type scale where 1 indicates strongly disagree, 2 indicates disagree, 3 indicates neutrality, 4 indicates agree, and 5 indicates strongly agree with the statement.[3] Idealism and relativism scores can be calculated by averaging ratings for items 1 to 10 and 11 to 20, respectively. The items are listed in Table 2.1.

TABLE 2.1 The Ethics Position Questionnaire.

	Item
1*	A person should make certain that their actions never intentionally harm another even to a small degree.
2	Risks to another should never be tolerated, irrespective of how small the risks might be.
3*	The existence of potential harm to others is always wrong, irrespective of the benefits to be gained.
4*	One should never psychologically or physically harm another person.
5*	One should not perform an action which might in any way threaten the dignity and welfare of another individual.
6*	If an action could harm an innocent other, then it should not be done.
7	Deciding whether or not to perform an act by balancing the positive consequences of the act against the negative consequences of the act is immoral.
8	The dignity and welfare of people should be the most important concern in any society.
9	It is never necessary to sacrifice the welfare of others.
10	Moral actions are those which closely match ideals of the most "perfect" action.
11	There are no ethical principles that are so important that they should be a part of any code of ethics.
12*	What is ethical varies from one situation and society to another.
13*	Moral standards should be seen as being individualistic; what one person considers to be moral may be judged to be immoral by another person.
14	Different types of moralities cannot be compared as to rightness.
15*	Questions of what is ethical for everyone can never be resolved since what is moral or immoral is up to the individual.
16*	Moral standards are simply personal rules that indicate how a person should behave, and are not to be applied in making judgments of others.
17*	Ethical considerations in interpersonal relations are so complex that individuals should be allowed to formulate their own individual codes.
18	Rigidly codifying an ethical position that prevents certain types of actions could stand in the way of better human relations and adjustment.
19	No rule concerning lying can be formulated; whether a lie is permissible or not permissible totally depends on the situation.
20	Whether a lie is judged to be moral or immoral depends upon the circumstances surrounding the actions.

* Item was included on the short form of the EPQ (EPQ-5).

The EPQ is not a disguised or indirect measure of a hidden psychological quality that individuals may not realize they possess; what the EPQ measures is obvious. People who mostly agree with the items in the idealism scale endorse relatively ardent beliefs about avoiding harm, and those who mostly agree with the items in the relativism score are skeptical about the possibility of formulating moral rules that apply across people, situations, and cultures. Since the average of the scores can range from 1 to 5, scores within the range from 1 to 3 indicate lower levels of idealism and relativism, whereas averages between 3 and 5 indicate higher levels of idealism and relativism. For both scales, about a quarter of the people who have completed the measure score below 3 for both scales, and an equal number above 4 for idealism and above 3.6 for relativism. The average scores on idealism and relativism, based on the responses of 30,230 adults who have completed the EPQ are 3.8 and 3.1, respectively (Forsyth, O'Boyle, & McDaniel, 2008).

Idealism and relativism are complex concepts, so any psychological inventory that purports to measure them should be circumspect in its claims of reliability and validity. To check for internal consistency, we conducted a second factor analysis of the measure, which reaffirmed that the items clustered into two coherent subgroups. We also calculated Cronbach's alpha—an index of strength of the relationships among the items—for both scales, and found that they were sufficient (0.80 and 0.73, respectively). We then administered the scales to a subgroup of respondents not once, but twice, to determine if their scores remained consistent over time. This test-retest reliability was adequate (0.47 for both scales), although only moderate in magnitude. This less-than-desired degree of consistency across time may indicate that the dimensions being assessed are unstable, but variations in the administrative procedures and questionnaire formats used for the two assessments may have influenced their responses. Cohen, Panter, Turan, Morse, and Kim (2014) report the test-retest correlations for idealism and relativism as 0.57 and 0.59.

Refinements and Revisions

The EPQ has been used to study moral judgments in organizations and businesses, schools and hospitals, and research laboratories. The results of these investigations, which are discussed in detail in subsequent chapters, support the convergent and divergent validity of the scale. Relativism, for example, is conceptually similar to Hogan's (1973) distinction between an ethics of conscience and an ethic of responsibility. He developed an instrument, the Survey of Ethical Attitudes (SEA) to assess this dimension, and relativism as measured by the EPQ is correlated, at −0.31, with the SEA. This result confirms the meaning of the relativism scale since low scores on the SEA are indicative of a rejection of societal regulatory standards in favor of an "ethics of personal conscience." Similarly, the idealism scale is related to an "ethic of caring" inventory that included such items as "Morality offers a way of solving conflicts so that no one is hurt" (Forsyth, Nye, & Kelley, 1988). The correlation between idealism and relativism in most samples is almost negligible; for example, −0.07 (Forsyth, 1980), −0.06 (Forsyth et al., 1988), +0.11 (Forsyth et al., 2008), and +0.04 (O'Boyle & Forsyth, 2019).

Since the EPQ's publication, a number of investigators have used exploratory or confirmatory factor analysis to determine if the EPQ measures two, and only two, latent constructs (e.g., Beebe & Guynes, 2006; Bhattacharya, Neelam, & Murthy, 2018; Chen & Liu, 2009; Cornwell et al., 2005; Cui, Mitchell, Schlegelmilch, & Cornwell, 2005; Davis, Andersen, & Curtis, 2001; Forsyth et al., 1988; Güğerçin & Ay, 2017; Johari, Sanusi, & Ismail, 2012; MacNab et al., 2011; Redfern & Crawford, 2004; Stefanidis & Banai, 2014; Stefanidis, Banai, & Richter, 2013; Tansey, Brown, Hyman, & Dawson, 1994; Ural, Gokturk, & Bozoglu, 2017; Vitell & Patwardhan, 2008). These investigations generally confirm the construct validity of the instrument, for the majority of the items cohere into two groups pertaining to idealism and relativism. For example, Tansey et al. (1994), in a study of individual differences in business professionals, found that all "twenty items loaded on the appropriate one of two factors and both factors combined explained 43 percent of the total variance" (p. 70). Similarly, in our re-analysis of the EPQ we found that a two-factor solution explained 42.4 percent of the variance, with idealism items all loading on one factor, and relativism factors loading on the second factor (Forsyth et al., 1988).

Several studies, however, suggested the original EPQ could be improved through additional scaling and psychometric analysis. Some investigators, after administering the EPQ, used only a subset of the 20 items from the full scale to measure idealism and relativism to increase the internal consistency of the scales. They found, for example, that certain items were not highly correlated with the other items, and so by removing those items they achieved higher internal reliability. When we meta-analytically reviewed a set of 83 studies that used the EPQ between 1980 and 2006 with 140 different samples, we identified 25 (18.1%) that used a shortened version of the idealism scale, and 30 (22.9%) that used a shortened version of the relativism scale (Forsyth et al., 2008).

Even more worrisome were several studies that suggested certain items on the EPQ were not closely linked to either idealism or relativism, but instead formed a coherent subcluster within these two domains. For example, MacNab et al. (2011), in a study of physicians in Canada, China, India, Ireland, Japan, and Thailand, reported that the original two-factor model of the EPQ based on idealism and relativism held for all but the Chinese participants. For this group, the EPQ seemed to measure four different aspects of moral thought: minimizing harm, protecting the welfare of others, individual relativism, and cultural relativism. Davis et al. (2001), using confirmatory factor analysis, reported the original two-factor model of idealism and relativism did not provide a good fit for their data (CFI = 0.78). But when they respecified the model, creating a third factor which included the two items from the relativism scale that pertained to lying (veracity), they reported an acceptable level of fit (CFI = 0.91). Güğerçin and Ay (2017) replicated this result, for they too identified a third factor that was separate from idealism and relativism that pertained to the morality of lies and lying.

These findings were reassuring, given they indicated that the EPQ accurately measures individual differences in idealism and moral relativism. However, they suggested that the original questionnaire could be improved to increase its reliability and validity. We therefore revised the original 20-item version of the EPQ, seeking two related, but not entirely compatible, goals. First, to ensure construct fidelity, we reviewed each item's association with one of the two central constructs measured by the EPQ—avoiding harming others (idealism) and skepticism about the usefulness of inviolate, transituational rules when making moral judgments (relativism)—to make certain the revised scale sampled fully the identified construct domains. Second, to maximize the predictive power of the measure, we eliminated any items that were not closely related to the core concepts of idealism or relativism and items that introduced novel elements that were not directly related to those constructs. For example, the majority of the items on the idealism scale emphasize harm-avoidance (items 1, 3, 4, and 6 in Table 2.1). Item 2, however, raises the issue of risk—"risks to another should never be tolerated"—but the word *risk* can mean different things to different people, including uncertainty, hazard, probability, and even danger (Holton, 2004). Likewise, Item 10 suggests one strive to reach the ideal of "perfect action," and makes no mention of harm at all. Among the relativism items, Items 19 and 20 both pertain to a specific moral rule—the prohibition of lying—rather than the usefulness of moral rules in general. Several other items on the relativism scale are similarly narrow in scope or include extraneous content, such as Item 18: "Rigidly codifying an ethical position that prevents certain types of actions could stand in the way of better human relations and adjustment." This item, in addition to using loaded wording ("rigidly codifying") does not pertain to the core focus of the relativism inventory: skepticism regarding moral rules.

After identifying items to review, we then used confirmatory factor analysis of the shortened inventory to verify that the remaining items were closely associated with idealism or relativism. The results of that analysis, shown in Figure 2-1, confirm the adequacy of the revised measure. The EPQ-5 includes items 1, 3, 4, 5, and 6 as measures of idealism, and items 12, 13, 15, 16, and 17 as measures of relativism. Both of the scales are internally consistent (Cronbach alpha = 0.87 and 0.83, respectively) and both correlate with the longer, original measures of idealism and relativism; rs = +0.95 and +0.93, respectively. The instructions and items for the EPQ-5 are included in Appendix A.[4]

A Taxonomy of Ethical Ideologies

Our initial analysis of people's intuitive beliefs about morality—their ethics positions—identified two dimensions of difference. First, some people—idealists—believe that an action, to be moral, should not cause harm. Others, in contrast, are more pragmatic, even more pessimistic, than these idealists: They

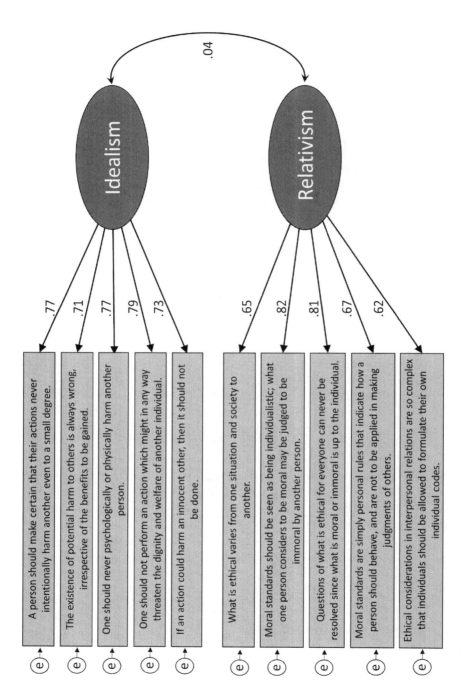

FIGURE 2.1 The factor structure of the EPQ–5.

do not agree that harm can always be avoided, and believe that in some cases positive results require some degree of harm to others. Second, some people—the relativists—take exception to the idea of basing moral judgments on fundamental moral rules that apply across people, situations, and cultural contexts. They do not agree with rule-based moralizers who based their judgments on ethical principles.

These two orientations are consistent, to a degree, with philosophical debates about the relative importance of principles versus consequences when defining what is moral. But ethics position theory does not assume that endorsement of principles as guides to morality requires, psychologically, the rejection of consideration of outcome quality, and vice versa. Individuals can range from high-to-low in their commitment to moral principles (relativism) and low-to-high in their concern for generating positive outcomes and avoiding harm (idealism), so these two aspects of moral thought are not mutually exclusive, either-or positions. Individuals can consider both principles and outcomes, only principles, only outcomes, or neither. The theory, therefore, does not only contrast idealists and pragmatists or relativists and those who are more principled. Instead, the theory assumes that idealism and relativism combine to influence people's moral judgments, actions, and emotions. Two equally idealistic individuals, for example, will not respond in similar ways if they differ in relativism, just as two individuals who are equally relativistic will not respond similarly if they differ in idealism. Just how these two qualities combine is specified in the theory's taxonomy of ethics positions.

Four Positions on Ethics

Ethics position theory is both a dimensional and typological theory. It assumes people range along two continua defined by their degree of idealism and relativism, but it also suggests individuals' positions along each continuum defines their ethical type. By dichotomizing idealism and relativism and crossing these two dimensions, we can identify the four ethics positions or ethical ideologies summarized in Figure 2.2: exceptionism (neither relativistic nor idealistic), subjectivism (relativistic but not idealistic), absolutism (not relativistic but idealistic), and situationism (relativistic and idealistic).

Exceptionists are relatively conventional in their moral orientation. They disagree with statements that suggest morality is purely personal, that universal moral rules do not exist, or that what is ethical varies from one situation and culture to another. But they are not idealistic, either, for they do not believe that harm can always be avoided, that innocent people can always be protected, or that risking other's well-being is always wrong. They were initially labeled exceptionists to indicate that they made exceptions to moral standards when necessary. Such a view corresponds roughly with rule-utilitarianism: a moral theory that suggests compliance with moral standards will generally yield the

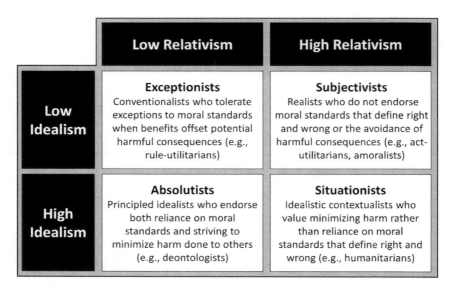

FIGURE 2.2 Four ethics positions as defined by variations in idealism and relativism.

greatest benefit for the greatest number, but that one must also be mindful of the practical demands of any given situation (Brandt, 1959). In hindsight, other labels—conventionalists, realists, conservatives, utilitarians—may more accurately describe the exceptionists.

Subjectivists are skeptical about basing moral judgments on trans-situational and transpersonal rules (high relativism); they agree with such statements as "Questions of what is ethical for everyone can never be resolved since what is moral or immoral is up to the individual." But, like exceptionists, they do not strongly endorse the mandate to "do no harm" (low idealism). Their reluctance to agree with such statements as, "One should never psychologically or physically harm another person," may reflect a level of realism with regards to the possibility of avoiding harm, but may also indicate they have adopted a relatively callous orientation with regards to shielding other people from harm.

This orientation—a rejection of harm-avoidance and universal moral principles—is consistent with several established theories in moral philosophy, including act-utilitarianism, egoism, emotivism, or even moral nihilism. The idealism scale includes items that explicitly reject balancing harm against gaining positive outcomes and subjectivists' disagreement with such items may indicate their utilitarian tendencies, and act-utilitarianism in particular. However, they may also believe that moral decisions are subjective, individualistic judgments that cannot be made on the basis of moral absolutes or consequences, and this view corresponds to an egoistic moral philosophy. This position maintains that no moral judgments can be considered valid except in reference to one's own behavior. The only moral conclusion possible is that all people should act to promote their own self-interest, rather than focus on producing positive outcomes for others. This teleological outlook admits that consequences must be considered when formulating moral judgments, but unlike the more idealistic ethics positions it does not insist that one strive to avoid harming others. Indeed, because each person must determine the weights and values of outcomes obtained, individuals will differ in their moral conclusions.

Absolutists, unlike both the exceptionists and the subjectivists, believe that one should strive to avoid causing harm to other people: They are high rather than low in idealism. They differ from subjectivists, however, because they also believe that people should act in ways that are consistent with moral standards. They endorse a kind of absolutism or universalism, as opposed to moral relativism or skepticism.

Philosophically, absolutism is similar to some, but certainly not all, deontological theories. Its emphasis on moral rules is consistent with Kant's concept of categorical imperatives: exceptionless universal moral principles that can be derived through reason rather than empirical evaluation. Absolutists differ from deontologists who stresses compliance with principles, however, because they react negatively to one specific consequence: harm. Kant, for example, famously argued that one must always tell the truth, even if the truth will cause innocent others to be harmed. If, for example, a friend of yours is fleeing from a murderer you can provide them with refuge in your house. But if the murderer asks you, "Is your friend hiding in your house?" you have no right, even in this instance, to lie to the murderer (Kant, 1873/1973). Absolutists, then, are not Kantians per se, but they instead are more similar to deontological consequentialists (e.g., Cummisky, 1996). These rule-consequentialists favor acting to promote the greatest good, but they also recognize that telling the truth, acting in a fair and just way, keeping promises, and so on are intrinsically good. Deontology, after all, is not just the study of principles, but the study of one's duties or obligations, as defined by standards, contracts, social position, and so on. For absolutists, avoiding harm is a duty.

Situationists do not believe that moral standards provide a bright line between what is morally good and bad (relativism), but instead base their moral judgments on the quality of the outcomes produced in a given situation and not the extent to which rules that traditionally define what is morally good or bad are violated or observed. They are humanitarian in their orientation— they are committed to promoting human well-being—but also skeptical about strictly adhering to traditional conceptions of morality. Their personal ethical ideologies are consistent, therefore, with skeptical philosophies of ethics such as Fletcher's (1966) situation ethics and James' (1891/1973) value pluralism. Fletcher argued that an action, to be moral, must be appropriate given the particular context; not necessarily good or right, but the fitting. James's value pluralism maintained that few actions can be judged a priori, for an action that minimizes harm or avoids it altogether is far more praiseworthy than an action that matches accepted canons of morality but yields little in the way of positive consequences. James (1891/1973, p. 157) believed that:

> In point of fact there are no absolute evils, and there are no non-moral goods; and the highest ethical life—however few may be called to bear its burdens—consists at all times in the breaking of rules which have grown too narrow for the actual case.

Classifying and Contrasting Ethics Positions

The ethics position theory typology classifies people into one of four categories; it assumes individuals in a category share certain features in common and that those features distinguish them from other types of individuals. The moral types are qualitatively different from one another and, to some extent, mutually exclusive. However, ethics position theory is a modal multidimensional species type of classification system (Buss & Poley, 1976), so one of the usual assumptions of typologies—that individuals in different categories are distinct from one another—does not apply to ethics position theory. Those classified as absolutists, for example, cannot also be situationists, but the two groups nonetheless share a common quality—a high level of idealism.

Theories that propose such typologies face unique methodological and empirical challenges. The primary methodological question asks: How can individuals be classified into each ethics position? With dimensional theories, in particular, it is necessary to identify some point along the continuum that marks the transition from one type to another. One approach, commonly used in self-report surveys, uses the response categories themselves to set the cut-point. Individuals are asked, directly, if they agree or disagree with the items on the EPQ, so those who agree with the items on each subscale—their average response is above the neutral point of 3.0—can be considered to be high idealists and high relativists, and those who disagree, on average, with the items are low idealists and low relativists. A data-centered approach, in contrast, bases the cut-point on the distribution of idealism and relativism in the sample or population. Individuals who are high in idealism, for example, score in the top one or two quartiles of the distribution, and those who are low in idealism score in the lower one or two quartiles. Neither approach, however, can satisfactorily classify individuals whose scores place them very near the cut-point itself. Those individuals with scores of 3.0 or ones that are close to the median score of the sample are difficult to classify into any of the types identified in the theory.

These two approaches would yield similar results if the median of the scales fell at the neutral point—neither agree nor disagree—of the response scale, but in most previous studies the data show a slight negative skew (e.g., Idealism,

$N = 2778$, $M = 3.83$, $sd = 0.76$, skewness $= -0.63$; Relativism, $N = 2778$, $M = 3.22$, $sd = 0.72$, skewness $= -0.30$). This skewness may occur because more people are idealistic and relativistic rather than pragmatic and principled, but it may also result from social desirability response bias. Both relativism and idealism scores are correlated, to a degree, with people's tendency to respond in a way which they believe others will accept as appropriate or desirable (Forsyth, 1980). In consequence, the scores on both scales may be slightly elevated.

The primary empirical problem concerns classification itself: Does the theory accurately describe distinct types that differ not just in degree, but in kind? Do people adopt one of four different types of ethics positions, and do their answers to the EPQ provide a clear indication of their position? The idea of distinct ethics positions, although a logical derivation from the theory's modal multidimensional specification of types, may not correspond to the natural groups that exist within the population. Rather than four categories, people may naturally cluster into fewer categories, more categories, or no categories at all. Although people vary in idealism and relativism, this variation may be so extensive that no natural categories exist at all. Individuals may vary from high-to-low in idealism and relativism along a continuum that should not be parsed into segments.

Fortunately, researchers have developed a number of statistical procedures to identify clusters of individuals within a more general population, including Bayesian expectation maximization algorithms, cluster analysis, latent class modeling, and taxonometric procedures (Waller & Meehl, 1998). When we applied one of these methods, hierarchical cluster analysis (HCA), to classify a large group of individuals who had completed the EPQ online, the results supported the ethics position theory's taxonometric approach. We first classified each individual, a priori, into one of the four ethics positions using the median of the distribution as the cut-point. We then used HCA (Ward's technique) to identify naturally existing subgroups within this sample. We next compared the four-group classification generated through cluster analysis with the a priori classification of individuals based on their ethics positions. The two classifications matched for over 90% of the cases. Most of the disagreements between the two classifications pertained to positions that are low in idealism—exceptionists were sometimes classified as subjectivists, and subjectivists as exceptionists.[5]

These findings offer empirical support for the classification of people into types based on their responses to the EPQ, but the theoretical implications and practical considerations of a taxonometric approach remain to be explored. The approach is consistent with ethic position theory's assumption that individuals develop distinctive ethical ideologies, and ideologies are, at least theoretically, discrete rather than dimensional; they are coherent belief systems that summarize a personal and socially shared understanding of some aspect of the interpersonal world—in this case, ethics (van Dijk, 1998). Classification, too, provides a way of describing how idealism and relativism combine to influence moral judgments. Ethics position theory identifies three possible relationships between ethical ideology and moral judgments: (a) Idealism influences moral judgment; (b) relativism influences moral judgment and; (c) idealism and relativism interact with one another to influence moral judgment. A modal multidimensional classification approach takes all three types of relationships, including the interaction, into account.

Dichotomization of variables that may be continuous rather than discrete is not without its limitations, however. A degree of precision in the assessment is reduced when individuals are classified as just low or high in idealism and relativism, particularly when the number of individuals who have mid-range scores is substantial. Those individuals who are numerically very similar to one another but on opposite sides of the cut-point will be classified as more different than they actually are. Dichotomization, too, is problematic when the relationship between variables is not a linear one or is so subtle that it will only be detected by maximizing the statistical power of the analysis. This loss of power to detect associations due to the reduction in variance in variables is one reason why dichotomizing continuous variables is often described as a "bad idea" (Royston, Altman, & Sauerbrei, 2006, p. 127). Therefore, alternative approaches, including the use of such statistical approaches as moderated multiple regression, should be used to supplement analyses that are based on the four ethical types.

Individual Differences in Ethical Thought

It's paradoxical. Two individuals who agree when discussing religion, art, literature, and so on can still manage to reach opposite conclusions when a moral judgment is to be made. Ethics position theory, in seeking to explain this paradox, suggests that this variance occurs because people differ in their philosophical stances regarding ethical issues, and that the position they take will influence the judgments they reach. Nearly everyone believes that morally good people avoid acting in ways that harm others and that they comply with their culture's ethical standards, but they nonetheless vary to a degree in their commitment to these two fundamentals.

Two different kinds of evidence lend support to this claim. First, exploratory analysis of people's moral beliefs identified two themes pertaining to harm and moral principles, and these themes and the moral types they describe were consistent with the major philosophical schools of ethical thought. At the very least, the theory seems to adequately describe variations in the ethical reasoning displayed by philosophers, and hence may also describe the ethical ideologies of lay persons who must find answers to ethical questions. Second, harm and principles are consistent themes in cognitive, development, and social psychological analyses of morality.

Once this premise is introduced, a means of accurately and reliably measuring these variations is needed. This chapter described that process, for it reviewed the development of the Ethics Position Question (EPQ). Although a comparatively simple way to measure morality—people are just asked to indicate their degree of agreement with a series of questions about avoiding harm and moral relativism—the data suggest that the EPQ possesses adequate psychometric properties, including moderately high internal consistency, reliability over time, and only small correlations with a measure of social desirability. In addition, confirmatory factor analyses and cluster analyses attest to the accuracy of the EPQ's meaning.

What remains to be done, then, is the testing of the predictive validity of the theory and its measure. One source of possible differences in moral thought was identified and operationalized, but these results only set the stage for subsequent investigations of individual differences in moral thought, emotion, and action. These studies, and their findings, are examined in subsequent chapters—beginning with work that compares the ethics position theories to other psychological theories of morality in developmental, personality, and social psychology.

Notes

1. As Milgram himself suggested, people's moral reactions to his work were influenced by the findings themselves. Milgram (1964, p. 849) asked if the ethical outcry was "based as much on the unanticipated findings as on the method? The findings were that some subjects performed in what appeared to be a shockingly immoral way. If, instead, every one of the subjects had broken off at 'slight shock' or at the first sign of the learner's discomfort, the results would have been pleasant, reassuring, and who would protest?" By experimentally manipulating the results of his study—some participants were told obedience levels were high but others were told that few obeyed—we confirmed Milgram's prediction. People judged the research to be more threatening and less moral the greater the obedience. We concluded Milgram was "at least partially correct in his feelings of 'victimization' at the hands of his own subjects" (Schlenker & Forsyth, 1977, p. 392).
2. The thread that ties all the idealism items together—avoid actions that could be harmful to others—is consistent with a type of consequentialism that is sometimes labeled negative utilitarianism. This perspective was noted by G. E. Moore (1903) in *Principia Ethica*, where he discussed the challenges faced when attempting to reconcile positive outcomes, such as pleasure and happiness, with negative outcomes, such as suffering and death. Karl Popper (1945/1994, p. 602), too, raises the problem in *The Open Society and Its Enemies*, when he writes "there is, from the ethical point of view, no symmetry between suffering and happiness, or between pain and pleasure. . . . In my opinion human suffering makes a direct moral appeal, namely, the appeal for help, while there is no similar call to increase the happiness of a man who is doing well anyway. . . . Instead of the greatest happiness for the greatest number, one should demand, more modestly, the least amount of avoidable suffering for all."
3. The EPQ originally used a nine-point scale that ranged from completely disagree to completely agree but other versions have used five- and seven-point scales. Meta-analytic review of variations in scale length did not reveal any systematic differences between longer and short response formats (Forsyth et al., 2008).

4. We conducted a confirmatory factor analysis to examine the responses of respondents who completed the survey online; $N = 10{,}945$, $\chi^2 = 695.46$, $df = 34$. The two-factor model's fit was excellent, as indicated by the following goodness-of-fit indicators: RMSEA = 0.042 (root mean square error of approximation), CFI = .985 (comparative fix index), SMRM = 0.038 (standardized root mean square residual), and NNFI = .985 (non-normed fit index).

5. Ward's hierarchical cluster analysis uses an agglomerative algorithm that calculates similarities, based on Euclidian distances, between possible clusters. It initially classifies the most similar persons into clusters, and then at each subsequent step identifies those individuals who are most similar to those clusters. The final step in the algorithm combines all clusters. Inspection of the magnitude of the squared Euclidean distances between the clusters combined in the final 12 steps in this process suggested that a four-cluster solution best fit the data because the magnitude of the Euclidian distances remained relatively constant as clusters are combined into fewer and fewer clusters until four clusters are combined into three. This step generated the largest acceleration of distance growth—indicating a substantial loss of specificity if clusters were combined.

3

MEASURED MORALITY

All morality consists in a systems of rules, and the essence of all morality is to be
sought for in the respect which the individual acquires for these rules.

—Jean Piaget (1932/1960, p. 13)

Complex phenomena often resist the limits of any single theoretical explanation, and moral judgment is no exception. Of the many theories that seek to
explain the processes that sustain moral thought, the four most prominent ones
are Kohlberg's (1983) cognitive developmental theory, Gilligan's (1982) ethic
of caring, Schwartz's (1992) theory of human values, and Haidt's (2012) moral
foundations theory. Cognitive developmental theory draws on moral philosophy to identify key stages in people's capacity to understand and resolve moral
conflicts. The ethic of care maintains that some individuals make moral decisions only after considering the harm their choice may have for other people.
Value theory identifies the motives and preferences that are the basis of evaluations of relative worth, and includes such core values as benevolence and tradition. Moral foundations theory argues moral judgments are guided by a set
of moral intuitions pertaining to care, fairness, loyalty, authority, and sanctity.
Each of these theories is similar in some ways to ethics position theory, but different in others.

* * *

No one explanation of morality has yet to gain widespread acceptance among
philosophers and psychologists who study the complexities of ethics. Some philosophers trace morality to the virtues exhibited by the very best among us,
including courage, temperance, and wisdom. Deontologists equate the moral

good with the morally principled. Utilitarians consider consequences when distinguishing between the good and bad, seeking to maximize the positive and minimize the negative. But the list continues: Egoists put self-interest at the center of their analysis, natural rights theorists link morality to respect for the universal privileges of all people, contractarians invoke the principle of presumed obligations to explain stable social exchanges, religious authorities turn to scripture as the ultimate authority on moral questions, and on and on.

Psychological analyses of morality, too, are equally numerous and equally debated (Giammarco, 2016). Ethics position theory traces variations in moral thought, emotion, and action to people's beliefs about consequences and the dictates of ethical principles but this theory is only one among many. In the 1960s and 70s, Lawrence Kohlberg (1963)—following a line of inquiry begun by the developmental psychologist Jean Piaget (1932/1960)—suggested that people's conception of morality changes as they progress through a series of developmental stages. In the 1980s, a second voice was heard in discussions of the psychology of morality: Carol Gilligan (1982), in her book, *In a Different Voice*, proposed that ethics is as much about relationships and interpersonal responsibilities as it is about rights and rules. Beginning in the 1990s Shalom Schwartz (1992, 2014) and his colleagues worked to identify the values that are recognized the world over, and the result is a comprehensive theory that organizes these motivationally distinct values based on their dynamic interdependencies. And in the 2000s, Jonathan Haidt (2001, 2012) and his colleagues proposed that morality and variations in morality stem from differences in people's valuing of five moral fundamentals: care/harm, fairness/cheating, loyalty/betrayal, authority/subversion, and sanctity/degradation. Here we review these four foundational approaches to the psychology of morality and compare them to ethics position theory.

Cognitive Moral Development

The cognitive-developmental approach to the dynamics of human maturation is one of the most influential theoretical perspectives on human development, in general, and moral development in particular. Cognitive-developmental theorists, such as Piaget (1932/1960) and Kohlberg (1963), shared a common focus on organism-environment interaction that results in the development of increasingly sophisticated cognitive structures and processes. This interaction leads to cognitive stages of development, which represent the restructuring of cognitive schemata into increasingly complex structures in a metastatic process. These cognitive changes reshape children's capacity to think and reason, and with these transformations come changes in how they make judgments about right and wrong. Whereas young children's moral thought is literal and egoistic, as people grow older they acquire the capacity to think about moral issues in cognitively sophisticated ways.

Piaget on Moral Thought

Piaget (1932/1960), the preeminent developmental psychologist, described with care the increasing complexity of children's morality as they developed the capacity to think theoretically and abstractly. Piaget theorized that the evolution of moral judgment in the child progresses through two major cognitive-developmental stages. He labeled the first stage moral heteronomy, drawing on Kant's (1785/2018) distinction between acting in accord with one's self-generated principles (autonomy) and compliance with external principles that define duty and responsibility (heteronomy). Heteronomous thought occurs when the child believes that what is good is obedience to adult's standards whereas acting in ways that are consistent with one's own desires and interests is wrong. The young child's intuitive moral philosophy is an absolutist one that brooks no possibility of a relativistic conception of ethics. Good is defined as conformity to moral standards, which are to be obeyed and not judged, questioned, or challenged. Moral judgments of others are based not on "the motive that prompted them, but in terms of their exact conformity to established rules" (Piaget, 1932/1960, pp. 111–112).

Gradually, increases in cognitive capabilities shift moral judgment to a higher stage. This shift is the result of a number of processes, particularly the reduction of egocentrism and the replacement of the morality of constraint with the morality of cooperation. The decrease in egocentrism is the result of a growth in cognitive ability which occurs as children shift their cognitive perspective to construe situations from other people's perspectives (Selman & Byrne, 1974; Wainryb, Brehl, & Matwin, 2005). The morality of cooperation, which subsumes the ideals of mutual respect for others in reciprocity governed interaction, is generated through egalitarian interactions with peers resulting in the internalization of rules and the reasons for their importance. In the children Piaget studied, this shift occurred between the years of seven and nine, and culminated in the attainment of the second stage of moral development, moral autonomy. Moral rules are no longer viewed as static and externally generated, but are internalized and modified in response to situational demands. The child's behaviors are governed by the adult morality of cooperation, so that behaviors are engaged in for their own sake and not because of contingent sanctions. Rules are seen as necessary for the maintenance of cooperation, but may be changed by mutual agreement.

Kohlberg's Stages of Moral Development

Kohlberg, like Piaget, believed that "age developmental trends in moral judgment have a formal cognitive base parallel to the structural base of cognitive development" (Kohlberg, 1969, p. 390). He investigated moral development by asking children of various ages to make judgments about people caught up in morally challenging situations. One of the best known of his dilemmas, involving a dutiful husband named Heinz, his desperately ill wife, and an entrepreneurial druggist, pitted the duty to preserve life against the moral prohibition of theft (Kohlberg, 1963, pp. 18–19):

> In Europe, a woman was near death from a special kind of cancer. There was one drug that the doctors thought might save her. It was a form of radium that a druggist in the same town had recently discovered. The drug was expensive to make, but the druggist was charging ten times what the drug cost him to make. He paid $200 for the radium and charged $2000 for a small dose of the drug. The sick woman's husband, Heinz, went to everyone he knew to borrow the money, but he could only get together about $1000 which is half of what it cost. He told the druggist that his wife was dying and asked him to sell it cheaper or let him pay later. But the druggist said: "No, I discovered the drug and I'm going to make money from it." So Heinz got desperate and broke into the man's store to steal the drug for his wife. Should the husband have done that?

Kohlberg's work led him to identify three distinct levels of cognitive development, and two distinct substages of development within each level. At the preconventional level, obedience to authority is stressed for hedonistic reasons such as maximization of personal gains or avoidance of punishment. Stage one thinkers accept without question imposed rules of conduct without interpreting their fairness or biases. Stage two thinkers shift toward self-interest, with personal gains valued more than the consideration of the needs of others. The hallmark of the second level, conventional thought, is conformity. Individuals who have reached this level of development strive to act in accordance with social norms, which they explicitly endorse. Stage three individuals seek social approval by careful conformity to socially defined ideals that prescribe and proscribe conduct. Kohlberg notes that intentionality affects responsibility delegations at this stage, but that too much emphasis is sometimes placed on motives, with the result that prosocial intentions can be cited as mitigating excuses for a careless act. Stage four is typified by increasing emphasis on authority and social order. At this stage "right behavior consists of doing one's duty, showing respect for authority, and maintaining the given social order for its own sake" (Kohlberg, 1968, p. 26).

The final level, postconventional or autonomous thought, moves toward increasing independence and away from obedience to existing societal impositions. Behavior is guided by inner principles, which may or may not be consistent with the personal dictates of one's moral community. Stage five morality is deontological, but with a degree of relativism as moral standards are not held to be inviolate and hence may be altered. Stage six morality emphasizes respect for others as individuals, for the equality of all, and of justice as equity, with behavior being guided by individually derived moral principles held by the individual to be comprehensive, logically consistent, and universally applicable (Krebs & Denton, 2005).

Measuring Cognitive Moral Development

Researchers have developed several methods for assessing individuals' cognitive moral development. Kohlberg, consistent with his initial methods, asked respondents to judge the morality of individuals facing a moral dilemma with no easily recognized solution. In addition to the Heinz dilemma, Kohlberg's Moral Judgment Interview (MJI) included vignettes involving a father who wishes to confiscate his son's hard-earned savings and two brothers who both steal money from others through outright theft or by bold deceit. An interviewer, using Kohlberg's scoring procedures, is to classify the 50 to 150 moral expostulations of the interviewee as representative of one of the 180 cells (30 dimensions by six stages) of the classification system. The results can then be summarized in terms of a global score of moral development or by a profile analysis which reports the number of responses at each stage (Colby & Kohlberg, 1987).

Most investigations of the theory, however, assess individual differences in cognitive moral development with Rest's (1979, 1983, 1986) Defining Issues Test (DIT). Respondents read a series of moral dilemmas and for each one indicate a preference for or the importance of statements representative of Kohlberg's stages. For example, after reading the Heinz dilemma, respondents indicate the importance of such statements as "Whether or not a community's laws are going to be upheld," "Isn't it only natural for a loving husband to care so much for his wife that he'd steal?," "What values are going to be the basis for governing human interactions?," and so on (Rest, Cooper, Coder, Masanz, & Anderson, 1974, pp. 493–494). Participants rate each item as to its importance and rank the four most important statements they believe determine "what ought to be done" (p. 494). Rest recommends the use of the P-score measure from the DIT, which is the sum of responses to those items indicative of post-conventional morality (stages five and six).

Researchers have confirmed the reliability and validity of the DIT as a measure of cognitive moral development (Rest, Narvaez, Bebeau, & Thoma, 1999). The developmental trends in scores are consistent with the prediction that children's moral thinking becomes more sophisticated over time, for levels two, three, and four decrease with age and P-scores increase. Scores on the DIT are highly correlated ($r = +0.68$) with morality scores from Kohlberg's MJI (global scoring method). DIT scores increase as individuals' understanding of morality increases, whether that gain is due to maturation, education, or a moral education intervention. Scores on the DIT are associated with other indicators of morality, such as certain forms of prosocial behavior and attitudes pertaining to social justice issues.

Ethics Positions and Moral Development

Kohlberg's cognitive developmental theory and ethics position theory are similar in that both seek to explain the puzzle of variability in people's moral judgments. Both draw extensively on moral philosophy by suggesting that people are, in a sense, intuitive moral philosophers. As Kohlberg (1968) explained in his article titled, "The Child as Moral Philosopher," people develop increasingly sophisticated cognitive schemas that allow them to resolve conflicts between roles, values, and social demands. Both models assume that morality serves to promote cooperation and minimize conflict, and that the most challenging moral situations—ones that pose true dilemmas for people trying to make the more moral judgment or choice—occur when traditional rules or norms pertaining to ethics are at odds with aspects of the situation that could cause others to be harmed in some way. Both, too, are primarily cognitive models of moral judgment, for they assume that the judgments of some individuals are guided by a deliberate and rational review of the relevant issues. For Kohlberg, morally mature people are principled: "Genuinely moral orientations tend to be linked to moral principles and it is moral principles which give rise to concepts of moral rationality" (1958, pp. 13–14). Similarly, ethics position theory recognizes that absolutists and exceptionists, more so than the relativistic situationists and subjectivists, rely on principles when making moral judgments.[1]

The two theories differ, however, in theoretical orientation, emphases, and assessment strategies. Kohlberg's theory takes a developmental approach. In consequence, Kohlberg ranks different moralities in terms of their sophistication and moral maturity. Ethics position theory does not consider any ethics position as more cognitively mature than another. The theories, too, differ in their emphasis on value-based principles of morality. According to cognitive moral development theory, individuals who explain their moral choices in terms of trust, respect, reciprocity, responsibility, duty, and even guilt are considered to be more morally mature than individuals whose choices are not guided by these specific principles, but ethics position theory is agnostic with regards to the specific content of individual's principles. Ethics position theory, too, stresses harm as the basis for variations in idealism, whereas Kohlberg's theory incorporates multiple social values, including justice, reciprocity, and fairness. Studies of the two theories also measure variations in moral judgment using different methods: One uses a story approach to tap respondents' reactions to hypothetical situations and the other asks individuals to indicate their degree of agreement with meta-ethical statements that pertain to idealism and relativism.

These theoretical and methodological differences explain why, for the most part, researchers who have measured both cognitive moral development using the DIT and individuals' ethics positions using the Ethics Position

Questionnaire (EPQ) have found little relationship between an individuals' moral maturity and their ethics position or their scores on the idealism and relativism scales (Cohen, Panter, Turan, Morse, & Kim, 2014; Forsyth, 1978; Ho, Vitell, Barnes, & Desborde, 1997; Ishida, 2006; Lawrence & Shaub, 1997). The correlation between idealism and P-scores on the DIT was -0.10 in one study (Ho et al., 1997), but negligible in others. Two studies do report a small, negative correlation between relativism and P-score (Cohen et al., 2014; Ishida, 2006), but others do not. Moreover, when we classified people into Stages 3 through 6 using the DIT and into one of the four ethics positions, analysis of the joint frequency distribution revealed no significant relation between the two measures (Forsyth, 1978). One researcher (Ishida, 2006) did find some evidence that absolutists—who are highly idealistic but not relativistic—have higher P-scores than the relativistic situationists, but other researchers have not replicated this result.

These findings support a tentative conclusion: An individual who displays post-conventional moral reasoning as classified by Kohlberg's stage approach could endorse any one of the four moral orientations identified by ethics position theory. Principled thought is the hallmark of conventional and post-conventional thought, and so relativists may be less likely to be classified as conventional thinkers compared to less relativistic individuals, but at the higher stages of Kohlberg's model—stages five and six—individuals' moral reliance on principles must be based on their individual acceptance of the rules rather than compliance with social standards. Such an outlook is consistent with relativism's emphasis on moral rules as personal, rather than transpersonal guidelines. As Rest and his colleagues (1999) explain, an individual who has reached the postconventional stage of moral reasoning realizes that "laws, roles, codes, and contracts are all social arrangements that can be set up in a variety of ways. Tradition, law, religious codes, or existing social practice prescribe certain behaviors. But solely the fact that these are the de facto arrangements does not entail that a person ought to behave in those way" (p. 306).

Kohlberg's cognitive developmental theory, too, emphasizes how individuals make their moral choices rather than the nature of the choices they make. Although some moral positions—ones that violate universal principles of justice, benevolence, and duty—may not fare well in terms of moral maturity when examined within Kohlberg' framework, any one of the approaches that define the four ethics positions could qualify as postconventional moralities. All the ideologies of the EPQ do, in a sense, accept certain principles, which can be distilled down to nothing more than "Cause no harm to others," "There are moral absolutes," "Look to the specifics of the given situation," and "Consider the action from your own viewpoint." Although the content of the principles determines the individual's ideology, the reasons for accepting the principles determine their stage of moral development.

In a Different Voice

Kohlberg deftly integrated theory and research findings from personality, social, and developmental psychology with moral philosophy to build a scientifically influential explanation for variations in moral judgments. But one of his colleagues, Carol Gilligan (1982), challenged a key assumption of his theory: its tendency to equate morality and justice. For Kohlberg (1969), morality is about legal and moral rules, fairness, rights of individuals and authorities, reciprocity, and distributive justice. The concept of justice, as he wrote in his dissertation, "helps concretize the concept of the moral by delimiting situations and attitudes to which or criteria of the moral may be applicable" (1958, p. 15). But Gilligan, in her own studies of people's explanations of the judgments they made when confronted with moral issues, explained that she heard a "different voice;" one that spoke not of justice, but of "an injunction to care, a responsibility to discern and alleviate the 'real and recognizable trouble' of this world" (Gilligan, 1982, p. 100).

An Ethic of Care

Gilligan suggested that Kohlberg's myopic focus was a consequence of the people he initially interviewed and his reliance on moral vignettes to structure his research. As he developed his theory, Kohlberg conducted a series of interviews with boys and young men, but he included very few girls and young women in his initial studies. Gilligan, in contrast, discussed issues of morality with both boys and girls, and as a result she drew conclusions that differed from Kohlberg's. Moreover, Gilligan and her colleagues eschewed reliance on people's reflections about hypothetical moral dilemmas, such as a husband's decision to steal a drug for his wife or a son's reaction to his father's theft of his savings. When researchers used Kohlberg's dilemmas to study the moral development of both boys and girls, they initially discovered that girls progressed up Kohlberg's scale of moral development more slowly than boys. But when Gilligan asked girls and boys to discuss moral issues they face in their own everyday lives and relationships, these sex differences disappeared or even reversed: "Hypothetical dilemmas, in the abstraction of their presentation, divest moral actors from the history and psychology of their individual lives and separate the moral program from the social contingencies of its possible occurrence" (Gilligan, 1982, p. 100).

Gilligan identified and contrasted two approaches to ethics in her work: an ethic of justice and an ethic of caring. She argued a morality based on justice, such as rights and duties, solves problems when individuals compete with others for resources, authority, and privileges, and so underscores individuality and the dispassionate application of moral rules. A morality based on caring, in contrast, solves problems created by interdependence, including maintaining and strengthening relationships, protecting and valuing others, and identifying ways to achieve mutually beneficial outcomes. Both ethics create obligations and respect for others, but through different routes. An ethic of justice creates obligations to principles, but an ethic of caring creates obligations to people and to relationships; an ethic of justice requires respect for principles, whereas an ethic of caring requires respect for other people. Moral problems, then, are not solved only through the impersonal review of the facts of the immediate situation, but interpersonal means, including sharing of viewpoints, empathizing with others, and exploring everyone's feelings. In consequence, morality arises "from the experience of connection and conceived as a problem of inclusion rather than one of balancing claims" (Gilligan, 1982, p. 160) and assumes that "inflicting hurt is considered selfish and immoral in its reflection of unconcern, while the expression of care is seen as the fulfillment of moral responsibility" (Gilligan, 1982, p. 73).

Ethics Positions and an Ethic of Caring

Gilligan's ethic of care and ethics position theory are similar in that both identify harm as one of the primary bases of moral thought and conduct. When individuals adopt an ethic of caring, they base their judgments and actions on their relationships with, and responsibilities to, other individuals. That ethic requires preventing, when possible, harm to others, and promoting their welfare by reducing their physical and psychological suffering. As one of Gilligan's respondents explained, "I personally don't want to hurt other people. That's a real criterion, a main criterion for me. . . . Not hurting others is important in my own private morals" (1982, p. 65). Similarly, individuals who take idealistic ethics positions—the absolutists and situationists—also emphasize the importance of avoiding causing harm to others in their descriptions of the moral viewpoint. When they complete the EPQ they endorse such statements as, "A person should make certain that their actions never intentionally harm another even to a small degree."

We examined the relationship between Gilligan's ethic of caring and ethics position theory's idealism by developing a brief self-report measure of Gilligan's ethic of caring (Forsyth, Nye, & Kelley, 1988). We based the items on the interviews Gilligan (1982) presents in her book, *In a Different Voice*. The items, which are listed in Table 3.1, dealt with such issues as responsibility to others, moral obligations, conflict resolution, selflessness, and caring for other people.

We averaged the items in Table 3.1 to create an overall index of individuals' endorsement of an ethic of caring.[2] As expected, individuals who expressed a stronger endorsement of an ethic of caring also tended to be idealistic ($r = +0.53$), and all of the individual items on the caring scale were correlated with the idealism—although they ranged in magnitude from +0.19 to +0.52. Moreover, relativism and an ethic of caring were also correlated, albeit much less

TABLE 3.1 Ethics of Caring Scale Items and their Correlations with the Idealism and Relativism Scales of the EPQ.

Item	Idealism	Relativism
Moral people strive to live in harmony with others.	0.26	−0.09
Morality is based on each person's responsibility to others.	0.29	0.03
We all are morally obligated to make the world a better place to live in.	0.40	0.01
Morality offers a way of solving conflicts so that no one is hurt.	0.52	−0.08
In moral solutions to conflicts, everyone benefits.	0.39	−0.14
Morality is based on responsibility to people.	0.30	0.04
Moral people are unselfish.	0.30	−0.34
We are morally responsible to other people.	0.34	−0.12
Morality means caring for other people.	0.34	−0.06
Moral actions sometimes require self-sacrifice.	0.19	−0.05

substantially ($r = -0.13$). In this case, however, the relationship was inverse: Relativistic individuals tended to be less likely to endorse an ethic of caring.

We further explored the relationship between an ethic of caring and the EPQ by classifying respondents into one of the four ethics position theory categories. Absolutists scored higher than all other groups, including the other idealistic group: the situationists. The situationists, however, had higher scores on the ethic of caring that the two low-idealism groups—who did not differ from one another. These differences suggest that those who expressed the strongest commitment to an ethic of caring were also slightly less relativistic. They were, therefore, more likely to be absolutists than situationists.

Men, Women, and Morality

Gilligan's ethic of caring theory was initially rooted in presumed differences between the sexes when making moral judgments. As Gilligan explains, her theoretical insights were "sparked initially by listening to women. The paradigm shift began with the recognition that empathy and caring are human strengths. The 'different voice' had been heard as 'feminine' because emotions and relationships were associated with women and seen as limiting their capacity for rationality and autonomy" (Gilligan, 2014, p. 89). Her work therefore suggested that men and women would likely differ in moral reasoning, as the sexes tend to define morality differently, but also because they make decisions differently. As Gilligan explains:

> Women's place in man's life-cycle has been that of nurturer, caretaker, and helpmate, the weaver of those networks of relationships on which

she in turn relies. But while women have thus taken care of men, men have, in their theories of psychological development, as in their economic arrangements, tended to assume or devalue care. When the focus on individuation and individual achievement extends into adulthood and maturity is equated with personal autonomy, concern with relationships appears as a weakness of women rather than as a human strength.

(Gilligan, 1982, p. 17)

Subsequent studies of men and women have confirmed what Gilligan suspected: women are, in general, higher in relationality than men—their values, attitudes, and outlooks emphasize and facilitate establishing and maintaining connections to others (Gore & Cross, 2006). Women expect more reciprocity and loyalty in their relationships as well as intimacy, solidarity, and companionship (Hall, 2011). However, Gilligan's second prediction—that these differences in relationality would manifest in differences in men's and women's morality—has not fared as well empirically. Although Kohlberg initially reported differences in moral development for men and women in his research, as he improved through revision his interview-based measures of morality, the sex differences he originally noted faded (Colby et al., 1987). Other investigations sometimes reported the sexes differed, but these differences were not consistent nor robust. Meta-analytic reviews suggest that the sexes differ to a degree, but the differences are not substantial ones. Walker (1984, 1991), in his meta-analysis of 79 studies that used Kohlberg's interview method to measure moral reasoning, reported only a slight difference between the sexes' overall level of moral maturity. Thoma (1986), when he examined 56 samples that assessed both men and women's morality using the DIT, reported that women outscored men, but only slightly. Jaffee and Hyde (2000) identified over a hundred studies that measured people's level of care orientation or justice orientation. Their analysis indicated that women scored higher in caring than men, and men were more likely to adopt a justice orientation relative to women—but, again, the difference was not so substantial that results indicate the ethical thought of women is uniquely focused on caring relative to men.

In the only study in which we directly measured respondents' endorsement of an ethic of care, we did not find men and women differed (Forsyth et al., 1988). We did, however, find support for Gilligan's prediction of a sex difference when we compared men's and women's responses to EPQ in a relatively large sample: 11,409 adults. To carry out this test, we relied on data gathered at the online survey site YourMorals (see Graham et al., 2011). Individuals who visit this site can complete a number of measures related to ethics, including the EPQ. They also provide background information about themselves, such as their gender, political orientation, country of origin, and so on. When we compared the responses of the women and men who completed the EPQ, we discovered the women's average scores for both idealism and relativism were higher than the men's scores. In consequence, when classified into one of the four ethics positions described in ethics position theory, more of the women were absolutists and situationists, whereas men were more likely to be exceptionists. Chapter 4 discusses these sex differences in more detail in its analysis of demographic differences in idealism and relativism, but in sum: they suggest women are more likely to base their moral judgments on the potential harm that may result from an action (idealism)—just as Gilligan predicted.

A Theory of Basic Human Values

Philosophical and psychological explanations for why some people are consistently generous, cooperative, and caring rather than selfish, cruel, and harmful inevitably make their way to differences in values. Plato, for example, valued justice, beauty, truth, and certain *aretê* (virtues) because they contributed to happiness and well-being. He maintained that his ranking of these qualities was based on objectively knowable facts, and that anyone who did not prize these values would likely act wrongly out of ignorance. Aristotle was less certain of the facticity of values, but he nonetheless based his theory of virtues on them. He valued courage over cowardice, friendliness over cantankerousness, wit over dullness, pride over vanity and his theory continues to influence ethicists' conception of character and moral strengths (Dahlsgaard, Peterson, & Seligman, 2005).

Social scientists, too, often trace differences in people's choices among various alternatives to their values: "a conception, explicit or implicit, distinctive of an individual or characteristic of a group, of the desirable, which influences the selection from available modes, means, and ends of action" (Kluckhohn, 1951, p. 395). Values are, as Rokeach (1979, p. 2) explained, "core conceptions of the desirable within every individual and society," which "serve as standards or criteria to guide not only action but also judgment, choice, attitude, evaluation, argument, exhortation, rationalization, and attribution of causality." Values provide the means of evaluating the relative worth and importance of the outcomes that may result from a course of action, and so serve to both motivate and guide individuals as they make choices among alternatives (Spates, 1983).

Schwartz Value Survey

Researchers have developed a number of methods for measuring values, but none are as theoretically sophisticated and well-validated as the Schwartz Value Survey (SVS). Schwartz and his colleagues assumed that values are evolutionarily adaptive, in that they facilitate the fulfillment of each person's basic needs, coordinate social interaction, and increase the overall welfare of the collective (Schwartz, 1992; Schwartz & Bilsky, 1987). Through review of previous studies of values and psychometric analyses of repeated surveys administered in a variety of cultural contexts, Schwartz came to identify ten values as fundamental and possibly universal. Respondents who complete the SVS rate each item from 0 to +7, where 0 indicates this value has low importance for the person and a 7 indicates supreme importance. A rating of -1 can be given to indicate opposition to the value. The ten values follow, with several of the items from the SVS that measure these values in parenthesis.[3]

- *Power*: Status, prestige, authority, and dominance over other people, including gaining and maintaining control over desired resources (social power, preserving my public image, wealth).
- *Achievement*: Completing challenging tasks successfully, thereby demonstrating one's competence and earning the deference or admiration of others (successful, influential, capable).
- *Hedonism*: Pursuing enjoyable, pleasurable activities and experiences that result in personal happiness (pleasure, enjoying food, sex, leisure).
- *Stimulation*: Enervating, exciting experiences and outcomes that elevate arousal, often through novelty, risk, or adventure (daring, a varied life).
- *Self-direction*: Sense of mastery, autonomy, and control over one's actions and outcomes (independent, freedom, curious).
- *Universalism*: Concern for the welfare of others and nature, including broad social values, such as justice, equality, wisdom, and peace (a world at peace, equality, broadminded).
- *Benevolence*: Treating other people in positive, caring ways during every day social interactions (honest, helpful, forgiving).
- *Tradition*: Respect, commitment, and acceptance of the customs and ideas that traditional culture or religion provide (avoiding extremes of feeling and action, holding to religious faith and belief).
- *Conformity*: Acting in ways that are consistent with social standards and avoiding doing things that will displease others (politeness, self-discipline, obedient).
- *Security*: Protecting oneself, one's loved ones, and one's community from threats by maintaining social order and stable exchange (family security, social order).

Schwartz (1992) indicates that some of these values are compatible; a person that highly values stimulation, for example, can also value hedonism, just as the person who values conformity can—without contradiction—also value tradition. However, other values are less congruent with one another, and so are less like to be considered important by the same individual; a person who values universalism, for example, would be less likely to also value power and achievement. Schwartz arranges the values in a circumplex model based on these complementarities and oppositions, with values varying along two dimensions: self-transcendence (e.g., universalism, benevolence) versus self-enhancement (e.g., power, achievement) and openness to change (self-direction, stimulation) versus conservation (e.g., tradition, conformity).

Values, Idealism, and Relativism

Some of the values Schwartz identifies and assesses, such as hedonism, universalism, and security, pertain more to issues of ethics and moral choice than others, so may also be related to either idealism or relativism. Speculating, idealism's emphasis on minimizing harm to others is consistent with the self-transcendence values of universalism, benevolence, and security. Idealists are harm-averse, and so should be more likely to agree that "working for the welfare of others" and ensuring "safety for loved ones" are important values. They are, as their name implies, idealistic, and so they may also resonate with the values in the universal cluster, which includes "a world at peace," "equality," and "wisdom." On the other hand, relativists should be less likely to endorse values that are more conservative. Relativists are skeptical about the importance of relying on standards when making moral judgments, and their rejection of traditional perspectives suggests they would be disinclined to endorse such values as "respect for tradition," "observing social norms," and maintaining the "stability of society."

These predicted convergences and divergences are consistent, in general, with the results of studies that have measured both values and ethics positions (e.g., Kung & Huang, 2013; Lanckneus, 2016; Strack & Gennerich, 2007). In our analysis of people's responses to the YourMorals survey, for example, we found that people's ethics positions were systematically related to all but one of the ten basic values clusters in Schwartz's theory (achievement). The strongest relations among the variables were between idealism and universalism and benevolence ($rs = +0.45$ and $+0.41$, $ps < 0.001$). Exceptionists and subjectivists considered universalistic and benevolent values to be less important than did absolutists and situationists. The interaction of idealism and relativism was also significant for respondents' ratings of the benevolent values, due to the significantly lower importance ratings of such values as honesty, helpfulness, and forgiveness by subjectivists ($p < 0.05$). Relativism, in contrast, was negatively correlated with both traditionalism and conformity, as predicted ($rs = +0.23$ and $+0.23$). Less expected was the significant positive relationship between ethics positions and the more self-gratifying values in Schwartz's theory: hedonism and simulation ($rs = +0.26$ and $+0.18$, $ps < 0.01$). For these value clusters, the interaction of idealism and relativism was statistically significant, indicating that individuals' values in these clusters were, to some degree, unique to each ethics position.[4] Subjectivists considered traditional and conformity values to be less important than situationists, who rated these values as less important than exceptionists, who rated these values as less important than absolutists. The subjectivists also valued hedonism more so than individuals in the other three ethics positions.

For those values related to stimulating experiences, exceptionists and absolutists rated these values lower than subjectivists, and situationists rated these values higher overall (see Figure 3.1).

The pattern and strength of these relationships between the EPQ and the SVS provide evidence of the validity of the ethics position theory as an account of individual differences in morality. In Schwartz's theory, universalism and benevolence are indicators of self-transcendence—putting others' needs before one's own needs—and individuals who were self-transcendent also tended to be idealistic: the situationists and the absolutists. Moreover, exceptionists, more so than all other ethical types, endorsed more conservative values, including tradition, conformity, and safety. The values endorsed by the subjectivists, too, were consistent with their personal moral philosophy, for they valued hedonism

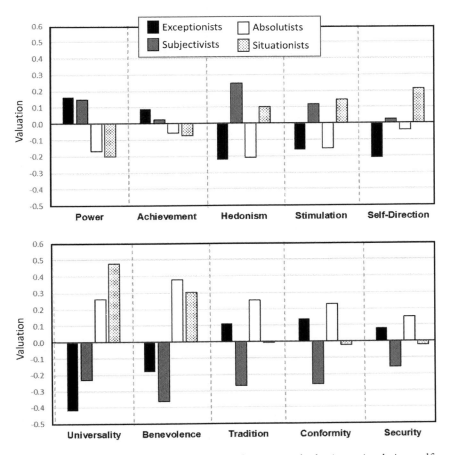

FIGURE 3.1 The mean Z-scores for power, achievement, hedonism, stimulation, self-direction, universality, benevolence, tradition, conformity, and security values of exceptionists, subjectivists, absolutists, and situationists.

and power rather than benevolence or conformity. Schwartz's model is based on years of careful investigation, so disparities between the SVS and the EPQ would raise questions about the EPQ's accuracy as a measure of sensitivity to harm and conformity to social norms. Fortunately for ethics position theory, the obtained relationships between the SVS and EPQ are consistent with the theoretical assumptions of both theories.

Moral Foundations Theory

For centuries the philosophical analysis of morality was also the rational analysis of morality. Philosophers since the time of Plato, Socrates, and Aristotle, when examining questions of right and good versus wrong and bad, considered first, and sometimes solely, the rational, logical bases of moral choice and judgment. Morality, they often assumed, balanced the too-human tendency to act on unbridled passions rather than measured reason. This view, however, was not shared by all. David Hume, in particular, argued that emotions, and not reason alone, are what motivates people to take moral actions, and emotions generate the intense reaction people often experience when they examine moral issues. Hume concluded that sentiments, passions, and affections are the primary "causes of all their effects; and consequently, the causes of pride and humility . . . and if not the sources of moral distinctions, are at least inseparable from them" (Hume, 1755/2007, pp. 14–15).

Hume's view was carried into moral psychology by theorists who included guilt, shame, sentiment, empathy, and other emotion-based processes in their accounts of morality (Moll, de Oliveira-Souza, Zahn, & Grafman, 2005). Freud, for example, suggested that human's actions are produced, in many cases, by strong emotional impulses that their conscious mind does not fully understand. People control these impulses, in part, by accepting societal standards as their own, and they experience guilt and shame when they fail to meet these expectations (Bornstein, Denckla, & Chung, 2013). Gilligan (1982), as we have seen, also suggested that objective analysis of rights and responsibilities is not the sole consideration when making moral judgments, for morality also depends on the emotion-based bonds of support and mutual assistance between people. The theory of moral foundations, developed by Jonathan Haidt and his colleagues, is also Humeian in that it pushes emotions to the forefront when explaining how people make their moral judgments (Haidt, 2001, 2012).

Five Foundations of Morality

Haidt and his colleagues, in their theory of moral foundations, argue that morality does not result from pondering dispassionately moral issues and subsequently rendering a moral judgment, but instead from moral intuition: "the sudden appearance in consciousness of a moral judgment, including an affective valence (good-bad, like-dislike), without any conscious awareness of having gone through steps of searching, weighing evidence, or inferring a conclusion" (Haidt, 2001, p. 818). Although people are quick to explain their moral actions and judgments by cloaking them in layers of logic, reasons, and rationales, these justifications are not the causes of the moral judgments, but are instead mere epiphenomena that present themselves after the fact.

The moral intuitions that determine people's judgments are not, however, unpredictable affect-laden valuations that arise capriciously from fluctuating emotional responses. Integrating anthropological analyses of morality (e.g., Haidt & Joseph, 2004), comparative studies of the bases of cooperation in primate populations (e.g., Brosnan, 2011), studies of the types of relational associations common in all cultures (e.g., Rai & Fiske, 2011), and their work examining people's moral reactions to harmless but culturally condemned practices (Haidt, Koller, & Dias, 1993), Haidt and his colleagues identified a common set of virtues, or foundations, that undergird systems of morality in cultures around the world: harm, fairness, loyalty, authority, and sanctity (Graham et al., 2013; Haidt, 2012; Haidt & Graham, 2007).[5] These core themes, Haidt maintains, are evolutionary adaptations that are further refined through social learning within any given cultural context.

The care/harm foundation is rooted in the universal need to protect and nurture those individuals who are unable to care for themselves. Kindness and compassion are the central elements of this moral foundation, which is activated when people learn that innocent others—and children in particular—are exploited, harmed, or suffering. The items on the Moral Foundations Questionnaire (MFQ), which Graham, Nosek, Haidt, Iyer, Koleva, and Ditto (2011) developed to assess these five bases of morality, ask people to indicate their degree of agreement with such statements as "Compassion for those who are suffering is the most crucial virtue" and "It can never be right to kill a human being" (Graham et al., 2011, p. 385).

The fairness/cheating moral foundation serves an essential interpersonal purpose by identifying and prescribing behaviors that promote cooperative relationships while inhibiting actions that could result in conflict and exploitation. Although individuals, in their day-to-day interactions with others, may be tempted to act in ways that maximize their own self-interests without concern for others, the fairness/cheating foundation's elements—justice, impartiality, equality (and proportionality), and trust—counter these self-serving tendencies. The MFQ items associated with this foundation include "Justice is the most important requirement for a society" and "I think it's morally wrong that rich children inherit a lot of money while poor children inherit nothing" (Graham et al., 2011, p. 385).

The loyalty/betrayal moral foundation explicitly recognizes that morality is as much a group-level process as an individual one. As a highly social species, humans evolved to live with other humans in small groups and tribes. Humans are therefore ready to cooperate with other humans in the pursuit of shared goals, but they are also ready to respond negatively to any human that is not a member of their group or tribe. Groups likely competed, forcefully, against other groups, claiming territories, plundering the resources of neighboring groups, and harming the members of those groups. Because outgroups were a substantial threat, the human mind developed the tendency to judge those who were loyal to their group positively but to condemn those who betrayed their group—especially during periods of group conflict. The MFQ items pertaining to the loyalty/ betrayal foundation include "People should be loyal to their family members, even when they have done something wrong" and "It is more important to be a team player than to express oneself" (Graham et al., 2011, p. 385).

The authority/subversion moral foundation recognizes the human penchant for living in stable, hierarchically organized social systems. Like other primates, human's groups tend toward hierarchy, as some members are able to influence others, but some members have little-to-no influence. This system of dominance and deference in human groups is an adaptive one, for it enhances survival by increasing group coordination and decision making, improving defense, and providing a means to resolve conflict. Because of these advantages, humans are instinctively prepared to accept, understand, and even prefer status differences. As a species, humans tend to respect authority and comply with social traditions, and those who do not accept the status order—the rebellious, the nonconformist, and the disrespectful—are not just viewed negatively, but as immoral. Items on the MFQ that measure this foundation include "Respect for authority is something all children need to learn" and "If I were a soldier and disagreed with my commanding officer's orders, I would obey anyway because that is my duty" (Graham et al., 2011, p. 385).

The sanctity/degradation moral foundation pertains to reverence and purity, on the moral side, and contamination and disgust, on the side of immorality. The most emotion-focused of the foundations, sanctity/degradation is also the most biological and least rational, for it is triggered by the threat of illness, infection, contamination, and death. Humans, to maintain their physical health, must identify, avoid, and expel pathogens, and the negative emotions that they experience when they encounter contaminants (e.g., unclean living areas, spoiled or fouled foods, diseased individuals)—disgust, revulsion, and even fear—energize and direct a self-protective response (Rozin & Haidt, 2013). Certain cultural institutions and symbols of purity elicit both moral approval and reassuring emotions such as reverence, awe, and a sense of security and well-being. This foundation is represented on the MFQ by such items as "People should not do things that are disgusting, even if no one is harmed" and "I would call some acts wrong on the grounds that they are unnatural" (Graham et al., 2011, p. 385).

Ethics Positions and Moral Foundations

Ethics position theory and moral foundations theory (MFT) share certain theoretical similarities. Both assume that morality is a culturally grounded mechanism that promotes self-regulation and cooperative relations while limiting selfishness and conflict. Both theories also trace individual differences in morality back to differences in tolerance of actions that cause harm to others and differences in respect for traditional, culturally approved conceptions of what is moral and what is not. Both theories, too, are consistent with Gilligan's (1982) predictions regarding sex differences in moral orientations. Just as women's responses to the EPQ suggest they are more likely than men to adopt moral positions that emphasize minimizing harm if at all possible, women are more likely to endorse more fervidly two of the five foundations on the MFQ: harm and fairness (Graham et al., 2011).

The theories differ, however, in the number of components that they use to fully explain these variations in moral judgment. Ethics position theory favors only two—idealism and relativism—whereas MFT includes five: harm, fairness, loyalty, authority, and sanctity. This disparity, however, may be more nugatory than substantive. As Haidt and his colleagues explain, the harm and fairness foundations are often closely associated with one another. They form, they suggest, the basis of a relatively liberal morality that functions to protect individuals from ill-treatment by other individuals, authorities, and social institutions. They label this twosome the individualizing foundations, since they serve to protect the personal rights and well-being of individuals in society. In contrast, they consider loyalty, authority, and sanctity to be the binding foundations, for they "are about binding people together into larger groups and institutions" (Graham et al., 2011, p. 369).

Their exploratory factor analysis of the MFQ items confirmed this two factor model. Although six factors had eigenvalues of 1 or more (the common rule of thumb for identifying the number of factors to retain for subsequent analysis), nearly all the items loaded on only the first two factors. Factor one was defined by the loyalty (ingroup), authority, and sanctity (purity) items, and factor two by the harm and fairness items. Confirmatory factor analysis also provided suggestive evidence of the close association of the individualizing and binding factors. A five-factor model, allowing each foundation to correlate with the others, provided the best fit for the data, but a two-factor hierarchical model, where individualizing and binding factors served as superordinate latent factors, accounted for significantly more of the variance than alternative models (Graham et al., 2011).

We quantified the degree of overlap between the five aspects of ethics identified in MFT and the two dimensions of ethics identified in ethics position theory by sampling the moral foundations and ethics positions of 9128 (37% women; mean age 36.2 years) who had previously registered at YourMorals online survey site and selected to take both the MFQ and EPQ (Forsyth, Iyer, & Haidt, 2012). (The majority of the respondents were residents of the U.S. (69.9%) and more liberal than conservative in their political orientation.

Our initial correlational analysis of the bivariate relationships between the five moral foundations of the MFQ and the two dimensions of the EPQ proved promising, as idealism scores were significantly correlated with the harm and fairness scales of the MFQ (*rs* = +0.58 and +0.42, respectively), but not with the three binding factors. Relativism, in contrast, was correlated with loyalty, authority, and sanctity; *rs* = −0.17, −0.24, and −0.37, respectively. A structural equations analysis of these two inventories also suggested that the five moral foundations are related, empirically, to the two factors identified in ethics position theory. A two-factor model, combining the individualizing factors of harm and fairness with idealism and the binding factors of loyalty, authority, and sanctity with relativism, fit the data relatively well. Items that measured idealism, care, and fairness were all significantly associated with the same latent factor as shown in Figure 3.2. Items that measured relativism, loyalty, authority, and purity were related to a relativism/binding factor.[6]

We also classified our respondents into one of the four ethics positions identified in ethics position theory, and used those groupings to predict

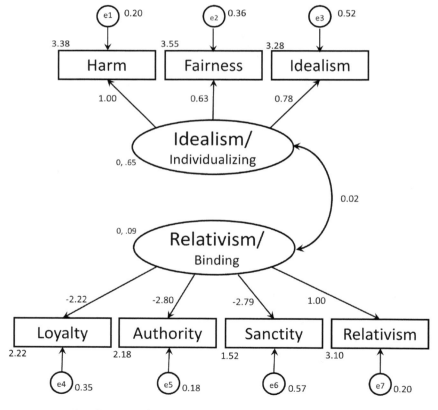

FIGURE 3.2 Confirmatory factor analysis results examining the relationships between the five factors of the Moral Foundations Questionnaire and the two factors of the Ethics Position Questionnaire.

their responses to the five scales of the MFQ. As the correlational evidence suggested, individuals who adopted one of the idealistic ethics positions—absolutists and situationists—had significantly elevated scores on the individualizing dimensions of caring and fairness. In contrast, relativists—situationists, and subjectivists—had lower scores on the binding dimensions. However, beyond this general difference, each ethics position had a unique profile across the five moral foundations. Exceptionists were not harm or fairness oriented, but more likely than all other ethics positions to value loyalty, authority, and sanctity. Subjectivists matched exceptionists relative disinterest in harm and fairness, but they also did not value loyalty, authority, and sanctity; they valued sanctity lower than all other groups. Absolutists and situationists concurred in their emphasis on harm and fairness, but diverged slightly in their weighing of loyalty and authority; absolutists were slightly above average, overall, in their emphasis on loyalty and authority. The two sets of idealists, however, diverged more substantially on sanctity; absolutists endorsed sanctity as a moral foundation, whereas situationists did not (see Figure 3.3).

These findings offer support for both theories. Both theories suggest that variations in ethics stem from two, more basic, sets of differences: concern for the well-being of other people (harm and fairness) and concern for social conventions that serve to regulate social behavior (loyalty and authority). Although clearly related, the results suggest that the ethics position theory's idealism and relativism and the MFT's caring, fairness, loyalty, authority, and sanctity are distinct constructs.

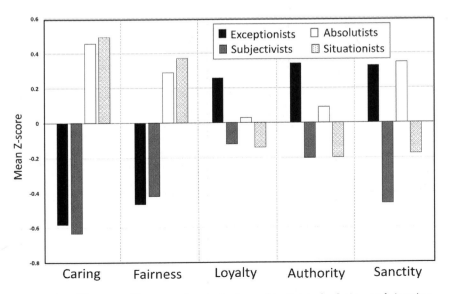

FIGURE 3.3 The mean Z-scores of exceptionists, subjectivist, absolutists, and situationists on the five factors of the Moral Foundations Questionnaire.

Five Moral Theories

The five theoretical analyses of moral psychology examined in this chapter each provide unique insights into the sources of moral differences. Both Kohlberg's theory of cognitive moral development and ethics position theory consider people to be natural moral philosophers—our life experiences have taught us to discriminate between what is right and wrong, and we have each developed the criteria that we rely on to make that distinction. Fortunately, Gilligan's ethic of caring, Schwartz's value theory, and Haidt's moral foundation theory counterbalance this emphasis on ratiocination by adding values, intuition, and feelings into the mix. Taken in combination, these five theories provide a fuller explanation for morality than any one taken separately.

Notes

1. Kohlberg is best known for his work on sequential stages in moral development, but he also identified variations in moral thought that were consistent with distinctions identified in moral philosophy (Colby et al., 1987), including "elements" and "types" at each stage of moral development. The four common elements in his revised scoring procedures included normative claims (consistency with moral rules or with socially defined role expectations), utilitarianism (consequentialism and welfare of others), fairness (equal treatment of all, reciprocity), and perfectionistic values (virtue and honor).
2. Factor and item analysis indicated that the ten items assessing an ethic of caring formed a unidimensional scale with an internal consistency of .85.
3. Schwartz continues to revise the list of universal values based on additional empirical findings. For example, an early list included spirituality (detachment, a spiritual life, accepting my portion in life) as a core value, but this value did not meet his criteria for universal significance (Schwartz, 1992). Recently he refined the list to draw distinctions between several of the values in the list and to identify those values that are growth- vs. protection-focused and social- vs. person-focused (Schwartz et al., 2012, 2014, 2017).
4. Ethics position theory predicts that, in some cases, the strength of the relationship between idealism and other variables will vary at different levels of relativism and vice versa. This predicted interaction of idealism and relativism can be tested in several ways, including moderated multiple regression, correlational analysis that include the idealism X relativism interaction term, and by classifying respondents into one of the four ethics positions and examining their responses using mean comparison procedures, such as analysis of variance.
5. Haidt and his colleagues continue to refine the labels and definitions of each of the five foundations. The original labels were harm/care, fairness/reciprocity, ingroup/loyalty, authority/respect, and purity/sanctity. A sixth foundation, liberty/oppression, is also being considered for inclusion in the theory (Haidt, 2012).
6. The analysis was based on the responses of 6,644 individuals, with $\chi^2 = 14310.74$ and $df = 719$. The model's fit was only adequate, as indicated by the following goodness-of-fit indicators: RMSEA = 0.053 (root mean square error of approximation), CFI = .849 (comparative fix index), SMRM = 0.060 (standardized root mean square residual), and NNFI = .836 (non-normed fit index).

4

INDIVIDUALS DIFFER

There is no fact more conspicuous in human nature than the broad distinction, both in kind and degree, drawn between the moral and the other parts of our nature.

—William Lecky (1919, p. 37)

No single quality, no matter how psychologically significant, defines a person. Beliefs, values, traits, attitudes, demographics, and ethics positions combine and recombine with other personal qualities in unique ways, but the results are not wholly unpredictable. To know a person's ethics position reveals something about that person's other qualities. Variations in idealism and relativism are linked to differences in age, sex, religiosity, and ethnicity. In terms of one's personal qualities, as idealism and relativism increase and decrease so do levels of agreeableness, conscientiousness, individualism/collectivism, conservatism, and empathy. And the darker qualities that are associated with less positive forms of social behavior are more often expressed as idealism decreases and relativism increases, so subjectivists are more likely to have elevated levels of Machiavellianism and psychopathy. For the most part, the relationships between the Ethics Position Questionnaire (EPQ) and other individual characteristics are theoretically congruent, and so provide evidence of the scale's concurrent, predictive, and discriminant validity.

* * *

Pat was one of the many people who took part in a Gallup Organization (2018) opinion poll about morality. One of the questions asked, "How would you rate the overall state of moral values in this country today—as excellent, good, only fair or poor?" Like the majority of the others surveyed (59%), Pat answered "poor," for Pat is constantly distressed by the daily news reports of others' moral indiscretions. It seems endless: the wars, shootings, crime, and corruption. Pat, even if provoked by others, would never act violently or intentionally harm another person, and believes that people who harm others should be punished. And even though many people these days seem to have turned their backs on traditional conceptions of morality, Pat is not one of them. Pat still believes that people should act in accord with fundamental standards of morality that define what is right and what is wrong. So Pat is disappointed in people, in general, and especially younger people—it is as if the overall state of morality in the country is declining.

Ethics position theory would consider Pat to be an absolutist; a person whose personal moral theory combines an idealistic outlook with a preference for the stability of moral standards that are transpersonal and transituational. But what more can be said about Pat? Is Pat older rather than younger, a man or a woman, friendly or unfriendly, conscientious or capricious, religious or irreligious, and prejudiced or open-minded? Can any of these qualities be predicted knowing Pat's ethics position?

The data are limited, but sufficient to offer some speculations about the basic qualities—other than their idealism and relativism—of absolutists, exceptionists, subjectivists, and situationists. The evidence reviewed in this chapter draws on the findings generated in empirical investigations of ethics that measured one or more characteristics of the respondents, such as their ages, their values, or their personality traits, but also their responses to the Ethics Position Questionnaire (EPQ). The chapter, when possible, also examines the responses of individuals who participated in the YourMorals research project, an online survey site developed by Ditto, Haidt, Iyer, Graham, Koleva, and their colleagues (Graham et al., 2013; Iyer, Koleva, Graham, Ditto, & Haidt, 2012; Koleva, Graham, Iyer, Ditto, & Haidt, 2012).[1]

Demographic Consistencies and Differences

People differ from one another in any number of ways, but among those defining distinctions are demographic qualities such as age, sex, education level, income level, marital status, occupation, religion, and so on. Some of these qualities are ones that are deliberately chosen or achieved through personal effort or experience, but others are relatively permanent characteristics that are ascribed to the person based on family background or biological features (Lipton, 1936). Nonetheless, individuals who can be classified into these aggregates often display similarities in other dispositional qualities, even though the processes that produce these similarities are identified more by speculation than by hard evidence. If it turns out that people who belong to some demographically defined aggregate are more likely to endorse one type of ethics position than another, the reason for this association will likely remain uncertain.

Age

Aging brings with it all kinds of physical and psychological changes, and those changes may include shifts in one's position with regards to sensitivity to the harm an action causes and its consistency with moral standards. Younger individuals tend to be more adventuresome both in their actions and in their judgments: they are more tolerant of ambiguity, and often question the status quo. Older individuals, in contrast, score higher in the need for closure and structure, and so are more likely to rely on principles and rules when they make moral decisions (Jost, Glaser, Kruglanski, & Sulloway, 2003). Older people are also more influenced by their intuitive reaction to events, and so actions that cause great harm can provoke a more intense, and therefore more negative, moral evaluation (McNair, Okan, Hadjichristidis, & de Bruin, 2019). From a cognitive developmental perspective, older individuals are more likely to have reached a stage of moral maturity where they base their reactions on principles—but ones that they themselves personally endorse, rather than those that are part of society's standards of morality (Rawwas & Singhapakdi, 1998). They therefore shift from conventional modes of ethical thought to a more post-conventional, idealistic one. Older people may also be members of a different generational grouping than younger people. Individuals in their late 20s and 30s, for example, are millennials, whereas those in their 60s are Baby Boomers, and the cultural experiences each generation shares may cause them to differ, in predictable ways, from the members of other generations.

Ethics position theory is not a cognitive developmental theory of morality, so it offers no firm predictions of how age might be related to either idealism or relativism. But, when people of varying ages complete the EPQ, older people tend to be more idealistic and less relativistic than younger individuals (e.g., Karande, Rao, & Singhapakdi, 2002; Kim & Choi, 2003; McNair et al., 2019; Marques & Azevedo-Pereira, 2009; Ramsey, Marshall, Johnston, & Deeter-Schmelz, 2007; Rawwas & Singhapakdi, 1998). For example, when we examined the level of idealism and relativism of 4,388 women and 6,996 men who completed surveys online at YourMorals, age was correlated with relativism ($r = -0.15$) and idealism ($r = +0.07$), but the two EPQ variables did not interact to predict age (see Chapter 3, Endnote 4).

When we considered age ranges—teenagers and college-aged adults (15 to 22 years of age), young adults (23 to 30), adults (31 to 40), older adults (41 to 60), and aged adults (60 to 100)—we found that aged adults were significantly more idealistic than the older adults, who in turn were more idealistic than all the other groups ($p < 0.05$). These five age groups were, however, more distinctly different with regards to relativism. Relativism declined with age, so the youngest respondents (14 to 22 years) were more relativistic than the young adults, who were in turn more relativistic than the adults, who were more relativistic than the older and aged adults (who did not differ significantly from one another).

Sex

Differences in the morality of men and women has been a topic of discussion for time immemorial, with some arguing women are more ethical than men, but others averring men are morally superior to women. Trait-based approaches, noting that men and women differ psychologically in instrumentality, competitiveness, sensitivity, and emotional understanding, suggest the sexes will likely also differ in ethics (Noddings, 1984). Gender socialization theories, such as Gilligan's (1982) theory of cognitive development, agree, but trace the differences to social processes, such as sex roles and differential socialization. More biological and psychodynamic approaches suggest that physiological differences between men and women produce differences in ethical orientation. Most people, if asked to compare men and women, agree that the sexes differ—but they just don't agree which sex is morally superior to other. Men tend to think men are morally superior to women, whereas women believe women deserve to be recognized as the more moral gender (Kidwell, Stevens, & Bethke, 1987).

Do men and women differ in idealism and relativism, and therefore, the positions they endorse regarding morality? The empirical evidence is inconsistent, and so offers no firm answer to this question. Some researchers report no differences between the sexes (e.g., Fatoki, 2014; Forsyth, 1985; Forsyth, Nye, & Kelley, 1988; Hadjistavropoulos, Malloy, Sharpe, & Fuchs-Lacelle, 2003; Kour, 2017; McHoskey et al., 1999) whereas others report sex differences (Donoho, Heinze, & Kondo, 2012; Friesdorf, Conway, & Gawronski, 2015). However, and as noted in Chapter 3, when we compared the responses of men and women who completed the EPQ online at YourMorals, women's scores were higher than men's on both idealism and relativism ($p < 0.001$). Of the 4,397 women who took part in the survey, 56.9% had idealism scores at or above the median, suggesting they were either situationists or absolutists. In contrast, only 36.9% of the 7,012 men in the survey were classified as idealistic. Sex differences were also apparent when we compared the frequencies of men and women in each of the four ethics positions described by ethics position theory; χ^2 (11508) = 462.55, $p < 0.001$. As Figure 4.1 suggests, more women were situationists rather than exceptionists, whereas more men were exceptionists and subjectivists than absolutists and situationists.

Ethnicity

Relatively few studies have examined the idealism and relativism of different racial and ethnic categories (e.g., Al-Khatib, Rawwas, Swaidan, & Rexeisen,

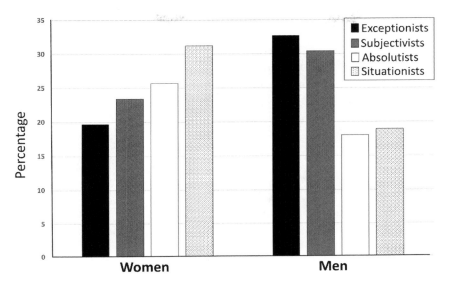

FIGURE 4.1 The percentage of men and women in each of the four ethical types described by ethics position theory.

2005; Marta, Heiss, & De Lurgio, 2008; Swaidan, Rawwas, & Vitell, 2008). We therefore examined the responses of the 7,420 men and women in the YourMorals survey data set who described themselves as Asian ($n = 331$), Black ($n = 86$), Latino ($n = 124$), White ($n = 6231$), or reported they belonged to an ethnic or racial category description that did not fit one of these four groups ($n = 648$). This analysis indicated Asians and Blacks were significantly more relativistic than Latinos and Whites ($p < 0.05$). For idealism, only Latinos differed from the other categories—these respondents were significantly more idealistic than individuals in all the other racial or ethnic groupings; $\chi^2 (7420) = 51.33$, $p < 0.001$.

Religious Orientation

The majority of the world's people base their moral beliefs and standards for ethical conduct on the traditions of their personal religious faith. Christians, for example, prize such virtues as temperance, fairness in dealing with others, charity, and faith in God. Islam similarly values honesty in interactions with others, justice, respecting others, temperance, and humility. These belief systems, by their very nature, tend to be principled rather than relativistic: Traditional religions in almost all human cultures, both past and present, explicitly set forth standards pertaining to sacred thoughts, beliefs, and actions (Paloutzian, 2017). Individuals who are spiritual may have strong existential and sacred beliefs, but commitment to Christianity, Islam, and other traditional religions generally requires acceptance of the moral standards of that belief system. Nearly all traditional religions also caution against causing harm to others. Principles such as "thou shalt not kill" and "do unto others what you would have them do unto you" are common in most religious codes and commandments.

This degree of codification in traditional religions and their general tendency to condemn actions that cause harm to others suggest that individuals who are more religious will be more idealistic but less relativistic and the empirical evidence supports this conclusion. Individuals who were more religious responded more negatively to vignettes that described actions that cause harm to others and are inconsistent with moral standards (Sims & Bingham, 2017). Women, more so than men, tend to be more religious—they attend services more regularly and also report praying more regularly—and this difference may be due to their higher levels of compassion and idealism (Penny, Francis, & Robbins, 2015).

More direct evidence comes from studies that have examined the correlation between idealism and relativism as assessed on the EPQ and religiosity. Oumlil and Balloun (2009), in a study of American and Moroccan business managers, found that relativism was negatively correlated with religiosity ($r = -0.33$), which they measured using the Wilkes, Burnett, and Howell (1986) religiosity scale. They also found that idealism and religiosity were correlated ($r = +0.40$). Other studies report similar findings (e.g., Barnett, Bass, & Brown, 1996; Chen & Liu, 2009; Singhapakdi, Marta, Rallapalli, & Rao, 2000; Voegel & Pearson, 2016; White, Peirce, & Jacobowitz, 2018). The correlations fluctuate in magnitude depending on the measures used and the population studied, but in most cases the correlation between idealism and religiosity is positive, but the correlation with relativism is negative.

The data collected as part of the YourMorals research project also indicate that religious individuals are more idealistic but less relativistic than individuals who do not describe themselves as committed to a religious belief system. Respondents in that survey indicated if they were currently practicing one of the traditional religions (Protestant, Jewish, Buddhist, Catholic, Hindu, or Muslim, $n = 1030$) or if they considered themselves to be "not religious" ($n = 1375$). Those individuals who reported they were religious had significantly higher scores on idealism (3.47 vs. 3.58) but lower scores on relativism (2.91 vs. 3.30) compared to those individuals who were not religious. In consequence, when classified into an ethics position, 69.3% of those persons who were relativistic but not idealistic—the subjectivists—indicated they were not religious; χ^2 (2403) = 59.03, $p < 0.001$. Situationists, who are both idealistic and relativistic, also tended to be less religious compared to the nonrelativistic ethics positions (exceptionists and absolutists), but these differences were not as substantial as the pronounced difference between subjectivists and all the other ethics positions.

Absolutists' religiosity and subjectivists' secularism also emerged in our meta-analytic review of differences in levels of idealism and relativism in countries whose citizens varied in their level of religiosity (Forsyth, O'Boyle, & McDaniel, 2008). Individuals who resided in countries whose citizens described themselves as less religious, such as Japan and China, were also more likely to be classified as subjectivists; the level of idealism was lower in these countries, but levels of relativism were higher. In contrast, in countries where a larger proportion of the population considered religion to be important in their lives, more of the residents were also classified as either situationists or absolutists. Chapter 7 discusses cross-cultural differences in idealism, relativism, and religiosity in more detail.

Personal Characteristics

Idealism and relativism are but two of the many ways in which individuals differ from one another, and these other variations in traits, dispositions, temperaments, attitudes, values, experiences, and so on each influence people's cognitive, motivational, and behavioral tendencies. But even though some of these personal qualities are independent of all others, some align to form networks (or complexes or profiles) of shared similarities. In consequence, individuals' ethics positions do not stand in isolation from their other personal qualities, but instead are systematically related to their attitudes, personality, values, and self-conceptions.

Personality Traits

Personality theorists believe that a person's enduring psychological and behavioral tendencies are caused, in part, by "the dynamic organization within the individual of those psychophysical systems that determine his unique adjustments to the environment" (Allport, 1937, p. 48). And while many different theoretical approaches have been taken in an attempt to better understand this complex and dynamic system, many personality scientists now believe that a small number of enduring dimensions of personality—traits—provide the basis for some of the most conspicuous differences between and similarities among people.

Personality researchers have studied hundreds of traits, but five of these traits have emerged with great regularity across measures, time, and cultures. The first of these traits, extraversion (E), describes the dispositional tendency to engage actively in social interactions with other people, and includes warmth, gregariousness, assertiveness, activity level, excitement-seeking, and cheerfulness. The second trait, agreeableness (A), comprises qualities that facilitate the development and maintenance of positive relationships with other people. People who manifest this trait tend to be more trusting, helpful, cooperative, modest, and compassionate than other people. They are also more likely to claim they are morally upright. Conscientiousness (C), the third trait, describes a person's basal level of persistence in the pursuit of tasks, and includes such related qualities as self-confidence, orderliness, meeting of obligations, achievement striving, self-regulation, and measured responding. The fourth trait, neuroticism (N) (or emotional stability), describes a person's basic reaction to life events. Those who have elevated levels of neuroticism experience more anxiety and distress than other people; they tend to consider the world to be more threatening and chaotic, and so tend to be anxious, depressed, self-conscious, and vulnerable. They also tend to be moodier and emotionally unstable, and so can respond in hostile, impulsive ways when they face challenging circumstances. Openness to experience (O), is the final group of related traits, and the more diffuse, for it includes a range of intellectually oriented qualities, such as imagination, fantasy, appreciation of art, openness to emotions and experiences, curiosity, and cognitive flexibility. Goldberg (1990), in his lexical analysis of the words used to describe people, termed these qualities the Big Five. Costa and McCrae (1992, 2013) incorporated these personality dimensions in their Five Factor Model (FFM) of personality.

Do variations in these five aspects of personality correspond to differences in either idealism or relativism? Theoretically, idealism corresponds to some extent with two subcomponents that define agreeableness: trust and tender-mindedness (compassion). This congruence suggests that idealists are likely to be high rather than low in agreeableness. Relativism, with its expressed skepticism of traditional moral rules, may also be consistent with aspects of openness, such as curiosity and cognitive flexibility, but negatively associated with neuroticism. However, researchers who have examined the relationship between personality and idealism and relativism report relatively few convergences. Khan, Akbar, Jam, and Saeed (2016), for example, reported a correlation of 0.30 between idealism and agreeableness, but this correlation was not significant given their sample size. They also reported that idealism was negatively correlated with neuroticism, as did Yuting (2009).

Given these empirical uncertainties, we examined the relationship between ethical ideologies and personality traits using the YourMorals dataset. A portion of the respondents in this project not only completed the EPQ, but also a short-form measure of the FFM (Costa & McCrae, 1992). The ten correlations were not substantial, averaging only +0.07. However, the largest correlation was between agreeableness and idealism: +0.30 ($n = 7472$, $p < 0.001$). The second highest correlation was between relativism and conscientiousness, but it was only 0.09 ($n = 7474$, $p < 0.001$). We also examined (in a moderated multiple regression analysis) the possibility that idealism and relativism, taken in combination, were related to the five FFM traits. Again, the only significant interaction effect was for agreeableness: $t (1, 7463) = 5.45$, $p < 0.001$. Further analysis indicated that one of the four ethics positions was particularly low in agreeableness: the subjectivists. Their agreeableness score was significantly lower than the agreeableness scores of the two idealistic ethics positions.

These findings are consistent, to some extent, with our analysis of the relationship between idealism, relativism, and the honesty trait (H-factor) identified by Lee and Ashton (2012) in their Hexaco theory of personality. These researchers concur with FFM's list of five factors pertaining to extraversion, agreeableness, conscientiousness, emotionality, and openness to experience, but they also believe that the FFM overlooks a cluster of personality traits corresponding to morality: honesty-humility. This H-factor, they argued, comprises four distinct facets pertaining to sincerity ("If I want something from someone, I ask for it directly, instead of manipulating them into giving it"), fairness ("I would still pay my taxes even if I would not get caught for avoiding them"), greed ("Having a high level of social status is not very important to me," reversed), and modesty ("I am an ordinary person who is no better than others").

When we administered the Hexaco and the EPQ to a sample of college students ($n = 188$), we found that honesty-humility was positively correlated with idealism ($r = +0.19$, $p < 0.01$) but negatively correlated with relativism ($r = -0.15$, $p < 0.05$; O'Boyle & Forsyth, 2018). The H-factor/idealism relationship was strongest for the fairness, sincerity, and modesty facets ($rs = +0.23$, $+0.17$, and $+0.17$, $ps < 0.05$), but nonsignificant for greed ($r = +0.04$). The H-factor/relativism relationship was strongest for sincerity ($r = -0.18$, $p < 0.05$), but nonsignificant for the other three facets. These findings are consistent with those reported by Cohen, Panter, Turan, Morse, and Kim (2014) in their study of moral character and workplace ethics. In their study, the honesty scale of the Hexaco was positively correlated with idealism ($r = +0.25$) but negatively correlated with relativism ($r = -0.32$).

Individualism and Collectivism

Some of the most value-laden concepts in moral philosophy—rights, justice, equality, and fairness—pertain to the master problem of social life: the balance between the needs and purposes of the individual and the needs and purposes of the collective. Individuals often seek what they personally require, such as power, rewards, and pleasurable experiences. Yet, because most people live with other people, they must often sacrifice their own outcomes so that others around them may benefit. Some never sink too deeply into the larger collective, for they remain individualists who are so self-reliant that they refuse to rely on others or concern themselves with others' outcomes. Other people, in contrast, put the collective's interests before their own personal needs, sacrificing personal gain for the greater good.

This distinction between the self-focused and socially focused virtues is consistent with the psychological and cross-cultural dimension of individualism-collectivism.

On the individualism side of this continuum is a tradition or worldview based on the independence and uniqueness of each person. Individualism assumes that people are autonomous and must be free to act and think in ways that they prefer, rather than submit to the demands of society. Each person is unique and self-governing and should strive to achieve outcomes and goals that will personally benefit them. Collectivism, in contrast, puts the community and its goals before those of each individual. Each person, if even recognized as an independent entity, is inseparably connected to the collective whole.

Individualism and collectivism describe cultural differences in customs, traditions, and world views, but when applied at the level of the individual rather than cultures they describe differences in people's self-conceptions, beliefs about rights and responsibilities, modes of dealing with conflict, and—quite possibly—ethics (Husted & Allen, 2008). Those who lean toward individualism—variously called individualists, independents, or idiocentrics—recognize each person's right to act in ways that maximize their personal outcomes, their independence, and their uniqueness. Collectivists, in contrast, stress their connections to others (Oyserman, Coon, & Kemmelmeier, 2002; Triandis, Leung, Villareal, & Clack, 1985). Collectivists are more likely to act in ways that are consistent with community standards, and to strive to do what they can to carry out their duties within that community. They are respectful of tradition, and are more likely to judge actions that disrupt the harmony of the group to be unethical. Individualists, in contrast, are not as emotionally attached to their community and its outcomes, for they put their own personal goals above the goals of the group; they find more enjoyment in personal success and competition.

A number of researchers have examined the relationship between collectivism, idealism, and relativism, but the findings vary considerably across samples. The majority of the studies use unidimensional measures of collectivism-individualism, so higher scores indicate a collective orientation and lower scores an individualistic orientation. In several of these studies, relativism was positively correlated with collectivism (Chaudhry & Stumpf, 2011; Swaidan et al., 2008; Smith, 2011; Vitell, Paolillo, & Thomas, 2003), although this relationship was negative in at least one investigation (Alas, Gao, & Carneiro, 2010) and nonsignificant in others (e.g., Smith, 2009). Idealism also predicted collectivism in some studies (e.g., Banai, Stefanidis, Shetach, & Özbek, 2014; Smith, 2009; Swaidan et al., 2008) but not in others (e.g., Chaudhry & Stumpf, 2011).

These inconsistent results suggest that the relationships between individualism and collectivism and ethics are unsubstantial, but they may also result from variations in each study's measurement and statistical procedures. For example, although individualism and collectivism are often assessed with a single instrument that assumes increases in individualism indicate decreases in collectivism, Triandis and his colleagues recommend measuring each one separately (Singelis, Triandis, Bhawuk, & Gelfand, 1995). Also, most researchers report the bivariate relationships among ethics positions and individualism/collectivism, but few explore the effects of the interaction of idealism and relativism. To explore these possibilities, we analyzed the responses of the 2,126 people who completed both the EPQ and separate measures of collectivism and individualism in the Your-Morals survey (Singelis et al., 1995). For these individuals and these measures, collectivism was negatively correlated with individualism ($r = -0.17$, $p < 0.001$), but the relatively small size of the relationship suggests that individualism is not simply the inverse of collectivism. Relativism was negatively correlated with collectivism ($r = -0.16$, $p < 0.001$), but uncorrelated with individualism ($r = +0.01$, ns). Idealism, however, was negatively correlated with individualism ($r = -0.27$, $p < 0.001$) and positively correlated with collectivism ($r = +0.26$, $p < 0.001$).

As these results suggest, individuals who endorse the more idealistic ethics positions—the absolutists and situationists—are less individualistic than those who endorse the less idealistic ideologies—exceptionism and subjectivism. However, for collectivism, idealism and relativism interacted to predict levels of collectivism; $t (1, 2122) = 3.44$, $p = 0.001$. The rank ordering, from most collectivistic to least, was absolutists, situationists, exceptionists, and subjectivists ($Ms = 3.8$, 3.7, 3.6, and 3.4, respectively, all differences $p < 0.05$).

Political Attitudes

Disagreement may sometimes flare up during discussions of moral issues, but spirited disputation is the hallmark of political discourse. Although political orientations are complex, they generally vary along a continuum from conservatism to liberalism. Conservative individuals tend to value tradition and heritage; they generally believe that customs and practices that have served adequately in the past should not now be altered. Although motivations for political outlook vary, conservatives are skeptical about progressive movements and values. They seek to conserve—to retain, rather than change. Liberal individuals, in contrast, are more likely to question the status quo. They are generally opposed to institutional and cultural practices that are restrictive, and they are committed to equality and greater liberty from traditional sources of governmental influence.

But these attitudes are not independent of moral beliefs (Sears & Funk, 1991). People do not choose the candidate and party based on a dispassionate review of their position on issues, but because they believe their party and the members of it are the most morally good. Conservatives and liberals take different positions on such issues as abortion, affirmative action, civil rights, climate change, the death penalty, euthanasia, gun control, health care, higher education, LGBTQ rights, immigration, science, the separation of church and state, and welfare, and these differences are sustained more by their divergent moral beliefs rather than the foundational principles of each party's political philosophy. And what might those differences be, when framed within the two dimensions of ethics position theory? To speculate, conservative individuals, given their preference for tradition, would more likely be lower in relativism than liberals, who would in turn be more idealistic than conservatives, given that they are generally characterized as the more softhearted and socially progressive of the two political orientations.

We investigated this possibility by comparing the EPQ scores of the 6,624 liberals, 1,135 moderates, and 1,455 conservatives in the YourMorals project. As expected, respondents who espoused political attitudes that were more conservative rather than liberal tended to also be less idealistic and less relativistic; $rs = -0.29$ and $-.021$. However, political orientation was also significantly associated with the interaction of idealism and relativism; $t (1, 9204) = 7.92, p < 0.001$. Since decreases in idealism and relativism were associated with an increasingly conservative political orientation, the majority (52%) of the respondents who described themselves as politically conservative adopted an exceptionist ethics position (see Figure 4.2). Some of the conservatives were absolutists (21.4%), but relatively few were subjectivists (16.8%) or situationists (9.1%). In contrast, the majority of the respondents who described themselves as politically liberal adopted one of the more relativistic ethics positions; either situationism (29.0%) or subjectivism (27.3%). The moderates were, as expected, moderate with regards to relativism, but tended to adopt ethics positions that were lower rather than higher in idealism—more were exceptionists and subjectivists (58%) rather than absolutists and situationists; $\chi^2 (9214) = 693.50, p < 0.001$.

These findings are consistent with the theory of moral foundations developed by Haidt and his colleagues (e.g., Graham, Haidt, & Nosek, 2009; Haidt, 2012). As noted in Chapter 3, individuals who adopt different ethics positions

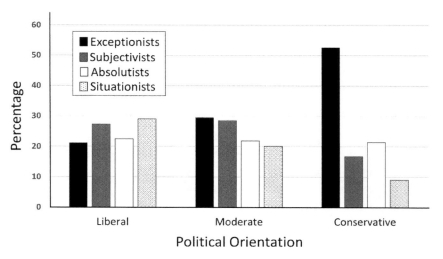

FIGURE 4.2 The percentage of each ethics position type who endorsed a liberal, moderate, or conservative political ideology.

also tend to differ in their endorsement of four of the five moral values identified in Haidt's moral foundations theory. Idealistic individuals tend to more strongly endorse the individualizing foundations (harm and fairness), whereas those who are lower in relativism (absolutists and exceptionists) are more likely to base their morality on the binding foundations (loyalty, authority, and sanctity). In addition, these differences in moral foundations are also closely associated with political orientation. Haidt and his colleagues have found that liberals' moral intuitions are more closely related to the harm and fairness foundations, whereas conservative individuals put more weight on the binding foundations (authority, loyalty, and sanctity) than liberals do (see Klein et al., 2018, for a report on the positive replication of these findings in a new sample of 6,966 respondents).

Empathy

Why do people, who so often act to only maximize their own gains, sometimes choose to give rather than take, to help rather than harm, to support rather than exploit? Philosophers as far back as Aristotle suggested that the answer lies in the uniquely human capacity to vicariously experience the suffering of others—pity, sympathy, compassion, empathy—for we are moved by "a feeling of pain at an apparent evil, destructive or painful, which befalls woe who doesn't deserve it" (Aristotle, 1935/350 BCE). Going beyond discussions of virtues, values, moral standards, and even the calculus of costs and benefits, both Hume and Smith moved sympathy into the center of their analysis of moral choice. Hume (1755/2007) believed that each person has the capacity to know what others are feeling, both intellectually and emotionally, but at the same time realizing that this feeling is caused by another person's emotion rather than one's own experiences. And Smith, in his *Theory of Moral Sentiments*, suggested the human capacity to resist continual selfishness emanated principally from "our fellow-feeling for the misery of others" (1759/2016).

Many psychologists, too, trace human's capacity to act in ways that promote others' outcomes back to empathy: the capacity to take other peoples' perspective on events, to see the situation as they see it, and to experience—or at least, understand—the emotions they are likely experiencing. If they are upset or fearful, then we become distressed and worried. If they are suffering, then we suffer as well. If they are happy, then we too are happy. Empathy, then, is responsible for guiding human action toward more morally commendable choices and away from actions that may harm others. Empathy increases not only altruism, care, and cooperation, but also reduces aggression, intergroup conflict, and prejudice (Batson, 2011).

Ethics position theory, and the items in the EPQ, do not directly address empathy, but idealism's emphasis on minimizing harm to others implicitly assumes that some individuals—the situationists and the absolutists—are more likely to calibrate others' experience of harm and suffering. This assumption is born out in studies that have assessed both individuals' levels of dispositional empathy and their ethics positions. Cohen, Davis, and their colleagues, for example, used Davis's (1983) Interpersonal Reactivity Index (IRI) to measure several forms of empathy, including empathic concern and perspective taking (Cohen et al., 2014; Davis et al., 2001). Items on the empathic concern (EC) subscale ask respondents to describe their tendency to feel sympathy or compassion for others experiencing a hardship using such items as "When I see someone being taken advantage of, I feel kind of protective towards them" and "I would describe myself as a pretty soft-hearted person." Items on the perspective-taking (PT) subscale address respondents' capacity to cognitively take the role of others, using such items as "I sometimes try to understand my friends better by imagining how things look from their perspective" and "I believe that there are two sides to every question and try to look at them both." These investigators discovered that both forms of empathy correlated significantly with idealism, with rs ranging from +0.17 to +0.41, but not with relativism.

We also confirmed this relationship when we examined the responses of the 3,477 people who completed both the EPQ and IRI in the YourMorals survey. Both empathic concern and perspective taking were positively correlated with idealism (rs = +0.46 and +0.22), but the correlations between relativism and empathy were relatively trivial (rs = −0.09 and +0.04, respectively). However, the interaction of idealism and relativism was significantly associated with both forms of empathy (ps < 0.001), prompting us to compare the empathy levels of individuals in the four different ethics positions. That analysis did not qualify our overall conclusions regarding idealism and perspective-taking empathy: The more idealistic individuals (situationists and absolutists) described themselves as more likely to consider others' viewpoints in comparison to the less idealistic respondents. The second form of empathy, empathic concern, varied more across the four ethics positions than did perspective taking. Subjectivists reported lower levels of empathic concern than all other respondents, including the exceptionists (who scored lower than situationists and absolutists in empathic concern). The rank ordering, from most to least empathic, was absolutists, situationists, exceptionists, and subjectivists (Ms = 4.0, 3.9, 3.5, and 3.3).

Darker Qualities

Of the billions of people in the world, some are more irritating than others. There are those who drive too slowly in the fast lane of the highway. Some let their dog bark at night to bother the neighbors. Some lack good table manners or a sense of decorum. But some individuals are not just irritating, annoying, and vexing, but socially aversive. Most people are cooperative, prosocial, and ethical. But some people use individually agentic, interpersonally injurious, and immoral strategies in their dealings with other people. Such qualities as agreeableness, collectivism, and empathy predict who will be more likely to respond negatively if an action may cause harm to others or is not consistent with social standards. But the dark traits, such as Machiavellianism, psychopathy, and authoritarianism, may predict who is unfazed by actions that result in harm to others or by actions that are inconsistent with social standards that define the difference between right and wrong (Moshagen, Hilbig, & Zettler, 2018).

Machiavellianism

The concept of Machiavellianism takes its name from the work of Niccolò Machiavelli (1532/1950), who offered some highly practical if morally suspect advice to those who wish to gain and hold power in turbulent contexts. Drawing on historical precedent rather than philosophical ideals, Machiavelli suggested that even a morally righteous man must make deliberate use of ruthless, amoral, and deceptive methods when dealing with unscrupulous men, for politics calls for shrewd analysis and manipulation. When Christie (1970) recognized that some people seem to regularly rely on Machiavellian principles in dealing with others he developed a personality measure to identify those who put more stock in expedience and self-gain than morality and service to others.

The Machiavellian personality is defined by three sets of interrelated values: an avowed belief in the effectiveness of manipulative tactics in dealing with other people (e.g., "The best way to handle people is tell them what they want to hear"), a cynical view of human nature (e.g., "It is safest to assume that all people have a vicious streak and it will come out when they are given a chance"), and a willingness to sacrifice relationships and moral principles to achieve their aims ("Never tell anyone the real reason you did something unless it is useful to do so"; Christie, 1970, p. 17). Machiavellians dismiss morality as a guide for their actions; they assume the ends often justify the means, even if the means will result in harm to others. As Christie (1970, p. 3) notes, Machiavellians appear to have a "utilitarian rather than a moral view of their interactions with others." They also explicitly reject moral standards as guides for action, for they believe "the biggest difference between most criminals and other people is that criminals are stupid enough to get caught" (Christie, 1970, p. 23).

A number of studies have examined the relationship between Machiavellians and ethics positions, and all have yielded the same basic findings: Machiavellians, given their pragmatic orientation and their rejection of standards as moral guides, tend to be less idealistic but more relativistic than most people (e.g., Cohen et al., 2014; Leary, Knight, & Barnes, 1986; McHoskey et al., 1999; Mudrack, Bloodgood, & Turnley, 2012). McHoskey and his colleagues, for example, in a study of college students found that increases in Machiavellianism were associated with lower levels of self-esteem, subjective well-being, hope, and—as predicted—idealism ($r = -0.45$). Machiavellianism was positively associated with relativism ($r = +0.25$), but also with nihilism: a sense of power-lessness, alienation, and lack of meaning in life. Leary and his colleagues' (1986) findings also suggest that Machiavellians are more likely to be subjectivists rather than exceptionists, situationists, or absolutists. In their study, Machiavel-lianism was negatively correlated with idealism ($r = -0.48$) but positively corre-lated with relativism ($r = +0.20$). The two highest negative correlations between specific items on the EPQ and Machiavellianism were "If an action could harm an innocent other, then it should not be done" ($r = -0.48$) and "One should never psychologically or physically harm another person" ($r = -0.43$). But for relativism, it was the items that pertained to veracity that were most highly asso-ciated with Machiavellianism: "No rule concerning lying can be formulated; whether a lie is permissible or not permissible totally depends on the situation" ($r = +0.35$) and "Whether a lie is judged to be moral or immoral depends upon the circumstances surrounding the action" ($r = +0.29$).[2]

Psychopathy

Studies of the darker side of human nature have identified one quality that is associated with a number of antisocial outcomes: psychopathy. Individuals with elevated levels of psychopathy, in keeping with its intimidating etymological roots—*psycho* (of the mind) and *pathy* (denoting disorder or dysfunction)—lack the kind of qualities that facilitate the development of authentic social relation-ships. Psychopaths are often interpersonally engaging and charming, yet they lack interest in other people and their well-being. One variety of this syndrome, termed primary psychopathy, is characterized by emotional coldness combined with an absence of sentimentality, impulse control, and concern for other peo-ple's well-being. A second form, secondary psychopathy, adds reactive hostility and a lack of conscientiousness, with the result that individuals with elevated levels of secondary psychopathy tend to adopt parasitic lifestyles, engaging in a variety of criminal activities to achieve their ends (Hare & Neumann, 2009).

Is any one of the four ethics positions more likely to display the antisocial tendencies of a psychopath? Psychologically, individuals who are psychopathic lack concern for other people's well-being; they would likely not agree that one should act in all cases in ways so that no one in harmed. They also lack concern for social regulatory mechanisms, and so tend to act impulsively without full consideration of the consequences of their choices. These two tendencies—the lack of care for others' outcomes and their disinterest in compliance with social standards—suggests psychopathy is negatively correlated with idealism but positively correlated with relativism—and that combination defines the subjectivists' ethics position.

The responses of the 857 people who completed both the EPQ and Lev-enson's Self-Report Psychopathy Scale (LSRP; Levenson, Kiehl, & Fitzpat-rick, 1995) in the YourMorals survey are consistent with this conclusion. Both primary and secondary psychopathology were negatively correlated with idealism ($r = -0.43$ and -0.08) and positively correlated with relativism ($r = +0.27$ and $+0.18$, respectively). Also, the interaction of idealism and relativism was associated with both primary and secondary psychopathology ($ps < 0.05$). Examination of the means for each ethics position indicated that scores on primary psychopathology increased from absolutists, to situationists, to exceptionists, and to subjectivists ($p < 0.05$). For secondary psychopathology, subjectivists had higher levels compared to absolutists and exceptionists, and the mean for the situationists fell intermediate and did not differ from any of the other ethics positions.

Authoritarianism

Prejudice is one of the more distinctively aversive social qualities people display in their social interactions. People do not only act in ways to sustain and protect members of their own community or social group; they also express negativity and inflict harm on members of outgroups. Although some people, due to personal experience, socialization, or some other psychological factor, display prejudice against a specific group, many show a general tendency to express negativity toward the members of all outgroups. Such negativity is captured in a number of psychological constructs, including authoritarianism, dogmatism, and social-dominance orientation (Duckitt, 2009). Authoritarianism, for example, was first studied by a team of social and personality psychologists in the 1940s (Adorno, Frenkel-Brunswick, Levinson, & Sanford, 1950). These researchers explored the belief systems of highly prejudiced persons through in-depth interviews, clinical case studies, and questionnaires. Their analyses revealed a distinctive pattern of values and beliefs that researchers labeled authoritarianism. Further analysis of this syndrome identified the three most central features of authoritarianism, particularly as it applies to individuals who are conservative in their political orientation (right-wing authoritarianism, or RWA). First, right-wing authoritarians tend to be high in conventionality. They feel that the status quo should be maintained at all costs and that conventional social standards should not be challenged. Second, they display signs of respectful submission to authority; they believe that children should mind their parents and that obedience is a virtue. Third, authoritarians endorse punitive aggression as a means of dealing with many social problems. They believe that the "world is a dangerous place" and that people should be punished harshly when they do things that threaten society's values (Altemeyer, 1988, p. 146). The basic premise of this approach to prejudice—that some attitudes are rooted deeply in the individual's belief system—has been supported in a wide range of studies (Duckitt, 2009).

Do individuals who adopt differing ethics positions also differ in their degree of authoritarianism? First, the conventionalism and submission components of authoritarianism both stand in contrast to a relativistic conception of morality. Relativists would be unlikely to agree that "The 'old-fashioned ways' and 'old-fashioned values' still show the best way to live" and "God's laws about abortion, pornography and marriage must be strictly followed before it is too late; violations must be punished" (Zakrisson, 2005, p. 870). Second, authoritarianism's emphasis on punishment of those who act in ways that violate moral rules is not consistent with an ethic of caring that characterizes idealism. Idealism, in theory, should be incongruent with a generalized negativity toward people who are members of other social groups. If one is sensitive to causes and consequences of harm being done to others, then how would one ever justify discriminating against others, since prejudice and discrimination cause suffering for those in the rejected group? However, some individuals with elevated levels of idealism are also stronger in their moral condemnation of those who act in ways that violate moral standards or cause harm to others. In consequence, and somewhat paradoxically, idealism may be associated with authoritarianism—at least for those who are also low in relativism (absolutists).

McHoskey (1996) explored these possibilities by administering both the EPQ and Altemeyer's (1988) Right Wing Authoritarianism (RWA) scale to a sample of college students. He discovered that RWA was positively associated with idealism but negatively correlated with relativism, and that this negative relationship was strongest for the conventionalism subscale of the RWA. Nicol and Rounding (2018) reported similar findings in their study of the relationship between ethics positions, RWA, and prejudice. Davis and his colleagues (2001), in their study of ethics positions and dogmatism—which tends to be related to authoritarianism—found that dogmatism was negatively correlated with both idealism ($r = -0.07$) and relativism ($r = -0.28$). Murthy and Bhattacharya (2015), however, reported just the opposite when they examined the relationship between dogmatism and a subset of the items from the EPQ.

These inconsistencies prompted us to investigate the relationship between authoritarianism, idealism, and relativism for the 2,404 individuals who completed both the EPQ and the RWA online at the MyMorals survey site. In that sample, both idealism and relativism were negatively correlated with authoritarianism ($rs = -0.24$ and -0.40). However, the interaction of idealism and relativism was also significant, which suggests both idealism and relativism must be considered conjointly when predicting respondents' level of authoritarianism. Consistent with the negative correlation between relativism and authoritarianism, the situationists and subjectivists were significantly less authoritarian than the absolutists and the exceptionists. However, within levels of relativism, individuals who adopted more idealistic ethics positions were less authoritarian than those who adopted less idealistic ethics positions. In consequence, situationists were less authoritarian than all other ethics types, and exceptionists were the most authoritarian.

Correlates and Characteristics

People who differ in their ethics positions diverge not only in their degree of idealism and relativism, but also in their personal qualities, traits, beliefs, and values. Situationists, besides being more idealistic and relativist than most people, are more likely to be younger rather than older, women rather than men, and persons of color—but these differences in ages, gender, and ethnicity are not particularly pronounced. Situationists are also less likely to be religious: 44.5% of the situationists described themselves as religious, compared to 47.2% and 50.8% of the exceptionists and absolutists. As for their likely personality traits, situationists are slightly lower in conscientiousness than absolutists and exceptionists, but they are also more extraverted, agreeable, neurotic, and open to new experiences. They are also more likely to endorse prosocial values such as justice and the fair treatment of others, but the acquisition of power is less important to them. Situationists are also more collectivistic rather than individualistic, and they are relatively empathic. They are also less likely to exhibit any of the darker psychological qualities, such as Machiavellianism or a sociopolitical orientation that is associated with prejudice (authoritarianism).

Absolutists are among the more benevolent individuals in our studies. Like situationists, they are idealistic, agreeable, open, empathic, and collectivistic. They endorse prosocial values such as benevolence and universality, they are highly empathic, and they are less likely to possess qualities that others find to be repellant (such as interpersonal manipulativeness). They are, however, more traditional than situationists. Absolutists are the most religious of all the ethics types. They endorse traditional values, such as respect for and conformity to social norms and practices. Moreover, as we will soon discover in Chapter 5, they are more likely to condemn individuals who act in ways that violate moral rules.

Exceptionists, like absolutists, are relatively traditional in their attitudes, values, and ideological beliefs. But unlike absolutists, they are pragmatic rather than idealistic, self-focused rather than benevolent, politically conservative rather than liberal, and individualistic rather than collectivistic. They are not particularly agreeable or open to new experiences, and they do not consider such values as equality, social justice, and environmentalism to be as important as respect for tradition, self-discipline, achieving wealth, and maintaining authority over others. They are not, by any means, antisocial in their orientation—they are not likely to be Machiavellians or have elevated levels of psychopathy—but they are relatively authoritarian. They may be prone to adopt a morality of expedience rather than caring (Schlenker, 2008).

Subjectivists, in contrast to all the other ethics types, are more varied in their values, beliefs, and behavioral tendencies. In terms of cognitive moral development, no one of the four ethics positions emerges as necessarily more likely to reach higher levels of moral maturity than another. However, subjectivists tend to be lower in their endorsement of an ethic of caring, and lower than all other groups on the moral foundations of caring, loyalty, authority, and security. Subjectivists are lower in religiosity, benevolence, traditionalism, collectivism, and authoritarianism, yet they are higher than all other ethics positions in hedonism. They are also lower than other ethical types in empathy and agreeableness, and these two qualities are two key markers of several of the darker personality traits, including psychopathy and Machiavellianism. It is no wonder, then, that subjectivists are more likely to have higher scores on both these qualities, suggesting they are the one ethics type that may be more likely act in less morally acceptable ways.

Notes

1. Individuals who register with the YourMorals project can complete a number of measures of individual differences, including the EPQ. The respondents are volunteers, the majority are residents of the U.S., and they usually find YourMorals. org "through publicity about psychological research or by typing keywords related to morality into an Internet search engine" (Iyer et al., 2012, p. 3). The majority of individuals who took part completed two surveys, but some (37%) completed multiple surveys of their values, personality traits, moral beliefs, and the EPQ. Because respondents selected which questionnaires they wished to complete from the site, the sample size varies depending on how many people completed any particular measure. The sample sizes, however, tend to be substantial, so even statistically significant findings should be interpreted with caution.
2. Leary et al. (1986) used the original, 20-item version of the EPQ in their research. That version includes the two items pertaining to lying (the veracity subscale); the relativism subscale on the shorter version of the EPQ (the EPQ-5) does not include those items.

5

MORAL THOUGHT

Vice may be defined to be a miscalculation of chances, a mistake in estimating the value of pleasures and pains. It is false moral arithmetic.
—Jeremy Bentham, *Deontology* (1834, p. 131)

When will a person judge an action to be immoral? Ethics position theory suggests perceivers begin by considering consequences and consistency with moral standards; an action that harms others or runs counter to traditional moral standards triggers moral scrutiny. But the theory also suggests the influence of consequences and standards is not equal across all people: Some individuals evaluate actions that cause harm more negatively than others, just as some people are harsher when judging actions that are inconsistent with moral standards. This tendency is evident in people's judgments of lies, broken promises, and thefts, in their positions on contemporary moral issues, and in the way that they process information as they formulate moral appraisals. Individuals' appraisals of an act, however, may not generalize to their evaluations of the person who carried out the action. If individuals are not responsible for their actions, then inferences about their ethics must be only tentative ones. Responsibility is the final link in the chain of reasoning that begins by raising the question "Is this a moral issue?" and ends with a moral judgment of a person.

* * *

Kimberly Davis, a county clerk in Kentucky, refused to issue marriage licenses to same-sex couples, citing God's authority. During the war in Iraq, American soldiers used "enhanced interrogation techniques" to extract information from captured enemy soldiers. David Gelernter (1998), who was badly injured by a bomb built by Ted Kaczynski, the so-called Unabomber, asked "What do murderers deserve?" His answer: the death penalty, for by "executing murderers, we declare that deliberate murder is absolutely evil and absolutely intolerable." Late one evening John Williams, a cab driver, shouted at a group of young men who had knocked an elderly man to the ground and were kicking him. When the men threatened Williams, he discharged his hand gun in their general direction, killing one of the young men.

An elected official who was morally opposed to same-sex marriages. Inconsistencies in moral judgments of torture during wartime. A person who believed that capital punishment is a moral necessity. The man who killed when he only meant to scare. These cases all invite moral scrutiny and judgment, but also debate. Some people sided with Davis, the clerk who broke the law by discriminating against people she believed violated the sanctity of marriage. Others condemned her. Some people believe that torture and capital punishment, although banned in most countries, are not just allowable but morally mandated in certain situations. In his first trial, Williams was convicted of involuntary manslaughter, but on appeal was found innocent. The appellate court believed that he was morally justified, for he had the right to use lethal force to protect himself and that his actions were therefore reasonable ones (*People v. Williams*, 1965).

Many are the sources of this variance in people's moral pronouncements, but ethics position theory singles out one of these causes among the many: individual differences in people's orientation toward harm (idealism) and moral standards (relativism). Actions that cause harm or are inconsistent with commonly accepted standards of morality trigger moral scrutiny, but the evidence reviewed in earlier chapters suggests people differ in their orientation toward both of these influences. Some people are more idealistic than others, for they believe that, "If an action could harm an innocent other, then it should not be done." Some people, too, believe that "what is ethical varies from one situation and society to another," but others disagree with such moral relativism. These two dimensions of variation, when combined, describe four ethics positions: exceptionism, subjectivism, absolutism, and situationism. But do these variations in ethical ideology predict differences in the moral conclusions people reach? Who is more lenient in their appraisals of others and who is harsher? Who is more likely to oppose, on moral grounds, abortion, capital punishment, same-sex marriage, and torture? Who is more likely to take into account mitigating factors before blaming others for their misdeeds, and who is stricter in their estimates of liability? This chapter reviews the evidence that suggests that a person's ethics position significantly influences their judgments of others' morally questionable actions, outlook on contemporary moral issues, and conclusions about praise and punishment.

Judging Right and Wrong

The formula for earning moral censure is a relatively simple one: If you cause harm to others and do so by breaking a moral rule, your action—and possibly you as a person—will be judged negatively. But the relative weights associated with these two key ingredients—harm and consistency with moral rules—depend in part on the evaluator's personal moral philosophy. In general, relativists tend to be more lenient when judging others, particularly in comparison to absolutists (if harm has been done), and in comparison to exceptionists (if moral standards have been violated).

Moral Leniency

Imagine you are on trial for doing something that society believes you should not have done; robbed a bank, divulged corporate secrets, tortured a terrorist, verbally assaulted a fellow citizen, caused an automobile accident with injuries, or the like. When you are offered the choice between having your case decided by the judge or by a jury of your peers, you take the jury option. You watch as each potential member of that jury is interviewed by your legal counsel. Knowing that people take different positions on moral matters, who do you hope make their way onto your jury? Does their ethics position matter?

Most of the studies that have examined this question reach the same conclusion: seek the relativists, avoid the idealists, and avoid the absolutists (nonrelativistic and idealistic) in particular (e.g., Barnett, Bass, & Brown, 1994; Barnett, Bass, Brown, & Hebert, 1998; Bartels, 2008; Etter, Cramer, & Finn, 2006; Forsyth & Pope, 1984; Giacalone, Fricker, & Beard, 1995; Kim & Choi, 2003; Smith & Lord, 2018; Tansey, Brown, Hyman, & Dawson, 1994; VanMeter, Grisaffe, Chonko, & Roberts, 2013; Vitell, Lumpkin, & Rawwas, 1991). Students who were classified as absolutists were more negative when evaluating other students who cheated compared to subjectivists, with situationists and exceptionists falling intermediate (VanMeter et al., 2013). Absolutists judged consumers who cheated merchants, say by switching price tags on merchandise or returning a product after using it, more negatively than individuals who adopted other ethics positions (Vitell et al., 1991). Absolutists, when asked to evaluate the ethics of research that involved deception, were more negative in their judgments than individuals who had elevated levels of relativism (Forsyth & Pope, 1984). Sports fans were more likely to judge certain behaviors, such as verbally confronting fans of the other team, causing disturbances during the game, and damaging cars in post-game celebrations, as more ethically suspect as their levels of idealism increased and their relativism decreased (Smith & Lord, 2018).

Researchers also confirmed this idealism-harsh/relativism-lenient effect when they asked individuals to judge the moral choices of protagonists in hypothetical moral dilemmas. What, for example, do you think about a druggist who charges people ten times the cost of making a life-saving drug, or the husband who broke into the drugstore and stole the drug to save his wife's life (Barnett et al., 1994, p. 477)? When Barnett and his colleagues put this question to a sample of college students, nearly all sided with the husband, commending him for his actions—idealism and relativism were unrelated to their judgments. But their appraisals of the druggist told a different story. Increases in idealism were associated with more negative moral judgments ($r = -0.44$), whereas their judgments were more positive as relativism increased ($r = +0.42$). Absolutists were the most negative in their appraisals, followed closely by the also-idealistic situationists. The exceptionists and subjectivists were significantly less negative, and their judgments of the druggist were nearly the same.

The sensitivity of absolutists also influenced their judgments when we had them read and respond to a story of a person who told a "white lie": a statement that is false, but is well-intentioned and generally benign in its consequences. We asked respondents to consider the hypothetical case of Pat, who is visiting a friend (Dale) in the hospital. Dale's doctors, before the visit, take Pat aside and explain Dale's condition is very serious, and caution Pat to avoid discussing the prognosis with Dale. But, when Dale asks for the details, Pat explains: "I don't think it is very serious, and I am sure that you will be up and around in a couple of days." The lie yielded some positive consequences, such as raising Dale's spirits, but also some negative ones as well (e.g., causing him to refuse to take needed medications). Absolutists, relative to others, rated Pat more negatively compared to individuals who adopted alternative ethics positions. Pat may have been well-intentioned, but those good intentions did not justify the moral inconsistency—at least in the eyes of the absolutists (Forsyth, 1978).

McNair, Okan, Hadjichristidis, and de Bruin (2019) also documented the relationship between idealism and harshness in moral judgment in their analysis of age-differences in moral thought. They asked participants to judge the morality of individuals who had to make difficult moral choices. For example (McNair et al., 2019, p. 50):

> You are a nurse who is in charge of a machine that controls drug dosage levels in patients' blood. Because of a technical failure, the machine is supplying a lethal dose of a drug to four patients. Another patient, in a single room, is hooked up to the same machine and has not undergone any variation in dosage. You press the button to block the drug supply to the four patients. You know that the overdose of drug will be redirected to the patient in the single room, who will die, but the other four will be saved.

They discovered that increases in idealism were negatively associated with moral judgments in such scenarios. Even though the utilitarian choices save more lives, the decision to harm another person still causes idealists to judge the action more negatively.

The empirical record is not pristine. Every study does not find that idealists are more negative in their judgments, whereas relativists are more lenient (e.g., Mudrack & Mason, 2013). But as Pan and Sparks (2012) conclude in their meta-analytic review of the predictors and consequences of ethical judgments (p. 85): "As idealism increases, ethical judgments become stricter," and "as relativism increases, ethical judgments become less strict."

Moral Beliefs

Differences in ethics positions are also systematically associated with variations in people's moral beliefs (Ditto & Liu, 2012). For example, is it ever morally acceptable to use torture to extract information from prisoners? Torture is banned by international treaty, but in some countries and communities, many condone its use in situations where lives are at risk. And what about the legal right for women to end an unwanted pregnancy through abortion? Some view abortion as a moral wrong, for it is prohibited by most religious authorities. So, even though U.S. citizens' attitude toward abortion has remained steady over the years—54% agreed that abortion should be legal in 1975, in 1995, and again in 2012 (Bowman & Marisco, 2014)—when asked about the ethics of abortion, more people say it is morally wrong (48%) than say it is morally right (43%; Gallup Organization, 2018).

Individuals who are relativistic take more liberal stances on a number of social issues, such as marijuana use, homosexuality, abortion, premarital sex, and extramarital sex (Forsyth, 1980; Singh & Forsyth, 1989). Consider, for example, the responses of the adults who completed both the EPQ and measures of moral beliefs as part of the YourMorals project.[1] Moderated multiple regression indicated that relativism was strongly and consistently associated with moral judgments pertaining to such social issues as abortion, capital punishment, and same-sex marriage. For example, exceptionists and absolutists, who are less relativistic than subjectivists and situationists, were more likely to believe that abortion, euthanasia, stem-cell research, the use of pornography, same-sex marriage, casual sex, having a baby outside of marriage, and homosexuality are morally wrong ($p < 0.05$). But respondents' levels of idealism mattered as well, particularly for issues that involved harm: torture, capital punishment, and medical testing involving animals. Regarding torture, situationists were more negative in their condemnation than exceptionists, and for both capital punishment and medical testing involving animals, absolutists and situationists were more negative in comparison to the exceptionists. And for two of the issues—using pornography and cloning—it was the subjectivists who were more generous in their moral judgments than individuals who endorsed the other ethics positions.

Differences in ethics positions also predicted respondents' support for regulatory policies related to each issue. For example, when asked about abortion, 82% of the subjectivists and situationists in our sample believed that abortion should be available to those women who want it, compared to 64% of the absolutists and 55% of the exceptionists. In fact, 26% of the exceptionists favored making abortion illegal, compared to only 6% of the situationists and subjectivists. Absolutists fell intermediate, with 22% favoring a legal ban on abortion. Conversely, the majority of the absolutists and situationists (56% and 58%) believed that torture is never justified, compared to 26% and 35% of the exceptionists and subjectivists.

Thinking About Right and Wrong

Studies of people making moral judgments and the positions they take on moral issues such as capital punishment and abortion support ethics position theory's most basic prediction: Individuals vary in their idealism and relativism, and these two dimensions of difference cause them to also vary in their attentiveness to the harm that results from an action and the consistency of the action with moral standards. But these studies do not test that assumption directly; what is needed, empirically, is evidence that shows that as levels of harm and rule-consistency vary, so do people's moral judgments at a rate predicted by their ethics position.

Moral Cognition

Moral judgments are similar in some ways to other types of social inferences. People are, in many ways, rational decisionmakers who gather data, process that data, and respond with a moral judgment that is based on the results of that processing. Therefore, to make a moral judgment people must procure information about the specific situation, but they must also retrieve relevant information, such as beliefs, values, and personal moral philosophy, from memory. But these two processes co-mingle. People's beliefs, values, and expectations influence what information they seek, just as the information they gather influences their judgmental conclusions (Guglielmo, 2015).

We examined these cognitive processes experimentally by manipulating both the consequences produced by an action and the consistency of the action with moral rules, and then tracking the influence of these manipulations on individuals' moral judgments. The 32 men and 32 women who participated were selected from a larger sample of approximately 325 individuals who completed the Ethics Position Questionnaire (EPQ) in a mass testing session. They scored one standard deviation above or below the median on the idealism and relativism subscales, and so could be classified in advance as exceptionists, subjectivists, absolutists, and situationists (Forsyth, 1985).

These participants then judged the morality of a series of actions that resulted in either positive or negative outcomes. These two-part vignettes described a person who, by acting in a way that was either consistent or inconsistent with a traditional moral rule, harmed or helped others. The person who violated moral principles stole things, lied, failed to do his duty, or broke a promise. In contrast, the one who acted in ways that were consistent with moral rules resisted stealing something that was not his, told the truth, did his duty, and kept a promise.

We manipulated the consequences of the action in the second part of the vignette: Half produced good outcomes for others and half caused harm. We also varied the intensity of the outcomes, so that some were only mildly beneficial or harmful, whereas others were extremely beneficial or harmful. Thus, each action produced one of four types of outcomes: extremely positive (e.g., "a child's life is saved," "a little girl gets the life-saving operation she needs"); mildly positive (e.g., "a team wins a football game," "a child gets a free ticket to a movie"); mildly negative (e.g., "a passerby's coat gets dirty," "a fishing rod is broken"); and extremely negative ("a little boy loses his eyesight," "a passerby is horribly disfigured"). We used eight different sets of standard conformity and consequences pairings, counterbalancing them across the four ethical ideologies. We also asked participants to judge the morality of a person who did or did not lie, steal, do his duty, and keep a promise, independent of any consequences. These ratings provide us with a baseline for determining if consistency or inconsistency of the action with moral rules influences judgments, independent of consequences.

Acting in accord with moral principles and producing positive consequences would likely be viewed by all as more morally commendable than violating moral principles and causing great harm. But ethics position theory predicts that (a) idealistic individuals would be more influenced by consequences and (b) relativists less influenced by the consistency of the action with moral principles. These tendencies would be indicated, statistically, by differences in the amount of variance accounted for by the main effects of the two manipulated variables (consistency with moral rules and consequences) and their interaction. If, for example, the relativists (situationists and subjectivists) were influenced more by consequences than by rules, the main effect of the consequences manipulation should be larger than the main effect of the rules manipulation for this group. Moreover, a statistical interaction between rules and consequences would indicate that information about consequences exacerbates or mutes the effects of rules on moral judgment (or vice versa). For example, because absolutists prize both principles and nonmaleficence, those who endorse this ethics position may judge actions that caused great harm and violated moral rules to be uniquely egregious—and this tendency would be indicated by a statistically significant interaction of conformity to rules and consequences.

The results were, for the most part, consistent with these predictions. The judgments of situationists were more influenced by consequences than the conformity of the action to moral rules; the consequence main effect accounted for approximately five percent more of the variance in their judgments than did the moral rules main effect. Absolutists, in contrast, were more influenced by moral rules than by consequences. They tended to rate actions that were not consistent with moral rules (e.g., lying, breaking a promise) more negatively and actions that conformed to moral rules (e.g., telling the truth, keeping a promise) more positively than did the situationists. However, like situationists, the interaction—although dwarfed in magnitude by the main effects of rules and consequences—was nonetheless significant. For both situationists and absolutists, the effects of consequence information depended, in part, on the conformity of the action to moral rules: Conforming to a standard had a greater impact on judgments when the consequences were relatively mild rather than severe.

The consequences and conformity to moral rules variables did not interact with one another to influence the judgments of those respondents who were low in idealism. Of all the participants, the subjectivists were the least influenced by the extent to which the action was consistent with moral principles—particularly in comparison to the absolutists—and they did not rate actions that resulted in mildly negative outcomes as negatively as did idealists. Exceptionists also rated actions that caused only minimal harm more positively than idealists, but their judgments were almost equally influenced by consequences and by the conformity of the action with more rules. Compared to subjectivists, exceptionists were somewhat less condemning of an individual who caused considerable harm by conforming to a moral rule, but this difference was not a substantial one. In general, when the consequences were extreme, ideological differences were not very pronounced. If, however, the consequences were mild, idealists—and absolutists in particular—were more favorable toward individuals who conformed to moral rules and less favorable toward nonconformists.

Moral Algebra

These findings suggest that individuals who differ in their ethics positions also differ in the way they integrate information about morality. Such a suggestion is not without precedent. Bentham (1789/1948), the moral philosopher, believed that moral judgment may require "cognitive algebra," for one must intuitively sum both the benefits and harms that will likely result from all available actions, and then choose that act that yields the maximum benefit for the maximum number. Bentham suggested that only the expected consequences should be fed into the moral calculus that determines judgments, but deontological approaches to morality suggest that people also consider the compatibility of the act with principles before reaching a moral verdict.

We investigated this combinatorial process by testing which of three different models best accounted for the moral judgments in our data set. The first model, an additive one, assumes that bits of information are combined in a linear fashion analogous to addition. Say, for example, you know a person told the truth, and that, on a scale from -3 (very immoral) to +3 (very moral), you rate truth-telling as a +2. Then, you discover that not only did the person tell the truth, but by telling the truth someone benefited, albeit in a relatively minor way. So, a +1 on the scale from -3 (very bad) to +3 (very good). An additive model predicts that the consequence information will result in an even more positive evaluation of the person: +2 plus +1 = +3.

An averaging model of information makes a different prediction. This model predicts information is not added, but averaged together to generate a final judgment. So, if the lie was rated as +2, but the consequences were only +1, then the evaluation may decline slightly once the relatively unimpressive consequences are considered along with the information about the act's consistency with moral standards: +2 plus +1 = +3 divided by 2 or 1.5.

A third model, a weighted-averaging model, offers yet an additional set of predictions about how this information can be integrated to reach a conclusion about morality. This model suggests that information is averaged, but that some information has more of an impact on the final conclusion than other information. More extreme or more unusual actions or attributes, for example, may be weighted more heavily than less extreme or more common ones. Or the consistency of the action with a moral rule may be of primary importance in determining moral judgments for some people, particularly in comparison to consequences, and so this information is weighted more heavily. As a result, the cognitive algebra may now suggest a new formula, such as (+2 x 2) plus +1 = 5 divided by 2 = 2.5.

We used Anderson's (2008) parallelism analysis to test the explanatory power of these three models of information integration. This method assumes that, if information is combined additively, and if each piece of information is equally weighted, then judgments will be a linear function of the input variables. Information about an action's consistency with moral principles will shift judgments upward (when consistent) and downward (when inconsistent), but the magnitude of that shift will be consistent across the various kinds of consequences (positive or negative and severe and mild)—so, if charted, the response lines will parallel one another. If, however, the change in ratings when the action produces positive rather than negative consequences differs depending on the consistency of the action with moral standards, then this nonparallel pattern is consistent with a weighted averaging model of information integration.

As shown in Figure 5.1, the ratings of idealistic individuals display nonparallelism, for the person who caused severely negative consequences by complying with moral standards did not receive the same level of leniency in comparison to those who caused only minor harm. Conformity substantially raised the moral judgments of situationists when the consequence was mildly positive or mildly negative, but conformity had much less influence on their evaluations when the consequence was extremely negative or positive. Absolutists' judgments followed a similar pattern if an action was consistent with a moral norm, but their judgments were more negative when they rated actions that violated

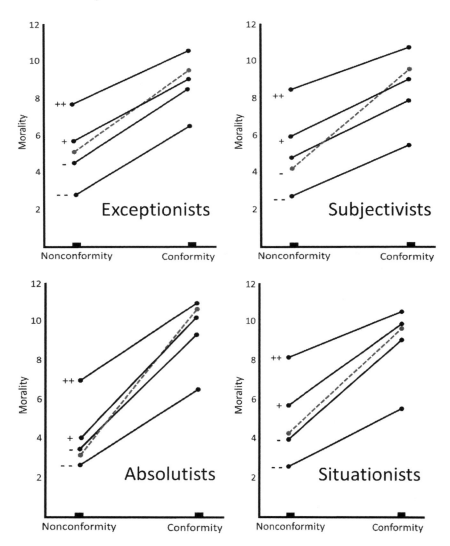

FIGURE 5.1 The mean ratings of eight different types of actions that varied in terms of their conformity to moral norms and the kinds of consequences they produced: very negative (− −), negative (−), positive (+), and very positive (+ +). The dotted lines represent judgments of conforming and nonconforming actions without consequences.

moral norms—except if the action yielded extremely positive consequences. These patterns are most consistent with a weighted averaging model.

In contrast to the idealists, subjectivists' judgments were best predicted by an averaging model of information integration. They rated actions that were consistent with a moral norm very positively, but when minor positive consequences were added to the mix, their ratings dropped—suggesting the relatively minor consequences were averaged with the highly positive information about moral norms. They also rated acting inconsistently with a moral norm very negatively, but when only minor negative consequences resulted from this indiscretion, ratings were more positive.

Unlike the other ethics positions, and somewhat contrary to expectations, exceptionists weighted the two types of cues equally in formulating their moral judgments. Their judgments showed strong evidence of parallelism, for each cue was integrated with the other cue in a cumulative, equally weighted fashion. The better the consequence, the more positive the moral judgment. The greater the conformity of the action to a moral norm, the more positive the moral judgment. The ratings of actions that were consistent with moral rules show some evidence of averaging (minor positive consequences lowered moral judgments of actions that were consistent with moral rules), but the effect was not statistically significant.

Moral Intuition

Why do individuals differ in their moral judgments and beliefs? Ethics position theory traces these differences back to a cognitive source—the way people combine information as they make their moral decisions—and the data support that interpretation. These findings, however, are also consistent with an intuitionist approach to moral judgment. Haidt (2012), for example, argues persuasively that moral judgments are largely determined by rapid, intuitive, gut reactions such that, "intuitions come first, strategic reasoning second" (p. 52). Discovering, for example, that an action causes harm triggers a negative affective response, and that response then drives perceivers' moral response to the event—either separate and apart from their rational analysis of the action's qualities or in a combined affect-intellective process (e.g., Cushman, Young, & Hauser, 2006; Nichols, 2018; van den Bos, 2018).

Intuitionism, then, suggests that individuals do not rely on a strictly rational moral calculus as they weigh risks, benefits, and principles, but are also guided by their implicit, intuitive reaction to events. Moreover, for many individuals—particularly those with a deontological orientation—this intuitive response is likely triggered by the degree of harm present in the situation.[2] We examined this possibility by recording how quickly participants judged the morality of persons who made difficult and, in some cases, high questionable choices in ethically fraught situations (O'Boyle & Forsyth, 2018). Examples of the vignettes include:

- Michael and Donna are wealthy. They have a child, who due to problems at birth is very limited intellectually. When an infant, the child develops a kidney problem that can be cured through an expensive medical procedure. Ernest and Donna decide to let the child die by denying him treatment for a kidney disease.

- Ernest promises his parents that he will stay home and babysit his younger sister. When friends come over and ask him to sneak away for an hour to listen to music, he tells them no: He must keep his promise. So Ernest is home when an electric problem causes the house to catch fire, and he saves his sister.

Individuals in the control condition read each vignette before rating the protagonist as moral or immoral. Other participants, however, made their judgments under conditions of cognitive load. Prior to reading the vignette, they were shown a seven-digit number, and were asked to remember it. After each vignette they were asked to recall the number or some combination of it (e.g., "What were the third and fourth digits of the number?", "Did five come before seven in your number?"). In terms of judgment, the manipulation of cognitive load served an inhibitory function. When under cognitive load individuals cannot process information as quickly, so they will need more time to make a decision (DeLeeuw & Mayer, 2008). They may also compensate for the increased cognitive demand by processing the available information differently than they would if working under less cognitively pressing conditions. They may, for example, shift to faster and more frugal methods for arriving at a decision, such as reliance on heuristics or intuition.

The vignettes we used in this study yielded a mix of good and bad consequences, so those who were more idealistic in their ethics positions did not differ in their judgments compared to those who were less idealistic. However, relativism was associated with moral judgments of those vignettes which involved violations of moral rules. As predicted, the relativistic situationists and subjectivists judged a higher proportion of the individuals who acted in ways that were inconsistent with moral rules to be moral rather than immoral, in comparison to the less relativistic absolutists and exceptionists. Over half of the relativists (56.5%) considered the majority of the individuals who violated rules to be moral, in comparison to only 35.6% of the low relativists.

As for response time, those participants who made their judgments more quickly tended to be more negative than participants who made their judgments more slowly, but this relation was not substantial ($r = -0.14$, $p = 0.05$). Response times did, however, vary across ethics positions, depending on cognitive load. In the control condition, the exceptionists made their judgments more slowly than both subjectivists and absolutists. The mean reaction time for situationists fell intermediate to all other ethics types, and did not differ from them. These findings suggest that exceptionists require more cognitive resources to formulate their moral judgments—which would be consistent with their utilitarian tendencies. Under conditions of cognitive load, however, it was the absolutists who made their judgments more slowly, particularly in comparison to the exceptionists and situationists. Their relatively slower responses may have been due to their need to integrate both information regarding the consequences and the consistency of the actions with moral standards, as they are the only ethics position that bases their moral judgments on both harm information and moral standards. These results are, in general, consistent with a dual-process approach to moral judgment. People's appraisals of right and wrong are surely influenced by moods, emotions, and psychologically subtle nudges that push their appraisals this way and that, but they are also based on thoughtful, rational deliberation (Johnson, 2014).

Judging Responsibility

Researchers have repeatedly confirmed that perceivers often base their understanding of other people on the things these other people do (Heider, 1958). We take note of others' actions, including the things they say, and draw inferences about their traits, beliefs, attitudes, values, and so on. If a person frequently misses deadlines, we question his conscientiousness. If an associate discriminates against the members of other groups, we may conclude she is a racist. If a person acts in ways that cause harm to others or repeatedly violates widely accepted rules that define what is moral, we question that person's moral character. Not every action, however, is fodder for some sweeping conclusion about another person's basic attributes. Even when a person's actions are characterized as immoral or moral, the link between the action and the individual may be too uncertain to support an inference about their moral worth.

Freedom, Foreseeability, and Purposiveness

You are back in the courtroom, and the assembled evidence indicates that you did, in fact, commit the crime you have been charged with by the prosecution. You did verbally assault a fellow citizen in the checkout line of the grocery store. You did refuse to issue a marriage license to gay and lesbian couples. You did cause the accident, and you did shoot an unarmed youth. All these actions will likely be viewed negatively—even condemned as immoral actions. But you yourself may not be colored by the quality of the actions you took or the consequences that resulted. Why not? Because those who are judging you may also believe that you cannot be held responsible for what you did or the consequences which ensued.

Responsibility defines the relationship between a person, that person's actions, and the consequences of those actions. When a person is judged to be responsible for an action that causes positive consequences, the person deserves credit, honor, rewards, commendation, and so on. But if the outcome is negative, responsibility implies blame, liability, obligation, culpability, guilt, punishment, and so on. An individual who is perceived to be responsible for something is judged to be answerable for that activity, or judged to be open to positive or negative sanctions as a consequence of being linked in some way to an event and its effects. Responsibility, then, is what knits together perceptually two evaluative processes—the appraisal of the action (which is determined, we have argued, primarily by the harm the action causes and the act's consistency with moral rules) and the moral appraisal of the person. Most people, and that includes legal authorities, would agree that if a person is not responsible for an action or its consequences, then no moral judgment can be made about the individual. In the person-as-moralist perspective, blame and praise are placed at the center of causal investigations of behavior and its consequences (Alicke, Mandel, Hilton, Gerstenberg, & Lagnado, 2015).

Responsibility, like morality, has received considerable attention from both philosophers and psychologists. Aristotle (350BCE/1935), for example, in his *Nicomachean Ethics*, suggested that a person should be held accountable only for voluntary acts. In recognizing the distinction between the voluntary and involuntary, Aristotle proposed that an act is freely produced only when it results from "proaireton," or deliberated choice. Jurisprudential theories similarly stress the importance of responsibility in the concepts of actus reus and mens rea, which suggest that both an action as well as the exercise of will is needed before a person can be said to be responsible for some occurrence and its consequences.

These conditions for the assignment of responsibility are consistent with psychological studies of the factors that influence perceivers' willingness to give credit or assign blame to others. Steiner (1970, p 189), for example, emphasized free choice among alternatives in his theory of responsibility allocation. As he explained, only when the perceiver believes the actor, "rather than other people, fate, or the press of circumstances, selects the outcomes he will seek and the means he will employ in seeking them" will the individual be held accountable. His work identified two primary factors that influence the perception of freedom: the actor's ability to perform the action and the restrictiveness of environmental influences. If individuals lack the ability to perform some behavior, say stop a runaway trolley car or staunch the bleeding from a gunshot wound, then it would be misleading to state that they freely or voluntarily chose to not stop the train or save a person's life. Nor could these people be held responsible if some force, whether external (e.g., a wall that could not be surmounted) or internal (e.g., disabling fear or revulsion), then they would not be perceived to be free to act. The bully from a broken family, the poorly trained technician who fails to properly repair the computer's operating system, and the psychopath who is neurologically unable to understand other people's feelings do not freely choose to bully, to mis-repair, or to injure.

A person's degree of responsibility is also influenced by the foreseeability of the consequences of actions, or the degree to which the individual should and could have been aware of the results of some action beforehand. Foreseeability depends upon two related questions: "Did the individual possess information concerning the nature of the act and the consequences it would foreseeably produce?" and "Should the individual have possessed this information?" If people did not foresee the consequences and are not seen as required to be familiar with them, then this ignorance leaves them relatively blameless. Although free to act in another manner since they possessed the ability to do so and the environment did not restrict them in any way, they are not seen to be as responsible as the individual whose actions produced foreseeably negative consequences. However, if the perceiver concludes that they could and should have been aware of the nature and consequences of his action—that a reasonable person would have known what would ensue from the action—then they will likely be held responsible, at least in part, for the outcome.

Responsibility is also influenced by the degree to which the behavior seems purposive. Behavior is described as purposive when the action was done deliberately to reach some specific goal. When individuals act with purpose, they are not behaving recklessly, randomly, or without considering what will result from their actions, but instead they are deliberately choosing to act in a certain way so as to cause certain and anticipated effects. They acted as they did "on purpose," and so likely cannot claim the outcome was not foreseeable or that they were not free to act in another way. Another adjective often employed, sometimes interchangeably with purposive, to describe such behavior is *intentional* (cf. Anscombe, 1957; D'Arcy, 1963).

Although in many instances behavior may "reek of purpose" and thereby allow a perceiver to assess goal-directedness directly, often purposiveness is revealed by the individuals themselves, as they clarify their motives to those who might judge them. These motive statements are a special class of performatives which give explanations of behaviors by providing a link between specific actions and anticipated consequences (Austin, 1962). As D'Arcy (1963) points out, the "for sake of" clause is a central part of every motive-statement since it mentions the desired objective. Motives are what link the action and the evaluations of the act, to the individual and the evaluation of the individual. From Mill (1863): "The motive has nothing to do with the morality of the action, though much with the worth of the agent. . . . Motive makes a great difference in our moral estimation of the agent, especially if it indicates a good or bad habitual disposition, a bent of character from which either useful or hurtful actions are likely to arise (pp. 26–27).

When the consequences of the act are negative, and people are seeking to avoid being judged negatively because of their association with the act, their description of their motives often take one of two forms: excuses or justifications. Excuses account for misfirings of human behavior through references to such things as inefficient deliberation prior to action, ignorance, or the press of internal or external causes. While the recognition of such factors may not totally absolve the doer of responsibility, the presence of such elements usually serves to mitigate responsibility to a degree which lessens the severity of the charge and/or punishment. In his *Plea for Excuses*, Austin (1962) notes that a person may admit that an act "wasn't a good thing to have done," but adds that it is "not quite fair or correct to say *baldly* 'X did A'" since there are extenuating circumstances which suggest that X's actions may have been partially accidental or unintentional (p. 556). The man who says that he meant to only scare the youths away from their victim, and never intended to actually harm them, may be judged to be less responsible than the individual who was enraged by the group's actions and wanted to harm them.

Motive claims can also alter the characterization of the action, and so work as a justification of behavior. Information which is interpreted as justifying an act indicates that, in the particular situation under review, a usually blameworthy act is in fact allowable or even praiseworthy. Thus a justification works to dispel the possibility that any moral wrong has been committed. For example, rather than claim he did not mean to injure, the man could instead say that the young men attacked him—they threw a brick at him which hit his automobile—and so he responded to their attack to protect himself. Excuses mitigate by reducing responsibility, whereas justifications absolve by redefining the action and its consequences as positive rather than negative.

Levels of Responsibility

Heider (1958), to bring order to the many and varied analyses of responsibility allocations, proposed a conceptually useful *levels of responsibility* theory based on intentionality, association, and external coercion. Heider suggested that the perceiver's first task is to determine if the actor is responsible or not responsible for the act; second, if judged to be responsible, the perceiver must then determine the degree of responsibility. In general, if the actor is seen to be related to the act through either association or commission, then little or no responsibility is assigned. If, however, the attributor perceives the actor's relationship to the act to be more complex than simple causation or association, then varying degrees of responsibility are attributed depending upon appraisals of freedom, foreseeability, and purposiveness (Shaw & Sulzer, 1964).

At the first level, that of association, people are held responsible for any actions or events which they are connected with in any way, no matter how remotely. People visiting another country might be blamed for the actions of their country's president, even though they did not vote for him and oppose his policies. Someone who has the same first name as a famous hero is treated more favorably by casual acquaintances. A person who was a teacher in a school where one of the students joined a terrorist movement is labeled a terrorist sympathizer. The individuals in these examples are associated with the outcomes, but they did not cause, foresee, or intend them. Associations may be based on similarity, ownership, or just proximity to the outcome or the actual individual who is responsible for the outcome, but the association is insufficient to warrant any blame or credit.

At the level of commission, people are held responsible for effects that they cause in a direct sense, even though the consequences were not intended or foreseen. In some cases, individuals are not considered to be sufficiently autonomous to be judged responsible for their behavior, as is the case with young children, individuals who are cognitively impaired, and those individuals who are compelled to act by some powerful internal or external force. Responsibility at this level is usually considered too low to warrant judgment, except in instances where commission alone is considered a sufficient condition for assigning blame. In a case of strict liability, for example, individuals who are not at fault—in the sense that they only caused the outcome but did not foresee or intend it—are nonetheless liable for any negative consequences that result from their actions. For example, engineers who designed a bridge do not intend for the bridge to collapse and kill people, but they are responsible—at the level of commission—for the harm the bridge causes if it should collapse.

At the level of foreseeability, individuals are held to be responsible for the produced event even though they may not have "set out to achieve it, either as a means or an end" (Hart, 1968, p. 120). Individuals who cause accidents—they don't put out their campfire and start a forest fire, drive through a traffic signal and hit another car, take the soccer team they coach into a dangerous cave where they are trapped—do not in any way wish to cause the harm they did, but they are nonetheless somewhat responsible.

At the fourth level, intentionality, responsibility depends not only on the demonstration of foreseeability of consequences, but on intentions as well. Responsibility allocation peaks when persons voluntarily perform a given action in order to achieve a certain foreseeable goal of a certain societally determined quality. They are fully culpable, at least for the consequences they were intentionally seeking. They may not, however, be held fully responsible for any side effects of the action that were neither desired nor intended. A person robbing a bank, for example, is seeking money, but during the course of the robbery a guard may be injured. The robber did not intend to harm the guard, but that outcome was foreseeable. Some actions, too, are means to an end—they are not the desired outcome, but rather an action that must take place if the actor's goal is to be realized (Alicke, Rose, & Bloom, 2011).

At the last level, justified commission, the person is held only partly responsible for intentionally done action due to the influence of various factors such as environmental coercion and duress. As Austin explains, the situation is "one where someone is accused of having done something, or (if that will keep it any cleaner) where someone is said to have done something which is bad, wrong, inept, unwelcome, or in some other of the numerous ways untoward. Thereupon he, or someone in his behalf, will try to defend his conduct or to get him out of it" (Austin, 1962, pp. 175–176).

Responsibility and Ethics Positions

Judgments of actions do not always elide into judgments of the persons who performed the action. For example, a lie, and especially a lie that causes harm, may be judged as morally wrong. But a person who lies is not always thought to be a liar. Moral judgments of actions inform judgments of individuals only when those individuals are thought to be responsible for their actions. Responsibility, then, is the final link in the chain of reasoning that begins with the raising of the moral question—Is this a moral issue?—and ends with a moral judgment of a person—This person is morally good (or bad).

We investigated the relationship between responsibility and moral judgment by asking individuals who differed in their degree of idealism and relativism to judge the morality of individuals who were responsible—at varying degrees—for either positive or negative consequences (Forsyth, 1981a). The scenarios we used were developed to vary responsibility across the five levels identified by Heider in his theory of responsibility: association, causation, foreseeability, intentionality, and justification (Shaw & Sulzer, 1964). Each one describes an individual named Perry who is linked with an action or event that results in a positive outcome (e.g., saving a drowning person, rescuing someone from a fire) or negative outcome (injury to an innocent person, loss of life). Some examples include:

> *Causation* (negative outcome): Perry called a boy and asked him to come over to his house to see his birthday presents. On the way to Perry's house the boy was struck by a car and was killed.
>
> *Intentionality* (positive outcome): Perry was watching a house that was burning down. As he watched, a small child appeared at a window and called for help. Most of the people there thought there was so much fire that no one should go in the house. Perry ran in and pulled the child to safety.
>
> *Justification* (negative outcome): Another boy tried to kill Perry with a large knife. Perry grabbed the knife and stabbed the other boy to death to keep from being killed himself.

As expected, increases in responsibility were associated with more favorable judgments of morality when the consequences were positive but more unfavorable judgments when the consequences were negative. At the higher levels of responsibility—foreseeability, intentionality, and justification—Perry was judged to be less moral when his actions resulted in negative outcomes rather than positive ones, but at the lower levels of responsibility—association and commission—outcome and morality were unrelated. Thus, moral evaluations were most extreme when Perry intended to cause the outcomes, and dropped down significantly at both the level of foreseeability and justification.

These relationships between responsibility and moral judgment varied, to a degree, with variations in ethics positions. At the lowest level of responsibility—association only—moral judgments were not influenced by the outcome across all the ethics positions. At the level of causation, Perry neither foresaw nor intended the outcomes, yet situationists considered him to be more moral when the outcomes he directly caused were positive ones; the other ethics positions were not influenced by the quality of the outcome. At the level of foreseeability, when Perry's actions caused negative outcomes which were foreseeable, absolutists judged the actor more negatively than did exceptionists, while the relativists' ratings fell intermediate. This same tendency held when Perry intended to produce a negative outcome—when his actions were deliberate and purposeful—but in this case both the situationists and the absolutists rated Perry more negatively than the exceptionists. This increased negativity in situationists' appraisals carried over to the last level of responsibility: justification. The situationists were more negative than all others when Perry's actions caused negative outcomes, even though exculpatory factors were present in the situation that moderated his responsibility for those outcomes. Given that the negative consequences described in the scenarios were quite severe—the killing of an aggressor in self-defense—the idealistic situationists were apparently less willing to forgive the harm done. Situationists, compared to others, also rated the outcome more negatively. Subjectivists, on the other hand, did not differentially evaluate Perry when his actions caused either negative or positive consequences but his behavior was justified.

Responsibility and Morality

Some actions raise no moral contestation. People don't debate the morality of molesting children, murdering a family member, valiant acts of heroism and philanthropy, or punishing in some way those who inflict great harm on others. But discussion of other issues are guaranteed to spark acrimonious debate. Any psychological theory of moral judgment, to adequately deal with the many factors which may affect such judgments, must take into account the ethics position of the judge, the circumstances which surround the act, the nature of the act, and the responsibility of the actor. Both philosophical analysis and psychological theories of moral judgment agree that the perceived goodness of others depends on the ethical quality of their actions, but these approaches disagree over the issue of what does (or should) determine the moral quality of the act. Ethics position theory, and the research examined in this chapter, resolves this disparity by focusing on (a) harm and moral standards, and how perceivers' combine these two pieces of information in their moral appraisals and (b) the individual's level of responsibility for the action and its consequences. Acting in ways that run afoul of rules that define what is and is not moral, and causing harm to others, will likely earn you moral condemnation, but only if you are responsible for your actions.

Notes

1. We examined the relationship between ethics position and attitudes pertaining to moral issues through moderated multiple regression and, when justified by the evidence of a significant interaction of idealism and relativism, by classifying respondents into one of the four ethics positions and examining their responses using both parametric and nonparametric procedures. For more information about the measures, see Graham et al. (2011) and Koleva et al. (2012).
2. Although aversion to harm is by no means a hallmark of deontology, as this perspective is studied in moral philosophy, psychological investigations of morality tend to focus on harm when they contrast a deontological perspective with a utilitarian one: "the nuances of deontological thinking have been typically boiled down to a blanket rejection of causing harm to an individual" (Reynolds & Conway, 2018, p. 1009).

6

MORAL BEHAVIORS AND EMOTIONS

It is, then, in the nature of the good man to do injustice voluntarily, and of the bad man to do it involuntarily. . . . That I, or any other ordinary man, go astray is not surprising.

—Plato, Lesser Hippias (376 BCE)

Moral thought and moral action do not always align. Do situationists chose to act in ways that minimize harm to others, even if they must act against commonly accepted standards of right and wrong? Do the absolutists, who prize the importance of avoiding causing harm to others and conforming to moral imperatives, act on these principles at all times? Do the exceptionists and subjectivists, with their emphasis on pragmatic acceptance of expediency, make choices that others condemn as immoral? Although differences seen in the judgmental tendencies of each position are congruent with people's descriptions of how they act, studies that directly assess moral choices when tempted to act immorally suggest that differences in idealism and relativism may not translate into differences in moral action. Absolutists, for example, tend to judge moral indiscretions more harshly, but they are as likely to act badly as those who endorse other ethics positions—although they do tend to experience higher levels of guilt following an indiscretion. Moral behavior, like all behavior, is not just a function of the characteristics of the person, but also the social situation where the action takes place.

* * *

Humans, by nature, have the capacity to act decently, yet they often act atrociously. Over 3,500 people have been awarded the Medal of Honor by the U.S. armed services for "conspicuous gallantry and intrepidity at the risk of life above and beyond the call of duty"—many of them posthumously. When surveyed, over 13% of married men and women admitted to having had sex with someone other than their spouse (Atkins, Baucom, & Jacobson, 2001). Since 1904, when philanthropist Andrew Carnegie created his award for heroism, over ten thousand people have received the Carnegie Medal for selfless acts of altruism. In the U.S., one in six boys and one in four girls will be sexually abused before they reach the age of 18 (Finkelhor, Hotaling, Lewis, & Smith, 1990). The average American household donates about $1,800 each year to charities (Brooks, 2006). People often tell the truth, but they also lie. Most people tell an average of two lies a day, and over the course of a week they lie to about a third of the people within whom they interact (DePaulo, 2004). The Center for Retail Research's study of retailers in 42 countries estimated the loss due to shoplifting, fraud, and employee theft to be $107.3 billion in any given year, which is more than one percent of all retail sales in those countries (Mannes, 2010).

Who can be counted on to act in ways that are morally commendable, and who is more likely to act in ways that are unethical? This question is ancient in its origins. For eons, humans needed to discern the moral integrity of those around them. Will my tribal leaders share with me in times of hardship or will they hoard? Who can be trusted to help defend our group against predators, and who will flee rather than fight? Who is kind, caring, and compassionate and who is dangerous—capable of harming others rather than helping them? People still ask these question in modern times: Will the person who is looking my way cause me harm? Will my spouse be faithful to me? Will my employee steal from the company? Will my colleagues do their fair share of the work when we collaborate on a project? Who has moral integrity and who does not? All difficult questions, which may be answered by considering individual differences in ethics positions.

Ethics and Moral Behavior

Long is the list of factors that can cause a person to act in ways that others consider to be immoral or moral. We may wish to resist temptation, but our capacity for self-regulation is sometimes weak and easily overwhelmed. Some of us, such as the authoritarians or the highly psychopathic, have little concern for others' welfare. Some people, motivated by an empathic concern for others, help even at a risk to themselves. We may be so self-absorbed that we put our own needs above the rights of other people. Situational factors, including organizational norms, an influential leader, or the appeals of one's peers, can also cause the morally good to falter and the morally suspect to act ethically. But among these many causes is a cognitive one: Individuals' judgment about the action under consideration. The student who does not think copying a few answers from another's test is wrong will be more likely to cheat. The citizen who respects speed limits will be less likely to speed. The person who believes that sharing one's wealth with others who are less fortunate is a moral duty is more likely to donate to charities. The spouse who does not think that infidelity is immoral is more likely to be unfaithful. A cognitive approach to moral behavior suggests that people who judge the act they are contemplating to be morally wrong will be less likely to follow through with the action, compared to someone who either fails to consider the morality of the action or, after review, decides the act is morally justified.

This basic premise—that moral judgment influences moral behavior—is acknowledged in nearly every philosophical, legal, and psychological analysis of moral behavior. In Plato's (360 BCE/1994) *Crito*, Socrates contemplates escaping from prison and the death sentence that awaits him, but he does not take action. Others urge him to break the law and save his life, but he cannot do so, for he believes that acting contrary to the ruling of the state would be immoral. He cannot engage in an action that is inconsistent with his moral judgment of that action. Aristotle (350 BCE/1935), in the *Nicomachean Ethics*, theorized that virtuous persons who engage in moral action do not do so merely to conform to conventional standards, but because they personally judge the action to be morally good. Although Hume challenged the assumption that moral reasoning, per se, motivates moral action, he did suggest that moral "passions" are required to motivate a person's actions, and such passions are experienced as moral evaluations. Moore (1903) concluded that before understanding moral action one must first understand moral judgment: "Ethics is undoubtedly concerned with the question what good conduct is; but, being concerned with this, it obviously does not start at the beginning, unless it is prepared to tell us what is good" (Moore, 1903, p. 2).

Within the law, the capacity to formulate a moral judgment—to be able to distinguish between what is right and wrong—is often required before one can be held responsible for an illegal action. Most legal systems assume that people who act contrary to moral principles should be punished. But what if, for whatever reason, a person is unable to make a moral determination prior to taking action? According to the M'Naghten rule, introduced in the British legal system in 1843, such individuals are not held accountable for their crimes: If at the "time of the committing of the act, the party accused was laboring under such a defect of reason, from disease of mind, and not to know the nature and quality of the act he was doing; or if he did know it, that he did not know he was doing what was wrong." The M'Naghten rule assumes that sane, law-abiding individuals first morally review their alternatives and then chose to act in ways that are consistent with community standards. The capacity to carry out this moral review is a necessary condition for legal responsibility.

Many psychological explanations of morality also assume moral judgments are the precursors of moral behavior. Rest's (1986) cognitive model, for example, recognizes that individuals sometimes act immorally because they fail to consider moral concerns when appraising the nature of the situation. If they reach a level of moral awareness, however, individuals then engage in the moral judgment process itself, and the result is a conclusion about the ethical justification of their choices. This stage, Rest suggests, is followed by an analysis of alternatives to action and their moral value (Treviño, Weaver, & Reynolds, 2006). In consequence, individuals who do not have sufficient time, motivation, or the cognitive resources to appraise a situation fully are more likely to err in their moral appraisal and so choose to act unethically (e.g., Gino, Schweitzer, Mead, & Ariely, 2011).

Given this hypothesized relationship between moral judgment and moral behavior, it stands to reason that individuals who differ in their ethics positions may also vary in their moral propensities. Individuals who differ in idealism and relativism often reach different conclusions about what is right and what is wrong, and these judgments may guide their subsequent behavior. Individuals who are idealistic, for example, claim that they consider an action that harms others to be morally wrong, and their judgments tend to be consistent with this moral value. As noted in Chapter 5, idealistic absolutists and situationists more strongly condemn individuals who act in morally untoward ways, particularly if their actions result in harm to others. They also tend to be more empathic, benevolent, and caring in their orientations towards others, all of which suggest they would be more likely to act in ways that are in accord with one of the key defining characteristics of moral acts: Do to others as you would have them do to you.

Variations in relativism, too, may also be associated with differences in individuals' conformity to moral standards. Relativists express skepticism regarding the importance of relying on traditional standards that define what is right and wrong when judging others, so they tend to be more lenient in their moral judgments. This leniency may prompt them to be less mindful of the relationship between their own actions and social conventions that determine ethics. Subjectivists, in particular, display a number of characteristics that have been associated with the tendency to engage in immoral behavior, such as psychopathy and Machiavellianism (see Chapter 4). They are also less likely to embrace such values as benevolence, traditionalism, collectivism, and religiosity, which are all qualities that are associated with acting morally.

Who Will Act Immorally?

The self-descriptions of exceptionists, subjectivists, absolutists, and situationists suggest that they will diverge from one another in morally charged settings, but the evidence pertaining to the unique moral integrity of any one of these four types is checkered at best. On the one hand, a substantial number of studies point to the same conclusion: People who are more idealistic and less relativistic are usually the ones who are less likely to cheat on tests, offer bribes during business negotiations, lie, file false receipts for business expenses, and so on. They are also more likely to act in prosocial ways, such as whistle-blowing, recycling, and rendering help to someone in need (e.g., Barnett, Bass, & Brown, 1996; Burnett, 2017; Douglas & Wier, 2000; Elias, 2002; Erffmeyer, Keillor, & Leclair, 1999; Greenfield, Norman, & Wier, 2008; Hastings & Finegan, 2011; Henle, Giacalone, & Jurkiewicz, 2005; Jones, Spraakman, & Sánchez-Rodríguez, 2014; Nayır, Rehg, & Asa, 2018; Shiyong, Shu, & Junxia, 2011; Singhapakdi, Salyachivin, Virakul, & Veerayangkur, 2000; Singhapakdi, Vitell, & Kraft, 1996; Smith & Shen, 2013; Valentine & Bateman, 2011; Vitell et al., 2003; Winter, Stylianou, & Giacalone, 2004). For example, when Tooke and Ickes (1988) asked people to indicate how frequently they act in ways that are inconsistent with conventional moral standards, such as taking recreational drugs, engaging in casual sex, stealing things, and using profanity, people who reported rarely doing such things were more idealistic but less relativistic. Studies of the errant actions of consumers also suggest relativists are more likely to stray. People commit a range of illegal and immoral behaviors when they are shopping for and buying products or services for personal use. They sometimes switch price tags on merchandise, to get a lower price. They misrepresent the value of items that are lost or stolen when making insurance claims. They download music files that are protected by copyright. They say nothing to their waiter if their restaurant bill is incorrect in their favor (Vitell & Muncy, 2005). And who is most likely to admit to these misdeeds? Relativistic consumers who are not idealistic (e.g., Arli & Leo, 2017; Vitell & Paolillo, 2003). Evidence also suggests that idealism (but not relativism) predicts who is more likely to lie when completing psychological assessments. Grieve and McSwiggan (2014) asked a community sample to complete the EPQ as well as items that asked about the morality of faking their answers on such surveys. Individuals who admitted that they planned to fake their answers on future psychological tests tended to be lower in idealism than those who planned to be truthful. The relationship was not a strong one, but then again: The study's findings suggest that it is quite likely some of the participants were not being truthful in describing their intentions to lie about how much they fake.

On the other hand, much of this empirical evidence about ethics and action comes from studies that have relied on people's own descriptions of their moral behavior, rather than measures of actual behavior. Most researchers do not directly measure immoral and moral behavior. They do not check to see if the person who claims to never lie speaks truthfully when tempted to deceive; if the self-described do-gooder actually renders aid to others; if the person who claims to be callous and indifferent to the suffering of others actually acts on their darker behavioral intentions. Instead, using survey methods, they ask individuals to estimate how frequently they have acted in moral and/or immoral ways in the past. Respondents might be asked if they cheated on a test, worked extra hours without pay, treated a colleague contemptuously, lied and gossiped, reported another person's immoral actions to a superior or the authorities, or misrepresented their expenses, and their responses are then correlated with their level of idealism or relativism. Alternatively, rather than relying on self-reports of moral action, researchers also measure respondents' behavioral intentions by asking them how they believe they would act in certain hypothetical situations. For example, the researcher may ask the following:

- You are a student in a class and see another student cheating. Would you turn in that student or just look the other way?
- You were mistakenly charged too little for an item you were purchasing. Would you keep the money or point out the retailer's error?
- A runaway trolley is heading down the tracks toward five workmen who will be killed if the trolley proceeds on its present course. You can push a switch to divert the trolley onto a side track, but there is a single railway workman on that track who will be killed. Will you push the switch?

Such measures may be valid indicators of how people actually respond in such situations, but they may also be influenced by individuals' need to perceive themselves in a positive light, their concerns about detection should they admit to such tendencies, and so on. As Haan, Aerts, and Cooper (1985, p. 48) explain: "there is often a great difference between people's 'knowing' morality and their acting morally, since the store of information, skills in social manipulation, and logical reasoning of well-educated people enable them to appear moral even when they might not be."

Moreover, even if people do not intentionally misreport their responses, most people consider themselves to be highly ethical, so their descriptions of their actions in morally turbulent situations may not always match their actual responses in such settings (Dunning, 2016). Absolutists, for example, may be committed to a personal conception based on avoiding harm to others and staying true to fundamental moral principles, and so they may tend to underreport instances when they acted in morally suspect ways. Similarly, subjectivists may claim that they have little regard for others' outcomes and moral standards, but in everyday situations they may yield to pressures to conform to social standards that require compassion rather than insensitivity. As a consequence, claims about one's moral actions may not accurately predict moral behavior (see, for example, Gerlach, Teodorescu, & Hertwig, 2019).

These uncertainties about the validity of self-reports of moral behavior prompted us to carry out several studies of how people respond when they are tempted to act immorally. In one study we asked college students who had previously completed the Ethics Position Questionnaire (EPQ) to take a test of social sensitivity in our survey laboratory (Forsyth & Berger, 1982). When students arrived for their individual appointments, they were greeted by a researcher who explained that the test they were about to take was a highly accurate indicator of social skill and competence, and that it predicted one's ability to make and keep friends. He also offhandedly ridiculed the previous student's performance by stating: "The last person only got four right out of twelve. See, look at all the mistakes. I am sure you can do much better than that." After these words of encouragement, the experimenter returned the scoring key to the work basket on the desk, explained he had some phone calls to make in another office, and left the subject alone in the locked room for fifteen minutes.

The social sensitivity test was high in face validity—it seemed as if it was a standardized measure of the ability to accurately assess the feelings and attitudes of another person from only a minimal amount of information about that person—but it was actually just twelve ambiguous multiple-choice items with no correct answers. Each item described a person in a common social situation, and the respondent was asked to select the most likely emotion the individual would experience. Although three alternatives followed each question, all three were equally likely. Hence, although the students were not observed while taking the test, cheating could be easily detected by checking their scores; if too many of their answers matched the answer key (say, six of the twelve possible), then they almost certainly cheated by retrieving the key from the researcher's desk. Thirty-six percent did obtain such scores, but neither idealism nor relativism scores predicted who would cheat: The cheaters included students from all four moral categories.[1]

Undeterred by these null results, we conducted a second study of students' willingness to cheat, but revised our procedures to better distinguish between those who resisted temptation and those who did not. The two students who volunteered to take part in each session were greeted by a male experimenter who told them the study investigated "dyadic analytic ability": The critically important ability to solve difficult cognitive tasks through collaborative problem solving. He then urged the two test-takers to try to do their best, and explained he would return in ten minutes to see if they had any questions about the task. The bogus test of analytic ability was actually a series of extremely difficult or impossible letter word jumbles that very few people would ever solve, such as "r o e e e e n t l n a v i" (environmental) and "t i b f u o o s c a n" (obfuscation). While working in the locked room, one of the students, who was actually part of the research team, broke his pencil point. Searching for a sharpener, he discovered the answer key in some papers on the experimenter's desk. When the experimenter returned, he expressed disappointment over the group's inability to solve the word problems, and told them they would have ten more minutes to make more progress. After he left, the researcher's confederate took several answers from the key after explaining he wanted the team to look good to the experimenter. He then urged the other student to do likewise. Without further prompting, 83% conformed and followed his lead by also cheating.

Again, however, ethical ideology failed to predict who would succumb to the temptation. No one ethical category was overrepresented among the cheaters.

These two studies suggest that differences among the ideologies are not so robust that they will emerge if given the chance. However, the two studies were limited, both methodologically and conceptually. In terms of the methods used, they involved a relatively small number of participants, who were tested in what was a very unusual situation for them; so unusual that personal characteristics such as ethical beliefs may not have influenced their responses. Moreover, we did not manipulate aspects of the situation that are related to the primary dimensions of variations identified in ethics position theory. Individuals who vary in idealism may not act differently if the harm that might result from a moral or immoral action is unknown. Similarly, although taking answers to a test is technically cheating, even individuals who were very low in relativism may not have considered their actions to be cheating in this impersonal, experimental situation.

This explanation for our null findings, post-hoc as it may be, is consistent with a *person X situation* approach to behavior. This perspective assumes that the influence of one's personal qualities on behavior is substantially influenced by aspects of the situation where the actions take place (Endler, 1975; Mischel, 1968). Individuals who are extraverted, for example, tend to be outgoing and personable, but they do not always travel in packs seeking out social activities. Rather, their extraversion influences their behavior depending on the situation. When socializing is appropriate, extraverts will display heightened gregariousness and warmth, but in many everyday situations their level of extraversion will not influence their actions at all (Fleeson, 2004). Similarly, individuals' level of moral identity, honesty, and cognitive moral development guides their responses over time and across situations, yet their actions in a specific setting may be inconsistent with their general behavioral patterns (e.g., Aquino, Freeman, Reed, Lim, & Felps, 2009; Zettler & Hilbig, 2010). Haan (1986), for example, found that individual differences in moral maturity explained nearly 50% of the variability in participants' behavior in some situations, but dropped down to only 9% in other settings. She concluded that moral action is "informed and influenced by variations in contexts" and by individuals' "own strategies of problem solving" when they confront a moral dilemma (Haan, 1986, p. 1282). The influence of the situation on trait-related behaviors was also in evidence in our meta-analytic review of negative social behaviors in work settings such as theft, substance abuse, harassment, incivility, and so on. We found that individuals who have elevated levels of psychopathy were significantly more likely to display counterproductive work behavior—but only in certain kinds of situations. Either these individuals had learned to manage their psychopathic tendencies in those settings or these qualities were not a liability in these contexts (O'Boyle, Forsyth, Banks, & McDaniel, 2012).

Persons in Situations

A person *X* situation approach, applied to predict the moral behaviors of individuals' who adopt different ethics positions, presumes features of the social setting may possibly enhance—or reduce—the causal impact of ethical ideologies on behavior. For example, absolutists and exceptionists stress the importance of moral rules, so they should be less likely to act in ways that are widely recognized as immoral. They should lie, steal, or cheat less frequently. But if they are not aware that their actions will violate moral rules, or the press of the situation is so great that they are not able to consider their personal values before they act, then the relationship between their positions' values and their actions will be nil. As Schwartz explains, "if a person construes a decision he faces to be a moral choice, relevant moral norms he holds are likely to be activated and to affect his behavior. When he fails to perceive that a moral decision is at stake, however, particular moral norms are unlikely to be activated" (1968, p. 355). Conversely, since the idealistic positions—situationism and absolutism—stress the need to achieve positive, humanitarian consequences, then individuals who accept these ideals might be tempted to engage in immoral action if such actions are the means to help others—especially if they are relativists (the situationists).

We tested this person *X* situation approach by again studying volunteer college students' resistance to moral temptation, but this time we also experimentally varied certain aspects of the situation (Forsyth & Nye, 1990). After assessing moral positions in an unrelated context, we contacted students and scheduled them to take part in a study titled "Understanding IQ." When they arrived at the research site, they were seated in a private room, before a video monitor displaying a 21-year-old student working on the written portion of an intelligence (IQ) test. The students were asked to watch the individual as he completed the oral portion of the test with the tester, and then formulate an opinion of his intelligence. Although students were led to believe that they were watching a student in the next room via a close-circuit video feed, in actuality they were viewing a previously prepared recording of a student performing very well as he completed the oral questioning.

After rating the IQ test taker, the researcher thanked the students and then asked them to perform an additional task as part of the study. Claiming that the project sought to understand the effects of feedback about intelligence on performance, the researcher asked the participant to meet with the test taker briefly and give him feedback about his score. However, the researcher explained that the test taker, for the purposes of the study, should be given only negative feedback: "You need to tell the other subject that his IQ score is about 80. You should add that you are surprised that anyone with such a low IQ could get into college and that you doubt he will be able to graduate."

We varied both the salience of moral norms and the consequences of the action by varying the wording of this request and explanation. First, the action was repeatedly described with the word *lie* for some participants, but as feedback for others. Second, some of the participants were told that the information would, in all likelihood, help the test taker improve his academic performance—that research indicated that this kind of feedback from a peer was highly motivating. Other participants, rather than being told the feedback would benefit the test taker, were instead just promised money ($3) if they would give the negative feedback to the test taker. We classified students who agreed to the request to lie as nontruthful; those who refused were classified as truthful.

As anticipated, the two situational variables—the salience of moral norms and the consequences of action—had a strong impact on moral action. While only 50.0% lied when they were offered $3 and were told that they would be lying rather than giving feedback, this percentage increased to 76.2% in the other three conditions. In addition, personal idealism influenced moral behavior, but in a surprising fashion. Although we predicted that idealists would resist telling a potentially harmful lie to another person, they were significantly more likely to lie than the low idealists. Fully 78.6% of the situationists and absolutists (high idealists) agreed to tell the lie, while only 62.5% of the subjectivists and exceptionists (low idealists) complied with the experimenter's request. In part, this difference was due to the low idealists' reluctance to lie when offered money. If told the other person would benefit, 75% agreed to lie; but if offered a small amount of money, only 46.5% of the low idealists agreed to lie. Moreover, calling the action a lie did not prompt the low relativists—who typically are more sensitive to violations of norms—to resist.

This study supports the commonsense notion that people who espouse lofty moral values may tend to behave the most immorally (Monin & Merritt, 2012). Although both situationists and absolutists endorse such beliefs as "One should never psychologically or physically harm another person" and "It is never necessary to sacrifice the welfare of others," both groups were willing to tell a total stranger a hurtful lie. While these findings are not too damaging for situationists since these individuals believe that lying is permissible in some settings, absolutists generally endorse conformity to moral standards, and are the harshest judges of others who have broken moral absolutes. Yet, when they themselves were tempted to lie, they were more likely to succumb. These findings are consistent with studies that suggest moral hypocrisy is common rather than rare (Batson, 2011).

A second explanation, however, is suggested by the participants' responses when they were asked to explain why they agreed to "give the information to the person" they observed. The students offered a range of explanations, including personal curiosity and a sense of duty, but more of the idealistic individuals said they agreed in order to help the experimenter. One wrote, "I agreed to give the information because I feel that by my participation I am contributing to help others better understand the way people act and/or react." Another, expressing a similar sentiment, explained "I just wanted to help the Psych Dept. with their research." Hence, they did not consider their behavior to be an antisocial act that harmed another person, but rather a prosocial act that helped someone. Their misstatements were lies, but "altruistic lies" (Price, 2010).

This interpretation is consistent with other studies that have explored people's reactions to the pressures they sometimes experience in psychological investigations. Milgram (1974), in his studies of obedience to authority, assumed that individuals capitulated to the experimenter's demands because their sense of autonomy and control was diminished; as agents of a higher authority, they no longer thought for themselves, but only carried out the experimenter's orders no matter what the cost. Subsequent studies, however, offer an alternative explanation—one based on cooperation rather than capitulation. The participants, rather than viewing themselves as subordinates taking orders from a superior, thought of themselves as collaborators working on a scientific study of learning. They identified more with the researcher, rather than the learner, and it was that identification that caused them to continue to administer shocks even when the learner protested (Haslam, Reicher, & Birney, 2014). This explanation suggests participants did not deliver the inaccurate information out of a sense of self-protective obedience, but because they believed they were helping rather than harming.

On the Ethics of Research

Even though people who vary in their level of idealism and relativism report acting differently in morally turbulent situations, our studies of actual moral behavior do not confirm these differences; Absolutists were, if anything, more likely to act in ways that were morally questionable compared to individuals who endorsed less idealistic ethics positions. These findings reinforce the importance of investigating moral behavior *in situ*, rather than relying only on individuals predictions about their actions. This discrepancy also offers some support for the decision to mislead the participants who took part in these studies. These studies created the potential for risk for participants, for they involve deception, invasion of privacy, and the withholding of consent. Society, in general, condemns deceptive practices, and researchers are not exempted from this standard. The participants themselves could freely choose to act in accordance with the dictates of morality, or they could instead decide to cheat or lie, but such situations are coercive ones, and some participants may have experienced anxiety after acting in morally questionable ways. Moreover, some participants also felt ashamed or guilty for what they agreed to do as participants in the study. We considered using alternative methods, such as role-play methods in which participants are asked to imagine themselves in a testing situation and self-report procedures involving retrospective reports of immoral action.

However, prior research suggested that such methods would tell us too little about how people actually act when tempted to cheat or to lie (Forsyth, 2001).

Still, the irony is inescapable: to study morality, we violated moral standards. Such work could be viewed as unethical, for it puts itself above, or at least outside, the regulatory social system that we were studying (see Chapter 8). This extra ethical objection, however, overlooks the intentions of the researcher. We were not seeking personal gain, but were impelled by a motivation that society applauds: the quest to expand our knowledge. In addition, given the potential for harm to participants, we were careful to thoroughly debrief all participants in these studies immediately after their sessions. Although the first few minutes of this interview probed for suspiciousness about the procedures, the bulk of the session concentrated on reassuring participants that their behaviors said nothing about their moral character. Participants were told about previous studies demonstrating the relatively large impact of situational factors on behavior, and their own reluctance to proceed with the experiment was noted. Lastly, when participants agreed to lie, their actions were likened to a mild social infraction, as when an individual watching a large group of people cross the street against the flashing "Don't Walk" sign decides to cross as well. All participants expressed retrospective approval of the research, and a number of participants requested copies of the conclusions. All studies were also reviewed and approved by a separate review committee, the Institutional Review Board. That review insured that the studies met federal guidelines for the protection of human participants (Forsyth, 2008).

Ethics and Moral Emotions

Why tell the truth rather than lie? Why keep promises and not break them? Why protect and serve rather than attack and exploit? Nietzsche and Kant notwithstanding, most philosophers have maintained that acting morally is a sure path to happiness (Wienand, 2009). For Plato, happy people conduct themselves in ways that are temperate, fair, and wise. Aristotle agreed that moral people are more likely to experience *eudemonia* (happiness), and added that acting in ways that are immoral is likely to provoke a range of negative emotions that are antithetical to happiness, such as shame, fear, and disgrace. Shame, he suggested, was the price paid for acting badly: "Young people should be prone to the feeling of shame because they live by feeling and therefore commit many errors, but are restrained by shame . . . the sense of disgrace is not even characteristic of a good man, since it is consequent on bad actions" (Aristotle, 350 BCE/1935). Similarly, psychological analyses of morality suggest that the emotional reactions people experience, both before and after they act in morally evaluable ways, substantially influence their subsequent moral choices and their sense of well-being (Tangney, Stuewig, & Mashek, 2007).

Acting morally or immorally, however, does not have the same emotional implications for everyone. The cynical Machiavellian who puts expediency before principle, the narcissist who feels entitled to far more than a fair share, and the psychopath who is devoid of concern for other people and moral principles are likely not plagued by feelings of guilt or remorse when they act immorally, nor do they swell with happiness when they act in ways that earn them moral praise (O'Boyle, Forsyth, Banks, Story, & White, 2015). Klass (1978), after reviewing a number of previous studies of individuals' feelings of guilt, shame, and self-esteem after breaking moral norms, concludes that "the same overt action seems to make some people feel better and others feel worse, and for still others, has no effects" (p. 766).

This variability in individuals' reactions following morally evaluable actions may be due, in part, to differences in individuals' ethics positions. Although differences in idealism and relativism did not prove to be strong predictors of how people acted in morally tempting situations, they may predict how people respond, emotionally, after they act in ways that are morally commendable or reprehensible. Who, for example, is more likely to experience shame after acting in a way that violates traditional moral principles pertaining to truth, justice, or fairness? A relativist, given their perspective on the importance of complying with moral principles, should be less likely to display such emotions as guilt or shame should they act counter to traditional moral standards. Relativists, however, should not experience as much pride should they comport themselves in ways that are consistent with moral principles; after all, they believe that what is ethical varies from one situation to another. In contrast, who is more likely to respond with negative self-recrimination if their actions cause others injury, and pride if their actions help others to escape from harm? Given more idealistic individuals are more committed to preventing harm to others, ethics position theory predicts they would be more likely to experience (a) negative self-relevant emotions such as guilt and shame if their actions cause others harm and (b) pride and other positive emotions if they are responsible for minimizing another's suffering.

Emotional Reactions to Moral Failures

We explored the relationship between people's ethics positions and their moral emotions in our studies of cheating and lying. We not only recorded people's moral choices—to cheat on a test or to tell a lie to another person—but we also asked respondents to describe their emotions on a series of adjective pairs, including sad-happy, upset-at ease, weak-strong, and nervous-calm. As expected, only one group of individuals' self-ratings were consistently influenced by their moral indiscretions: the absolutists. The more they cheated, the more they rated themselves as weak, bad, dissatisfied, and sad. The absolutists rated themselves more negatively (significantly weaker, more negative, less likeable, and more dirty in comparison to one or more of the other ethics categories) after they cheated when pressured to do so by another person (Forsyth & Berger, 1982). When they agreed to lie absolutists rated themselves as less moral, honest, friendly, good, and so on, particularly compared to situationists (Forsyth & Nye, 1990).

Other researchers have also documented absolutists' higher levels of guilt, overall, relative to others (Arli & Leo, 2017; Cohen, Panter, Turan, Morse, & Kim, 2014). Cohen and her colleagues, for example, developed the Guilt and Shame Proneness Scale (GASP) to assess individual differences in peoples' tendency to experience negative emotions, such as shame and guilt, after committing a private transgression (Cohen, Wolf, Panter, & Insko, 2011). Items on the GASP scale include, "You lie to people but they never find out about it. What is the likelihood that you would feel terrible about the lies you told?" and "At a coworker's housewarming party, you spill red wine on their new cream-colored carpet. You cover the stain with a chair so that nobody notices your mess. What is the likelihood that you would feel that the way you acted was pathetic?" They also developed measures of three related constructs: Guilt-repair orientation (tendency to make amends after a transgression), shame proneness (tendency to experience negative emotions for transgressions that may result in public censure), and shame withdrawal-orientation (the tendency to withdraw from the situation after engaging in some morally inappropriate behavior). When they administered both the EPQ and the GASP to 1,020 employed adults as part of their Work Experiences and Character Traits project, they found that guilt proneness was positively correlated with idealism ($r = +0.33$) but negatively correlated with relativism ($r = -0.21$). These relationships also held for guilt-repair orientation and shame proneness, but not for shame withdrawal orientation (Cohen et al., 2014).

Emotional Reactions to Moral Successes

Aristotle suggested that negative emotions, such as shame, guide individuals away from moral temptation, but he also suggested that positive emotions, including happiness, are the rewards people accrue by acting morally. His insight is consistent with studies of individuals who act morally, for their emotions tend to be positive ones, including pride, joy, happiness, and contentment. For example, individuals who perform a pro-social action—donating blood—usually experience such negative emotions as nervousness, fear, regret, and even anger before they make their donation. But after giving blood, they describe themselves as relieved, relaxed, self-satisfied, warm-hearted, carefree, playful, and happy (Piliavin, Callero, & Evans 1982).

Ethics position theory, however, suggests that the warm glow of morally good behavior may depend, at least in part, on one's ethics position. Relativists may be as likely as nonrelativists to keep their promises, tell the truth, and abide by other traditional standards of morality, but they may not experience as much pleasure from doing so compared to absolutists. For absolutists, what may matter most is the inherent goodness of one's intentions, for a "good will is good not because of what it performs or effects, not by its aptness for the attainment of some proposed end, but simply by virtue of the volition, that is, it is good in itself" (Kant, 1788/2014). Others, however, may respond as consequentialists might, for an action that results in positive outcomes is far more praiseworthy than an action that matches accepted canons of morality but yields little in the way of positive consequences.

We investigated these possibilities by arranging for individuals who differed in ethics positions to work on tasks that would yield a monetary payoff if completed successfully (Forsyth, 1994). We told some participants that they could keep whatever money they earned. Others, in contrast, were charitably motivated: they were told that their earnings would be donated to a charity. After the task was completed participants were given information about their level of performance. If successful those who were working for themselves received their pay, but if they were working for a charity their pay was donated to a worthy cause. Those given failure feedback were told that they did not meet the minimum standards needed for payment. After receiving their feedback, they rated their affect, morality, and their self-esteem.

As predicted, idealistic individuals who stress the importance of fundamental moral principles—absolutists—put intentions before consequences. Although they reported feeling more upset by the testing situation in comparison to other participants, absolutists felt the most positive about their own morality when they were working for a charity rather than themselves. Working for a good cause was sufficient to garner moral approbation, irrespective of the overall success or failure of the effort. As Kant proposed, their virtue lay in their volition, rather than its successful fruition.

Situationists, who are more relativistic than their absolutist counterparts, did not rate themselves as positively when working for a charity, but otherwise they responded similarly to the absolutists. All participants reported more positive self-esteem when they succeeded rather than failed, but this asymmetry was particularly pronounced for the high idealists. Absolutists' and situationists' thoughts were also more negative in content when they failed rather than succeeded, reflecting their greater concern for achieving positive outcomes. Low idealists' did not show such a negative preoccupation after failure. The idealists, when working for a charity, were also more likely to report thoughts pertaining to the charity—either remorse over failing it or happiness over helping it—and when working for their own benefit they reported more self-reflective thoughts. Low idealists rarely mentioned the charity and reported few self-reflective thoughts.

Exceptionists, however, responded unexpectedly. Like participants in all ethical categories, their global self-ratings, including overall affective, attractiveness, and self-esteem, were influenced more by performance than motive or personal moral philosophy: When they succeeded they rated themselves more positively and when they failed they rated themselves more negatively.

Exceptionists, however, reported feeling distressed when laboring for a charity rather than themselves. They also did not feel particularly moral when working for a charity; indeed, they felt most morally virtuous when they performed badly when working for personal gain. Exceptionists also reported more positive thoughts in the self-motivated conditions rather than the charitable conditions.

These findings extend previous studies of ethics position theory by suggesting that absolutists are more extreme in their reactions in moral settings. When they themselves break a moral principle, they react with greater distress and discomfort. When they are working for a good cause, in contrast, they respond positively no matter what consequences they produce. Subjectivists and exceptionists, in contrast, display only muted moralistic reactions. Their reactions to their own moral and immoral behavior are governed more by their own personal outcomes than by consequences for others or the degree to which the action matches a moral principle.

Moral Happiness

This analysis of moral behavior and emotions closes by considering one final question: Who is happiest? Both philosophical and psychological analyses of ethical judgment and action assume morality provides the foundation for a healthy, happy life. Plato, for example, wrote that virtue is "the health and beauty and well-being of the soul," and those that fail morally will likely end up unhappy, unfulfilled, and physically unwell (Plato, 376 BCE/1973, p. 136). In psychoanalytic theory the individual's personality and eventual adjustment as an adult hinges upon the development of a moral outlook or conscience. In the clinical realm, psychological health is often defined as the ability to discriminate between right and wrong, to avoid infractions of societal rules and principles, and to become capable of fairly judging the behaviors of others. Positive psychologists, such as Peterson and Seligman (2004), suggest that virtues and character strengths are the markers of psychological well-being, just as the symptoms of psychiatric disorders are the markers of dysfunction.

Given the moral judgments, actions, and emotions of people who adopt different ethics positions vary, who is most likely to experience higher levels of well-being and happiness? Will it be the absolutists, for they display more of the characteristics associated with traditional conceptions of morality? They are no more likely to resist moral temptation—the studies reviewed in this chapter suggest they are as likely to cheat and lie as most people—but they are more likely to experience shame if they should veer from the moral path. Does their proneness to guilt cause them to experience less happiness, even though this ethics position incorporates two of the defining elements of a moral focus: concern for others well-being and respect for traditional moral standards? Or perhaps the situationists are happiest of all, for they too are concerned with others' well-being, but they are less judgmental than the absolutists.

Very few studies have directly assessed the causal chain leading from variations in ethics position to happiness and well-being. Kernes and Kinnier (2005) found that the professional psychologists they studied tended to be either absolutists or situationists, but they found no significant relationship between idealism, relativism, and their measures of happiness, life-satisfaction, and well-being. Giacalone, Jurkiewicz, and Promislo (2016), in their study of the well-being of MBA students, found that idealism was associated with higher levels of hope, personal growth, and a sense of meaning in life. Suggestive evidence also comes from our analysis of cross-cultural variations in ethics. As discussed in the next chapter, we identified patterned variations in ethics positions across countries, with an exceptionist ethic more common in Western countries, subjectivism and situationism in Eastern countries, and absolutism and situationism in Middle Eastern countries. These patterns were systematically related to variations in levels of happiness, as indexed by the Marks, Abdallah, Simms, and Thompson (2006) ratings of global happiness levels. Happiness scores were highest in the countries where more of the citizens reportedly endorsed an exceptionistic ethic (e.g., Canada, Austria, Belgium), but lowest in countries whose mean idealism and relativism scores suggested an absolutist ethic (e.g., Egypt, South Africa, Poland). The two clusters of relativistic countries fell intermediate (Forsyth & O'Boyle, 2012).

The responses of the 4,388 people who completed both the EPQ and the Diener, Emmons, Larsen, and Griffin (1985) Satisfaction with Life Scale (SLS) in the YourMorals survey also suggest that exceptionists are happier than most, but that absolutists, too, are happier than individuals whose ethics positions are more relativistic. Only relativism scores were correlated with SLS, and examination of the means indicates that satisfaction with life scores were highest for exceptionists and absolutists compared to situationists and subjectivists ($p < 0.05$). Exceptionists and absolutists also tended to describe their overall mental health more positively than situationists and subjectivists. People who described their mental health as "excellent" tended to be low in relativism, whereas those who rated their mental health as "poor" were more likely to be high in relativism ($p < 0.001$).

So who, among the four ethical types, is likely to be happiest? The evidence, although relatively meager, suggests that exceptionists—who embrace traditional moral principles but are not as troubled by others' misfortunes—are the happiest ethical types of all.

The Uncertainty of Moral Action

The link between moral beliefs and moral behavior has long-intrigued psychologists. As early as 1928, Hartshorne and May, in their *Studies in the Nature of Character*, reported some surprising inconsistencies among moral values and moral actions. These researchers developed thirty-three measures of deceit—cheating, lying, and stealing—and administered these tests to hundreds of children. Although some of the children behaved immorally more consistently than others, in many cases the situation, and not the characteristics of the children, determined who would yield to temptation. Furthermore, when Hartshorne and May extended their studies by searching for other aspects of the children's moral outlook that would better predict their actions, their efforts proved fruitless. They measured their moral values, the sophistication of their ethical knowledge, and their judgments about moral dilemmas, but all were only weakly related to actual conduct.

Despite the counterintuitive nature of the Hartshorne and May findings, subsequent researchers have frequently reaffirmed the disparity between moral thought and moral action, and studies of the relationship between ethical ideology and action are no exception. Although absolutists and exceptionists rely on moral rules when making moral judgments, they were as likely as the situationists and subjectivists to break those rules. And absolutists and situationists, although they morally condemn actions that may cause harm to others, agreed to do something that could have caused harm to another person. But just at one's ethics position explains some of the variance in people's moral judgments, ethics positions explained some of the variance in how people respond, emotionally, after they act in ways that are inconsistent with moral standards. Absolutists, in general, were more likely to evidence signs of shame when they acted immorally, whereas situationists responded the most positively in terms of moral emotions when their actions were morally admirable. Moral behavior, then, remains difficult to predict, even when we are informed about individuals' ethics positions.

Note

1. In order to study moral behavior rather than just retrospective accounts of moral behavior, researchers themselves must sometimes withhold information about the situation from participants. In such cases, researchers must meet more stringent regulatory guidelines for the protection of human participants in their research.

7

THE GEOGRAPHY OF ETHICS

> The value which we attribute to our own civilization is due to the fact that we participate in this civilization, and that it has been controlling all our actions since the time of our birth; but it is certainly conceivable that there may be other civilizations, based perhaps on different traditions and on a different equilibrium of emotion and reason, which are of no less value that ours.
> —Franz Boaz (1911, pp. 208–209)

The diversity in moral judgments at the individual level also manifests itself at the cultural level, for what is considered moral differs to some extent from one culture to another. These geographical variations are determined by a host of factors, but among them are differences in cultural norms pertaining to harm and compliance with social standards. By comparing the responses of people in countries on the Ethics Position Questionnaire (EPQ), we identified systematic variations in idealism and relativism in different world regions: People living in Western nations, such as the U.S., are less idealistic than those living in the Middle East, whereas people living in the Eastern regions of the world express higher levels of relativism compared to Westerners. These variations are also associated with other cultural differences, including power orientation, individualism, religiosity, autonomy, and the rule of law. These findings suggest that themes that influence individuals' moral judgments—idealism and relativism—express themselves at the group, organization, and even the cultural level.

* * *

Just as individuals vary in their moral judgments, actions, and emotions, so do the world's diverse societies differ in what they define as ethical and unethical. Among the Yanomamo, men settle arguments with axes, and no one considers that to be a bad thing. In some countries, the left hand is morally suspect, and is not to be used for eating, greetings, and so on. The judicial system in the U.S. continues to end the lives of individuals convicted of certain crimes through lethal injection, but the majority of nations consider the death penalty to be unethical. German Nazis somehow believed that killing all their fellow citizens whose religion was Judaism was morally acceptable. At one time, among the Chambri (also known as the Tchambuli) of Papua New Guinea, husbands were encouraged to physically assault their wives. The Jains consider it to be morally wrong to kill any living thing, including insects. In some parts of Europe incest is not just legal, but also morally acceptable. What is considered right, just, moral, and good among Canadians, the Tsimane, or Pawnee may be viewed as morally suspect by the Shuar, Australians, or Tibetans.

These variations in standards and practices across the world's societies are the result of any number of historical, environmental, political, and social factors, but among these causes are two social exigencies that resonate with ethics position theory: minimizing harm to the members of one's community and encouraging compliance with the group's standards. The theory suggests individuals vary in their moral judgments, actions, and emotions because they also vary in their personal moral philosophies: Some people are more attuned to moral standards than others, just as some are more sensitive to the possibility of harm. But morality is as much an interpersonal process as an individualistic one, and so these person-level differences may correspond to distinctions that are manifested at a collective-level: the society where individuals live. This chapter examines this possibility by identifying variations in the moral responses of people who live in different parts of the world.

Idealism, Relativism, and Culture

The German philosopher Johann Gottfried von Herder, writing in the 18th century, was intrigued by differences between the peoples of the world. Von Herder was a student of Kant, but he disagreed with Kant on one critical point: the likelihood of identifying fundamental moral principles that were transituational and inviolate. For von Herder, morality was defined by one's society, and societies varied tremendously in their beliefs, practices, concepts, and even their affective sensations. As a result, "A good, honest man who only knows the world from the market-place, from the coffeehouse, and most out of the *Hamburg Correspondent*, is as amazed when he comes upon a story and discovers that the manner of thought and taste change with climate, with regions of the earth, and with countries" (1887/2002, p. 247). It was as if each society cultivated its citizens, each in a unique fashion, so von Herder used the word *culture* to describe the distinctive ideas, customs, and social patterns of any particular community.

Von Herder also recognized, however, that beneath these differences in moral practices and customs are regularities—tendencies that are manifested in all surviving communities of *Homo sapiens*. As different as the Australians may be from the Tsimane, both these societies have regularized methods for ensuring the well-being of their members and promoting stable interpersonal relations among them. In both Australia and the rain forests of Bolivia where the Tsimane live, people must coordinate their actions with those of others in the community, and the cultures of these communities have developed to facilitate such coordination. When members act in ways that will cause considerable harm to the survival prospects of others, processes are initiated that function to remedy the damage done. All people who live socially, interacting in at least rudimentary ways with other people, must set boundaries for acceptable behavior, cope with conflict, encourage collaborative exchanges, identify priorities, and define each individual's connection to the larger community.

Yet, just as some individuals are more wary of harmful possibilities and actions that are contrary to moral standards, the world's cultures vary in the surveillance of and sensitivity to harm done to others and their reactions to those who act in ways that are inconsistent with accepted moral practices. Pinker (2011), in his review of the worldwide decline in violence that has occurred since the Middle Ages, notes that violence levels are place-specific. For example, the Yanomamo, as described by Chagnon (2013), are as likely to inflict harm on others as they are to avoid it. In contrast, The Tiwi of Australia consider causing physical harm to others to be morally wrong, and so resolve conflicts through a series of group sessions where the offended vent their grievances—but only peacefully (Fry, 2007). The majority of the people in some societies are quicker to offer care and protection to those in need than the majority of people in other societies (Feygina & Henry, 2015). In Rio de Janeiro and San Jose, for example, a man in need on a public street was helped by passersby over 90% of the time, whereas he received help less than 50% of the time in Singapore, New York City, and Kuala Lampur in Malaysia (Levine, Norenzayan, & Philbrick, 2001). In many Asian countries Confucianism guides people's moral choices, and this philosophy emphasizes benevolence, humility, and care and love for others (Bond & Hwang, 1986).

Societies vary, too, in the strength, clarity, and reach of the norms that define proper and improper conduct. In some societies the line between what is considered good and decent is a bright one, and those who cross it can expect corrective interventions (Zhao & Cao, 2010). Austria, for example, is a place known for its predictable orderliness. Austrians share a common religion, language, and set of values. When in public, Austrians tend to be formal and moderate in their actions, and dress to fit the requirements of any given situation. They are careful to be on time for meetings or social events, and those who fail to be punctual can find that their invitations will dwindle. They tend to be serious and do not readily embrace informality. Slips in decorum, in style of dress, or inattention to the required details of a social event may earn the slipshod miscreant public censure. Their social and moral standards are enduring.

Other cultures are more laissez-faire in their reactions to those who act in ways that are inconsistent with accepted moral standards. Spain, for example, was for many centuries a relatively conservative and paternalistic culture, but political changes in the 20th century culminated in the liberalization of expectations, values, and standards. The Spanish people still honor their traditions, but they are relatively easygoing and tolerant of those who do not follow the norm. Traditional modes of action are valued less than creativity and well-being. People do not have one set of rules about what is correct behavior in a given situation, and so they often tolerate those who act in ways that deviate from the norm (e.g., Bobowik, Basabe, Páez, Jiménez, & Bilbao, 2011).

Ethics position theory is based on the psychology of individual differences, but the two aspects of morality that account for some of the variance in individuals' moral judgments—concern for consequences and conformity to traditional moral standards—may also account for some of the consistencies and contrasts across cultures. We explored this possibility by summarizing statistically the results of prior studies that have examined these two dimensions of ethics worldwide (Forsyth, O'Boyle, & McDaniel, 2008). Our research led us to conclude that levels of idealism and relativism rise and fall across regions of the world, and that these variations are consistent with other cultural patterns, such as differences in collectivism and time perspective.

Cross-Cultural Variations

Researchers have used, with some success, the Ethics Positions Questionnaire (EPQ) to predict how people respond in a variety of situations. These studies suggest that, in general, idealism is associated with firm moral convictions, whereas relativism suggests ethical leniency. For example, Al-Khatib, Vitell, and their colleagues, in a series of studies conducted in different nations, explored how consumers respond when they benefit at the expense of others or as a result of morally questionable or illegal activities. This work finds some differences among the nations they investigated, but in studies conducted in Egypt (Al-Khatib, Dobie, & Vitell, 1995), Romania (Al-Khatib, Robertson, & Lascu, 2004), the U.S. (Vitell & Paolillo, 2003), Saudi Arabia (Al-Khatib, Stanton, & Rawwas, 2005), Austria (Rawwas, 1996) and Japan (Erffmeyer, Keillor, & LeClair, 1999) idealistic individuals more often responded negatively when consumers took advantage of a retailer's error, whereas relativists were more lenient. Al-Khatib et al. (1995), for example, found that Egyptians who were more idealistic reacted more negatively to situations where some might benefit but others are harmed, but individuals who endorsed a more relativistic ethics position found such situations to be more tolerable.

Some work, however, suggests that levels of idealism and relativism, and their relationship to moral reactions, vary across cultures. Americans, for example, scored lower on the EPQ scales when compared to residents of Australia

(Singhapakdi, Marta, Rao, & Cicic, 2001), Thailand (Singhapakdi, Vitell, & Leelakulthanit, 1994), Malaysia (Axinn, Blair, & Thach, 2004), and Spain (Vitell et al., 2003). Davis, Johnson, and Ohmer (1998) found a predominance of exceptionists among the Americans they studied, but a higher percentage of the participants from Indonesia were subjectivists. Deering (1998), in a comparison of British and American pre-service teachers, found higher levels of idealism and relativism among the British. Al-Khatib et al. (2005) reported that consumers in Saudi Arabia were more idealistic than those in Kuwait or Oman. Rawwas, Vitell, and Al-Khatib (1994), noting that social stability and internal conflict may influence ethics positions, discovered that residents of Lebanon were less idealistic and more relativistic than residents of Egypt, and they could predict differences in the leniency of moral pronouncements by considering these variations. These findings suggest that cultures may vary in their idealism and relativism, just as individuals do.

Mapping Morality

These culture-based differences prompted us to review, systematically, as many of the published and unpublished studies that used the EPQ to measure idealism and relativism that we could locate (Forsyth et al., 2008). We used various search engines, backward reference searching, and direct contact of researchers to identify 139 samples drawn from 29 different countries, for a total sample of 30,734 respondents. Slightly over half of the studies were conducted in the U.S. (52.9%), and another 21.4% were studies of people who lived in other Western countries (e.g., the United Kingdom, Australia, and Ireland). The remainder were studies of people living in the Eastern countries (Asia and the Pacific Rim, 15.7%) and Middle Eastern countries (10.0%).

These studies suggest the theory passed the first test required of any systematic attempt to compare cultures. The great variety in languages and customs is a reminder that one cannot assume that one cultures' concepts and expressions will be understood by people who were raised in another culture (Flanagan, 2017). Words that are part of nearly all the world's languages, such as *self, honor,* and *happiness,* have different meanings in different places. Conversational gestures, such as a clenched fist or touching your forefinger to your thumb, mean very different things in one country than another. Even basic psychological processes, such as the perception of color, the understanding of sounds used in speech, and judgments of distance, are substantially influenced by one's culture. We developed ethics position theory and the Ethics Position Questionnaire (EPQ) in the U.S. prior to the introduction of Internet-based cross-national survey methods. The participants were all recruited from the same geographic area of the U.S., and so can be considered WEIRD: They lived in a Western, Educated, Industrialized, Rich, and Democratic society (Henrich, Heine, & Norenzayan, 2010). The factors that influence WEIRD individual's moral judgments may be very different from the factors that influence the moral judgments of the non-WEIRD.

Fortunately, the two core concepts in ethics position theory—concern for harm and conformity with moral principles—seem to be understood similarly in most cultures. When researchers translated the EPQ into different languages (e.g., Dutch, Japanese, Russian, Korean, and Thai) and examined the items through exploratory and confirmatory factor analysis, they discovered the items clustered naturally into two groups: those pertaining to idealism and those pertaining to relativism (e.g., Cornwell et al., 2005; Cui, Mitchell, Schlegelmilch, & Cornwell, 2005; Rawwas, 2001; Vitell & Patwardhan, 2008). In some studies, certain items—particularly the more lengthy, wordy ones—were not sufficiently correlated with the two basal concepts to be included in that culture's version of the EPQ. Overall, however, the majority of the items that asked individuals about their position with regards to harm covaried, as did the items pertaining to social standards that define what is morally right and wrong.

Our confidence in the use of previously published studies to estimate each nation's level of idealism and relativism was also bolstered by the correspondence between our meta-analytic results and the responses of individuals who completed the EPQ online at the Your.Morals website. This website used only an English-language version of the EPQ, but respondents were residents of dozens of countries, including Thailand, Israel, Spain, China, and India. When at least 20 people from any nation had completed the survey, we calculated the mean level of idealism and relativism for that country. These scores were modestly correlated with our estimates of idealism and relativism drawn from the meta-analytic review ($r = +0.43$ for idealism and $r = +0.41$ for relativism).

So where are idealism and relativism highest and where are they lowest? By plotting each country into a two-dimensional space based on idealism (on the vertical axis) and relativism (on the horizontal axis), we generated the map of morality shown in Figure 7.1. Near the bottom portion of this map are the countries that are lower, overall, in idealism: Belgium, Israel, New Zealand, Hong Kong, and China. Near the top, in contrast, are the more idealistic countries, such as Egypt, Spain, Brunei, and Poland, with such countries as Saudi Arabia, United Arab Emirates, and Ireland positioned closer to the midpoint. Turning to relativism, Canada, South Africa, Belgium, and Israel were all relatively low in relativism, whereas Brunei, the United Kingdom, Ireland, and Indonesia were among the most relativistic countries in the sample. The majority of the countries, however, fell intermediate between these extremes (e.g., Korea, Malaysia, and Austria).

A country's location on the morality map was related to its geographic location on the world map. We classified the countries into one of three world regions: East, Middle East, and West, and then tested for differences in idealism and relativism of the countries in these regions. People living in Western

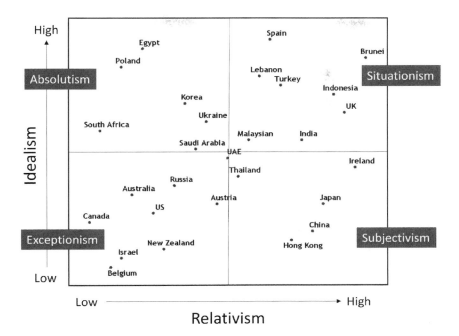

FIGURE 7.1 The average level of idealism and relativism in 28 nations, and the classification of those nations into one of the four ethics positions identified in ethics position theory: exceptionism, subjectivism, absolutism, and situationism.

nations, such as the U.S., Canada, and Austria, were significantly less idealistic than those living in nations located in the Middle East (e.g., Egypt, Lebanon). The scores for nations in the East—Asian countries such as Thailand and India—fell intermediate to and not different from either the Middle East nations or the Western nations. Relativism, too, varied systematically across these three regions. People living in the Eastern regions of the world expressed higher levels of relativism compared to Westerners, with Middle Easterners falling intermediate to and not different from either group.

To further explore these country-level variations in morality we also classified each nation into one of the four ethics positions: absolutism, situationism, exceptionism, and subjectivism. Five nations (20%) were absolutist in their ethics position: Egypt, Korea, Poland, South Africa, and Ukraine. Eight countries (32%) of the nations were classified as situationists, for their idealism and relativism scores were above the median: Brunei, India, Indonesia, Lebanon, Malaysia, Spain, Turkey, and the United Kingdom. The four subjectivist nations (16%) were China, Hong Kong, Ireland, and Japan. The remaining nations (32%), Austria, Australia, Belgium, Canada, Israel, Russia, New Zealand, and the U.S., were classified as exceptionist countries. Thus, exceptionism and situationism were the most common ethics positions at the national level, displayed by two-thirds of the countries in the survey, and subjectivism and absolutism were nearly equally endorsed by the remaining nations.[1]

Consistent with regional differences in idealism and relativism, a majority of the Western countries shared exceptionism as their national moral philosophy. None of the Eastern nations were classified as exceptionists: instead, most were evenly divided between situationism and subjectivism, the highly relativistic positions. All the Middle Eastern countries were idealistic, but they were divided between absolutism (Egypt, Saudi Arabia) and situationism (Lebanon, Turkey, United Arab Emirates). A 3 (region) X 4 (ethics position) frequency analysis, χ^2 (6, $n = 28$) $= 17.63$, $p < 0.01$, offered statistical support for these clusterings: residents of nations in different regions of the world tended to endorse different ethics positions.

Cautions and Limitations

Considerable methodological caution is required before embarking on a cross-cultural analysis of any social and psychological process. First, as with all empirical efforts, we would be more confident that Figure 7.1's moral map reflects the actual levels of idealism and relativism in the population of these countries if the reported statistics were based on larger samples, multiple studies, and more representative samples of the residents of these countries. For some countries, we could locate only one study that provided the necessary information to use in the meta-analysis, and as a result the nuances of that study's sample and procedures may have determined the location of that country in the moral map. As studies are added to the database, the location of each country may shift accordingly, and in proportion to the size of the current database. With so many respondents for such countries as the U.S., Australia, and Hong Kong their location should not change with each new study. However, other countries whose locations are based on fewer data points may move their location.

Second, a number of countries' averaged scores on idealism or relativism were very close to the median. For example, Saudi Arabia's idealism score was very near the midline, and so this country could be classified as either absolutist or exceptionist. Similarly, United Arab Emirates' scores for both idealism and relativism were near the midline, so additional information about the citizens of UAE would be needed to determine, with more certainty, the ethics position of that nation.

Third, this analysis uses nationality as a proxy for culture, and so does not take into account the variation in cultural beliefs within any specific nation. The customs of the people living within a nation's boundaries vary in enumerable ways, so broad generalizations about any country's customs will fail to do justice to the unique variations within any given country.

Moral Positions and Cultural Complexes

Each community of human beings that exists in the world—from the A'ani of the Great Plains of the U.S. to the Zulu living in the South African province of KwaZulu-Natal—is unique in any number of ways. But our meta-analytic review of the responses to the EPQ, collected from people living around the world, suggests that variations in idealism and relativism that define individuals' moral positions may also describe moral differences between nations. Morality, however, is but one of the distinctive features of any society. For example, the Japanese people are more likely to adopt a relativistic outlook on what is right and wrong, but they are unique in many other ways. But, just as people can be compared to one another in terms of certain traits and characteristics—some are, for example, more extraverted or idealistic than others—so can cultures be compared along certain dimensions. Some societies, for example, are more hierarchical than others are, for members are nested in tiers that differ in terms of prestige, honor, or influence. Some societies, too, are more collectivistic than others, for they tend to focus on groups within the society first, and only then consider the individuals who compose those groups.

These systemic variations, while the subject of analysis for as long as people's travels brought them into contact with groups of humans whose cultural practices that seem surprising, unusual, or simply wrong, are the central focus of geographical psychology. This field is "concerned with the spatial organization of psychological phenomena and how individual characteristics, social entities, and physical features of the environment contribute to their organization" (Rentfrow & Jokela, 2016, p. 393). Researchers in geographical psychology have identified a number of social trends that are spatially patterned and, as the following analysis indicates, many of these regularities are associated with the shifting emphasis on harm and moral standards that occurs as one travels from one country to the next.

Hofstede's Theory of National Cultures

Organizational psychologist Gert Hofstede (1980) was one of the first researchers to explore cross-cultural variations empirically. His theory of national cultures recognizes the uniqueness of each culture, but at the same time draws comparisons among them by considering five key aspects of culture: power, individualism, masculinity, tolerance of uncertainty, and perspective on time (Hofstede, Hofstede, & Minkov, 2010). Some cultures, he suggested, are more hierarchically organized than others. Ones that are low on the *Power Distance Index* (PDI) strive to minimize inequalities in the distribution of power within society; all members of the culture are thought to be of equal worth and equal potential. But when PDI is high, hierarchy is accepted as the natural order of things. *Individualism* (IDV) contrasts group-centered and more individualistic cultures. Individualism assumes people are autonomous, and must be free to act and think in ways that they prefer, rather than submit to the demands of the group. Collectivism, in contrast, stresses the fundamental importance of relationships, with moral obligations based on respect, trust, and a sense of community. *Masculinity* (MAS) refers to the extent to which masculinity and its associated elements—competition, assertiveness, machismo—is manifested in the culture's practices, relative to values that are stressed in traditional conceptions of femininity (e.g., compassion, solidarity, relationality). Countries with higher scores in masculinity are also, in many cases, places where gender roles are traditional ones. *Uncertainty Avoidance Index* (UAI) describes the extent to which the culture's practices minimize uncertainty and ambiguity, generally by developing extensive social and legal guidelines, emphasizing security, and adopting religious or philosophical beliefs that define how one should behave. People living in societies with a *Long-term Orientation* (LTO) culture have a longer view of things: They are less concerned about what was and is, but are focused more on what will be. These cultures value persistence and a steady pace toward goals that are far in the future, in contrast to cultures that stress immediate outcomes, including leisure, luxury, and protection of status. *Indulgence* (IND) is a sixth aspect of cultures that Hofestede and his colleagues have identified as they have continued to investigate cross-cultural differences. This dimension pertains to permissiveness, leisure, and general optimism with regards to outcomes. Cultures with high scores on this dimension are indulgent: Residents are less restrained in their actions, and more likely seek positive outcomes for themselves. In restrained societies, people are more likely to control their hedonistic impulses, and generally have a more pessimistic view of the future.

We discovered systematic relationships between Hofstede's national cultures and each nation's level of idealism and relativism.[2] Two of the six cultural dimensions—masculinity and uncertainty avoidance—were significantly associated with idealism (see Figure 7.2). The relationship between masculinity (MAS) and idealism was consistent with findings from previous studies that indicated women had elevated scores on idealism: As idealism increased among the residents of a country, levels of masculinity declined. In consequence, individuals living in idealistic nations, such as Egypt, Spain, and Turkey, are more likely to be concerned with other people's well-being. They are more tender-minded rather than tough, and the skills and strengths traditionally associated with femininity are valued equally with those associated with traditional masculinity. In contrast, countries whose citizens reported lower levels of idealism—such as Japan, the U.S., and New Zealand—scored higher on MAS, and so were more likely to (a) value the skills and strengths traditionally associated with manliness (e.g., logic, physical strength, toughness, and so on) and (b) assume these qualities are more typical of men rather than women.

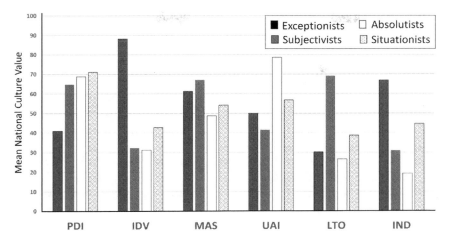

FIGURE 7.2 Mean national culture values (Hofstede, 1980) for nations classified into one of the four moral positions defined by ethics position theory: exceptionists, subjectivists, absolutists, and situationists. PDI = Power Distance Index; IDV = Individualism; MAS = Masculinity; UAI = Uncertainty Avoidance Index; LTO = Long-Term Orientation; IND = Indulgence.

The relationship between idealism and uncertainty avoidance (UAI) was not predicted, however. Individuals living in a culture that is high in uncertainty avoidance "actively seek to decrease the probability of unpredictable future events that could adversely affect the operation of an organization or society" (House & Javidan, 2004, p. 12), and a moral code is one way to achieve this security. We expected UAI to be negatively correlated with relativism, rather than idealism. Instead, it was the harm-sensitive idealistic countries (and absolutist countries, in particular) that were more likely to express less tolerance of uncertainty and ambiguity. Hofstede suggests that countries that have elevated levels of uncertainty avoidance generally impose stricter regulations on its citizens to assuage their need for regularity and routine, but our findings suggest this regulatory zeal may be motivated more by the desire to minimize harm rather than a reverence for standards themselves.

Countries that differed in their ethics positions also differed in power distance (PDI), individualism (IDV), long-term orientation (LTO), and indulgence (IND), but for these dimensions idealism and relativism combined so that one type of ethics position tended to differ from the other positions. For PDI, IDV, and IND, it is the exceptionist countries that stand apart from the others. These countries, which include most of the western nations, resist differentiating between people based on rank or privilege—at least, relative to people who live in all other cultures. These countries, however, are also individualistic and indulgent. IDV and IND are, in fact, significantly correlated in our sample;

$r(28) = +0.73$, $p < 0.001$. People raised in individualistic countries are more likely to put personal outcomes before group-level ones; they are competitive and self-focused rather than collectivistic and communal. Similarly, those living in indulgent cultures are less restrained when seeking gratification, and so are more likely to value positive personal experiences. In our sample, exceptionist nations had higher scores than all other nations, and situationist nations had higher scores than absolutist nations. Subjectivist nations fell intermediate to, and did not differ from, nations whose citizens tended be classified as absolutists and situationists.

The subjectivist nations did, however, stand apart from most other nations in their long-term orientation. Relative to absolutists and exceptionists, they were more likely to value personal steadiness, carefully ordered relationships, and the quest for distant goals. These differences are consistent with previous studies of the cultural beliefs of Western and Eastern cultures (Minkov et al., 2018).

Religiosity

The world's nations differ in their idealism and relativism, but these variations follow a geographic pattern; Western countries differed from Middle Eastern countries, which in turned differed from Eastern countries. But these regions do not only differ in their location, but also in their religions. The spiritual traditions of people living in Eastern countries are rooted in Shintoism, Hinduism, Zen, Buddhism, and Taoism. People who live in Middle Eastern nations, such as Saudi Arabia, Lebanon, and Egypt, are primarily Muslim, and they are therefore more likely to adopt the ethical principles and perspectives of the Quran and the teachings of the Prophet Muhammad. In Western nations, the majority of the religiously faithful are Judeo-Christians.

These religious orientations could explain, in part, the regional differences in idealism and relativism. Eastern faith traditions tend to be more contextual, relational, and dynamic but less dualistic and principle-focused in comparison to Western, Judeo-Christian philosophies. Buddhism, for example, is the dominant spiritual tradition in many parts of Asia, and despite the clear direction of its teachings it maintains that what is right and wrong, morally, is a decision that must be made in a specific context. Buddhism offers suggestions for making moral choices, but its principles are not cross-situational and cross-temporal rules that define the morally good. Eastern philosophies stress change rather than constancy, as illustrated in the ancient Chinese symbol T'ai-chi T'u, or Yin/Yang. The notion of Yin/Yang suggests that what is wrong can be transformed into what is right, and that both good and evil contain within them elements of the other. This committed relativism results in a general skepticism of conventional knowledge and reasoning since the human intellect can only dimly comprehend the spiritual world (Tan, 2002; Xing, 1995).

Islam urges compliance with the moral teachings of the Quran, and so those who accept this faith will tend to be less rather than more relativistic (Abeng, 1997). Islam also enjoins its followers to provide service to their community. Powerful social mores that govern interactions within Islamic society are based, in part, on the value placed on helping others, forgiveness, compensating others for their losses, and service to the community at large (Marta, Attia, Singhapakdi, & Atteya, 2003). These cultural tendencies may explain why individuals from Middle Eastern countries endorse moral philosophies that are more idealistic but less relativistic.

We examined these predicted relationships among idealism, relativism, and religious beliefs by drawing data from two sources: the PEW Research Center 2018 Global Attitudes and Trends database and the World Values Survey project. Our analysis of the PEW data indicated that people living in more idealistic countries tended to also be more religious ($r = +0.43$). Only 47.3% of the residents of subjectivist countries reported a religious affiliation, compared to 92.1%, 87%, and 75.6% of people living in situationist, absolutist, and exceptionist countries. Similar differences emerged when people were asked if their religion was important to them. Only 11.7% of the people in subjectivist countries considered religion to be important to them, compared to 58.1%, 48.2%, and 24.7% of people living in situationist, absolutist, and exceptionist countries.

This connection between religion and ethics positions was also evident in people's responses to the World Values Survey. In his analysis of that survey, Inglehart (1997) identified consistent differences between countries in traditional/secular-rational values (TSV) and survival/self-expression values (SSV). People who live in traditional societies, he suggested, have "high levels of national pride, favor more respect for authority" and "accept national authority passively." They "emphasize social conformity rather than individualistic striving [and] believe in absolute standards of good and evil" (Inglehart & Baker, 2000, p. 25). Cultures with low scores on the TSV dimension also tend to be ones where the populace adopts traditional religious beliefs, such as believing in God and Hell and gaining strength from their religious beliefs.

Consistent with ethics position theory, both idealism and relativism predicted nation-level scores on the TSV dimension. People living in countries classified as subjectivists were more likely to embrace secular-rational values, whereas individuals living in the idealistic countries (situationists and absolutists) were more traditional in their religious views. Those in exceptionist countries reported beliefs that placed them at the midpoint on this continuum. Exceptionist countries, however, had higher scores than all other groups on Inglehart's survival/self-expression values (SSV) dimension. This dimension "taps a syndrome of trust, tolerance, subjective well-being, political activism, and self-expression that emerges in postindustrial societies" (Inglehart & Baker, 2000, p. 25).

Regulation and Autonomy

In Brazil and Russia, requesting monetary compensation for smoothing out a business transaction is standard practice; in the U.S. soliciting and accepting a bribe would cross a moral boundary (Baughn, Bodie, Buchanan, & Bixby, 2010). In some countries, individuals scrupulously conform to governmental regulations pertaining to business practices, but in others these rules are flouted or even nonexistent (Ferrell, Gresham, & Fraedrich, 1989). Most colleges and universities in the U.S. require students pledge that they have not cheated on their tests, but rules about cheating are not strictly enforced in other countries (Miller, Agnich, Posick, & Gould, 2015). Many companies that are headquartered in Germany and the United Kingdom have formal codes of conduct that define corporate principles, ethics, and regulations, but these codes are more rare in other parts of the world (Langlois & Schlegelmilch, 1990). In Confucian countries, the principle of *wu wei* requires a laissez-faire approach to dealing with those who have acted in morally questionable ways, for they believe conflicts, problems, and other unpleasant social experiences will resolve themselves without intervention.

These cross-cultural variations have been examined both by Schwartz (2014) in his studies of cultural value orientations and Pelto (1968) in his work on cultural "tightness." Schwartz and his colleagues, after administering the Social Values Survey (SVS) worldwide, identified variations in autonomy and embeddedness. In cultures that value autonomy residents are free to make choices about most aspects of their lives—the food they eat, the leisure activities they pursue, the work they undertake, and so on. Each person is encouraged to seek their own ideals and positive experiences. Residents of other countries, in contrast, tend to stress embeddedness: the maintenance of status quo through restraint and conformity to tradition. Similarly, Pelto (1968) drew a distinction between tight and loose societies. In tight societies, such as the Puebloans, the Hutterites, and Japanese, norms governing social and moral conduct are both clear and comprehensive, and those who act contrary to these standards are sanctioned. Other societies, such as the Skolt Lapps of Finland or the Thais, are loose societies. Social and moral norms are guidelines rather than inviolate rules, interpersonal dealings are relatively informal and less constrained, and those who do not conform are tolerated rather than punished (Gelfand, Nishii, & Raver, 2006).

These cultural tendencies, although not specific to moral standards, are conceptually similar in some ways to variations in idealism and relativism. Cultures that are more idealistic are, in general, more caring, spiritual, and humane, but at the same time they are stronger in their condemnation of those whose actions harm others. Relativistic cultures, too, should be more likely to be tolerant cultures—after all, relativists do not believe moral rules are transituational and transpersonal.

To clarify the relationship between idealism, relativism, and normative robustness we examined the levels of cultural autonomy and cultural tightness-looseness in countries that we had previously scored for idealism and relativism.[3] We drew the data on each country's level of autonomy from Schwartz's (2014) survey of cultural value orientations, where he identifies two types of autonomy: intellectual and affective. Cultures that encourage intellectual autonomy value such qualities as creativity, open-mindedness, and exploration of ideas. Those that encourage affective autonomy encourage their citizens to be relatively open in their social lives, pursuing positive, growth-promoting experiences. For a culture's level of tightness-looseness, we relied on Uz's (2015) analysis of the European Values Study Group and World Values Survey Association (EWVS, 2006) integrated data set. His domain-specific index is based on the degree of variance among the residents of a specific country on such issues as prostitution, abortion, divorce, euthanasia, and suicide, with countries with lower variance identified as tighter and those with more variance as looser.

Our analysis indicated that relativistic countries tend to be higher in cultural autonomy and looseness, but that idealism moderates this relationship (see Figure 7.3). Countries that were lower in relativism, such as Egypt and Saudi Arabia, but also relatively idealistic—the absolutists—were the countries with the highest levels of normative restraint, as indicated both by their low level of cultural autonomy and looseness. More unexpectedly, the exceptionist countries, which are not relativistic nor idealistic, were the countries that were more normatively relaxed. The residents of countries with relatively high levels of relativism—the situationist and subjectivist nations—displayed moderate levels of normative constraint, but they fell intermediate to and did not differ from the exceptionist and absolutist countries.

These findings are not entirely consistent with the results of our study of cross-cultural differences in codes of ethics (Forsyth & O'Boyle, 2011). In that project we examined the regulatory standards in the businesses and corporations located in eleven different nations to determine if these codes were consistent or inconsistent with the country's overall levels of idealism and relativism. We indexed the extensiveness, application, and content of each country's ethical codes for commerce using the statistical information provided by the Ethical Investment Research Service (EIRIS). EIRIS examines the extent to which corporations establish and strive to act in ways that are consistent with positive moral practices. The EIRIS bases its analysis on public documents about companies, and in some cases surveys specific companies for information about their ethical practices and outlooks. We focused on the elements in the EIRIS indices described by Scholtens and Dam (2007) in their analysis of codes of ethics: degree of codification, culture, implementation, corruption, and human rights.

That study indicated that a nation's average relativism was negatively correlated with the degree to which businesses within that nation codified their

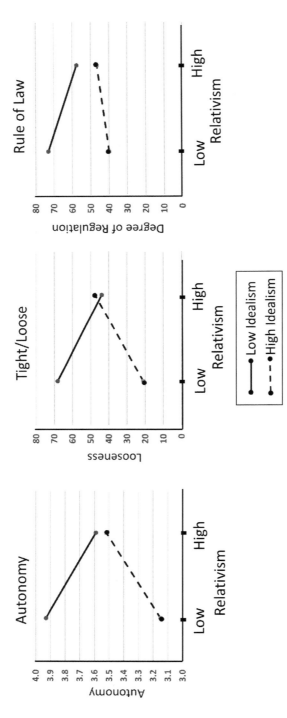

FIGURE 7.3 Mean levels of cultural autonomy (Schwartz, 2014), tightness-looseness (Uz, 2015), and rule of law for nations classified into one of the four moral positions defined by ethics position theory: exceptionists, subjectivists, absolutists, and situationists. Higher scores indicate higher levels of autonomy, looseness, and formal regulations.

ethics. The firms that were headquartered in the five countries that were lower in relativism—Canada, Australia, Belgium, U.S., Austria, and New Zealand— had more extensive ethics codes than the four more relativistic countries in the sample: Spain, UK, Hong Kong, and Ireland. Japan and Austria fell inter- mediate between these two clusters. More codified countries were also the same countries that tended to be higher in autonomy and lower in normative tightness.

This inconsistency between degree of relativism and regulatory standards may result from inadequacies in the data used to determine ethics positions and normative restraint. However, these relationships could also result from the increased need for more formal regulatory mechanisms in societies where cultural norms are less restrictive. Absolutist nations do not require extensive ethics codes, for their normative culture already provides the necessary level of restraint.

We explored this possibility by examining patterns of correlations among country-level indexes of regulatory policies and social values. To assess regu- latory standards, we retrieved data from the World Justice Project (https:// worldjusticeproject.org), which annually indexes each's nation's formal regu- lations pertaining to constraints on government power, corruption, human rights, and civil and criminal justice. This project's Rule of Law index was positively correlated with both Schwartz's (2014) index of autonomy ($r = +0.66$, $p < 0.01$, $n = 42$) and Uz's (2015) index of cultural tightness-looseness ($r = +0.58$, $p < 0.01$, $n = 42$). Exceptionist nations, which are characterized by higher levels of autonomy and cultural looseness, also had significantly elevated scores on the Rule of Law index (see Figure 7.3). Absolutist nations, in contrast, were not only lower in autonomy and looseness, but they were also lower in the rule of law. The relativistic nations fell intermediate to and did not differ from the other nations in the averages on the index of the rule of law.

Cross-Cultural Conclusions

In most societies people are praised for resisting temptations and enticements, and may even be celebrated as moral heroes if they act in particularly com- mendable ways, such as saving others' lives. But they are morally condemned if they deceive and deliberately manipulate other people or cause them substantial harm. This cross-cultural agreement, however, often falls short of unanimity. Some countries tolerate actions that are vilified in others, whereas actions that invoke no more censure elsewhere are considered morally wrong. It seems that what is judged to be moral and immoral often depends on where one is rather that what one has done.

A geographical approach to moral variations confirms that aspects of moral- ity that explain some of the variance in individuals' moral judgments also account for consistencies and contrasts across cultures. When we mapped the ups and down of idealism and relativism across cultures, a pattern emerged: The majority of subjectivist countries were located in the East, the exceptionist countries were in the West, and the absolutist and situationist countries were more evenly distributed around the world. The East was 88.8% subjectivist or situationist, the West 78.5% absolutist or exceptionist, and the Middle East was 100% absolutist or situationist.

But there's more. These geographical variations in morality also predicted cross-cultural differences in collectivism, social stratification, time-orientation, religion, and values. Residents of exceptionist nations (low idealism and relativism countries such as Australia, Canada, New Zealand, and the U.S.) differed from other countries not just in location, but also in values, religiosity, and regulatory codification. The individuals living in nations that we classified as exceptionist ones were individualistic rather than collectivistic, indulgent rather than restrained, and they leaned toward self-expression values rather than traditional (survival) values. Opposed to hierarchical social systems that create inequalities among people, people in exceptionist nations also valued traditional conceptions of the sexes and they were relatively religious. These countries were also normatively looser rather than tighter, yet they were also more regulated—at least, as indicated by their more extensive codes of ethics for businesses and their higher rankings in the rule of law index.

Residents of the subjectivist nations (low idealism and high relativism countries such as China, Hong Kong, and Japan), like exceptionists, held traditional conceptions of the sexes' social roles and did not value the minimization of uncertainty and ambiguity in their cultural practices. They were not religious, at least in the Western sense, for they favored a secular-rational perspective over a traditional, faith-based outlook, but they were collectivist—as were most non-exceptionist countries. As relativistic cultures, residents of subjectivist nations valued autonomy to a moderate degree, but they were not characterized by a particularly high level of regulatory tendencies or cultural tightness. Subjectivist nations were, however, highest in their long-term orientation. Given their longer view of history and change, they were more accepting of diversity in people's interpretation of what is valued and what is not.

People living in the idealistic cultures—the absolutists (countries that are highly idealistic but low in relativism such as Egypt, Saudi Arabia, and Ukraine) and the situationists (high idealism and relativistic countries such as India, Malaysia, Spain, and the United Kingdom)—were similar to each other in many respects. They recognized and accepted status differences within their societies, yet they were also collectivistic. They were less likely to assume men and women's roles in contemporary society were distinctively different, and they were also more religious, leaning away from secular beliefs towards more traditional ones. They were also considerably more likely to express discomfort with uncertainty. Absolutists, however, were unique in their level of avoidance of uncertainty as well as their particularly low levels of indulgence. Perhaps in response to that uncertainty and stoicism, they did not value autonomy as much as people living in the exceptionist nations. Absolutist nations were also tighter than all others—the variance in these nations when reporting their values was low—so they have less need for extensive regulatory requirements.

These findings clarify, to a degree, the conceptual meaning of the dimensions of the ethics position theory. EPQ classifies individuals who agree with such items as "One should never psychologically or physically harm another person" as idealists, but the current findings suggest that they tend to be more traditional, conservative, and religious as well. Similarly, the theory assumes people who agree with such statements as "What is ethical varies from one situation and society to another" are relativists, but the current results suggest that they are also collectivistic, logical/rational, less uncertainty-averse, and possibility less traditionally religious.

In closing, the limitations of this analysis bear repeating. We relied on data of unknown representativeness, using in some cases the responses of a few hundred people to speculate about the values of millions. As research continues, the classification of countries may change, in some cases dramatically. The classification may also change when the cultures themselves undergo change. Many of the world's cultures are experiencing significant social change, as traditional cultural practices give way to ones influenced by technological and economic pressures. As Durkheim (1951) explained in his theory of anomie, in some cases the normative structures of a society become fragile, and fail to provide clear guidance to its members: "When society is disturbed by some painful crisis or by beneficent but abrupt transitions, it is momentarily incapable of exercising this [moral] influence. . . . The limits are unknown between the possible and the impossible, what is just and what is unjust, legitimate claims and hopes and those which are immoderate" (Durkheim, 1951, pp. 251, 253). One result of such change is uncertainty about the norms and standards that serve as guides for both moral and nonmoral behavior, so any estimate of a country's moral norms made at this time may be inaccurate at a different period in the country's history (Zhao & Cao, 2010).

Our analysis used nationality as a proxy for culture, and so does not take into account the variation in cultural beliefs within any specific nation. Each nation of the world includes within its boundaries innumerable subgroups and indigenous populations whose values may have little similarity to those expressed by other citizens of that county. To categorize all the people in any one country as just one moral type is to oversimplify. The majority of the people living in India may be situationists, but in all likelihood a substantial proportion are subjectivists, absolutists, or exceptionists, just as many of the people living in the U.S. are situationists rather than exceptionists. It is best, then, to resist generalizing wildly about the morality of the residents of any country, including one's own. As the historian of moral philosophy, William Lecky (1869/1919, pp. 138–139) puts it (perhaps too unreservedly):

> it is possible to find, even in a nation whose citizens are "habitual liars and habitual cheats," people whose lives are adorned by the consistent practice of some of the most difficult and most painful virtues: Trust in Providence, content and resignation in extreme poverty and suffering, the most genuine amiability and the most sincere readiness to assist their brethren, and adherence to their religious opinions which no persecutions and no bribes can shake, a capacity for heroic, transcendent, and prolonged self-sacrifice.

Notes

1. Several nation's scores (Saudi Arabia, UAE, Thailand) were so close to the midpoint for either relativism or idealism that their classification into one of the four ethics positions is uncertain.
2. These analyses were based on a series of 2 (idealism: high or low) X 2 (relativism: high or low) sample-size-weighted least squares analyses of variance. The findings are consistent with those reported in Forsyth et al. (2008), but some differences resulted from the use of the updated nation data retrieved from www.hofstede-insights.com, including the addition of the indulgence dimension.
3. The relationships between ethics positions and value orientations (Schwartz, 2014) and cultural tightness-looseness (Uz, 2015) were tested in 2 (idealism: high or low) X 2 (relativism: high or low) least squares analyses of variance, followed by Duncan's multiple range post-hoc tests when appropriate. In these analyses both the main effect of idealism and the interaction of idealism and relativism were significant; Fs (1, 19 and 13) = 13.75 and 14.34 (cultural autonomy) and 4.49 and 6.18 (cultural tightness-looseness), all $ps < 0.05$.

8

ETHICS IN CONTEXT

The utility of moral and civil philosophy is to be estimated, not so much by the commodities we have by knowing these sciences, as by the calamities we receive from not knowing them.

—Thomas Hobbes, *Elements of Philosophy* (1839)

The natural variability in people's moral judgments of actions that cause harm and are contrary to moral standards, once recognized, provides insight into the moral problems and conflicts that arise in everyday social contexts. In workplaces, individuals often reach widely disparate decisions that have moral implications and this disparity is determined, at least in part, by differences in idealism and relativism. Those who are in positions of leadership must frequently make choices that could result in negative, harmful consequences that are normatively questionable, and their more idealistic followers may take exception to their choices. Students in school settings, although honor-bound by integrity codes, may nonetheless act in ways that are inconsistent with their teachers' less relativistic expectations. Scientists, too, must be certain to use procedures that are consistent with moral standards, otherwise risk reproach from those who put moral principles before scientific ones. Thus, the analysis of morality is a supremely practical pursuit, for it provides insights into and reveals possible solutions to the most enduring problems of human existence.

* * *

Few problems in life cannot be traced to the sometimes uncertain line that separates the morally acceptable from the morally dubious. Politicians push proposals that are consistent with their party's preferences, overlooking the harm they cause. Businesses promulgate codes of moral conduct, yet too frequently corporate executives choose expedience and profit over what is fair and just. Leaders make choices that will benefits some, but rarely all. Students swear to follow their schools' honor code, but some will stray. Researchers in their quest to explore, study, and understand sometimes push past the boundaries that define moral sensitivity. As people navigate their way through their personal and professional lives they constantly confront the disappointing discrepancy between what is the morally correct thing to do and what they have actually done.

Moral philosophy and moral psychology offer no obvious solutions to this issue, but their analyses of morality's complexities are not mere intellectual exercises. At least, so said the pragmatic philosopher and psychologist John Dewey (1900, 1922; Dewey & Tufts, 1909). Concerned with the ineffectiveness of the educational practices of his day, the level of conflict between the world's nations, and social policies that created rather than countered human suffering, Dewey required theories in both moral psychology and philosophy meet a standard beyond the norm: Not only must they be logically coherent and empirically successful, they must also be practically significant. To study what Kant had to say about moral imperatives or why individuals who value honesty sometimes tell lies is not just intellectually intriguing. Dewey believed moral psychology and philosophy are laden with practical potentiality. From Dewey (1922, pp. 11–12):

> It is not pretended that a moral theory based upon realities of human nature and a study of the specific connections of these realities with those of physical science would do away with moral struggle and defeat. It would not make the moral life as simple a matter as wending one's way along a well-lighted boulevard. All action is an invasion of the future, of the unknown. Conflict and uncertainty are ultimate traits. But morals based upon concern with facts and deriving guidance from knowledge of them would at least locate the points of effective endeavor and would focus available resources upon them.

What, then, is the practical significance of a theory of ethics positions? The theory suggests that people monitor the degree of harm that might result from an action and the consistency of actions with moral standards, but individuals, communities, and cultures vary to some extent when they weigh these two moral directives. Recognizing these two aspects of morality, researchers have used the theory to frame and explain inconsistencies, paradoxes, and problems in a variety of contexts. This chapter selectively samples the results of that work, focusing on four domains: business, leadership, education, and research.

The Ethics of Business

Probably for as long as humans have worked together in the pursuit of joint goals have people done things that others find to be morally objectionable.

Collective endeavors require considerable cooperation, for production, manu-facturing, distribution, management, marketing, finance, and so on are too demanding for a single person. But working with others is the quintessen-tial mixed-motive endeavor (Di Norcia & Larkins, 2000). Infighting, power struggles, and disputes are common rather than unusual in work settings, for the drive for power, promotions, and prominence pits one against another. Businesses also compete against other businesses, for the success of one business may mean that other businesses may fail.

These mixed motivations—to cooperate and to compete—combine to cre-ate pressures to act unethically, and many business professionals are not able to resist these pressures. For example, the executive officers of the energy company Enron manipulated the company's accounting records to disguise the company's debt level. Their actions drove the company into bankruptcy. The CEO of the electronics giant Tyco used company funds to support an extravagant lifestyle. The top-level executives at one of the largest banks in the U.S., Wells Fargo, failed to intervene when many local bank managers were opening up unneeded accounts for customers and billing them monthly charges for those accounts.

These sensational moral failures are matched by the parade of ethically question-able and counterproductive work behaviors that occur each day in the world's boardrooms, factories, offices, warehouses, and retail establishments. The list of ways in which people misbehave when at work is long, and includes minor infractions and irritations—wasting resources, taking credit for others work, hiding one's mistakes and failures, gossiping, deliberately overcharging cus-tomers, damaging equipment and merchandise, ignoring safety regulations—and far more serious and more immoral actions: selling of merchandise that is known to be defective, false advertising, sexual harassment, bullying, assault, sabotage, and endangering co-workers (Bennett & Robinson, 2000). These negative behaviors are sometimes personal, for they are directed at specific people (e.g., bosses or co-workers), but sometimes they harm the organization itself (Dalal, 2005).

The most serious of these workplace infractions are universally condemned, but as is the case with moral judgments in general, people often disagree when judging the rightness and wrongness of many common business practices. Some even argue that business is, to some extent, exempt from the moral con-ventions that apply in other contexts (e.g., Carr, 1968). Lying, for example, is considered morally wrong in nearly all non-business situations, but isn't the use of manipulative communication strategies during negotiations and transactions just business as usual? Given that one of the defining features of a lie is the intent to mislead someone, if no one actually expects others to speak truthfully, then are lies even lies? In many cases, too, when business professionals act in morally questionable ways, they do so for the good of the organizations where they work. Are their actions therefore laudable, for they are acting in ways that are morally reprehensible for what they consider to be a good cause. So, should we expect the same level of moral goodness from people when transacting business as we expect from individuals in everyday contexts? Ethics position theory suggests the answer may depend, in part, on one's personal moral philosophy.

Judgments of Questionable Business Practices

The divergence is one of degree, but it is nonetheless a reliable one: Idealists are harsher and relativists are more lenient when judging the morality of other people's actions (see Chapter 5). Many of the studies that support that conclusion are ones that focused on misbehavior in business settings. When asked to evaluate such actions as deceitful negotiating, using offshore shadow companies, sexual harassment, tolerating illicit methods of accounting, insider trading, violations of fiduciary duties, punishing whistleblowers, overcharging customers, taking care of personal business on company time, and blaming co-workers for one's own mistakes, increases in idealism were associated with more negative judgments of such indiscretions. Relativism, in contrast, predicted more lenient evaluations of such indiscretions (e.g., Abou Hashish & Ali Awad, 2017; Al-Khatib, Malshe, Sailors, & Clark, 2011; Bowes-Sperry & Powell, 1999; Douglas & Wier, 2000; Karande, Rao, & Singhapakdi, 2002; Keyton & Rhodes, 1997; Nayir & Herzig, 2012; Shaub, Finn, & Munter, 1993; Singhapakdi, Vitell, & Franke, 1999).

This tendency has been corroborated across a number of business contexts, including finance, marketing, accounting, and advertising. Clouse, Giacalone, Olsen, and Patelli (2017), for example, asked a national panel sample of office workers to evaluate the morality of various financial misdeeds, including sharing privileged information about salaries and bonuses, offering CEOs excessively high compensation, misrepresenting one's credit history, and so on. They discovered that increases in idealism predicted more negative moral judgments whereas relativism was associated with leniency. Barnett, Bass, Brown, and Hebert (1998) asked marketing professionals to evaluate individuals who did such things as offered bribes to secure an account or divulged privileged information to advance their career. They discovered that as idealism increased and relativism decreased, perceivers' judgments became increasingly negative: Absolutists were the most severe in their judgments, whereas the subjectivists were the most lenient. Kung and Huang (2013) also confirmed the idealism-harsh/relativism-lenient effect in their study of accounting practices. They asked the senior auditors in major accounting firms how they would respond if they encountered evidence of unethical (and often illegal) bookkeeping practices when working with a client (e.g., misreporting debit to avoid publicizing declines in profit, shifting transactions to subsidiaries, stock manipulations). As predicted, idealistic auditors were more likely to condemn the actions of clients that violated moral norms, while relativist auditors were more permissive (Nasir, Sallem, & Othman, 2014).

Ethics and Counterproductive Work Behaviors

People who condemn others' actions may themselves act unethically when they get the chance, just as those who say they are morally tolerant never stray. But when people working in business contexts are asked if they have acted immorally in the past, or if they think that they would likely act immorally in the future, the idealism-harsh/relativism-lenient effect becomes the idealism-ethical/relativism-unethical effect. As Kish-Gephart, Harrison, and Treviño (2010) concluded after reviewing meta-analytically the factors that influence workplace ethics, idealism is "negatively related to unethical choices" and "a relativistic moral philosophy was positively related to unethical choice" (p. 4).

Consider, for example, counterproductive work behaviors, or CWBs. These forms of workplace deviance are deliberate actions that run counter to the normative standards of the organization, and in consequence undermine the productivity, social relations, and general well-being of the organization and its members. Some of these actions, such as acting rudely or leaving work early, are relatively minor, but others are more significant: stealing equipment, using illegal drugs, or hate speech. The target can be the organization itself, people in the organization, or both (Bennett & Robinson, 2000). Some researchers distinguish among various types of CWBs by considering the cause of the behavior, including anger, injustice, revenge, and retribution (O'Boyle, Forsyth, & O'Boyle, 2011).

CWBs cause harm to others and they violate organizational norms: Two characteristics that likely link them to individual differences in ethics positions. Confirming that association, Henle, Giacalone, and Jurkiewicz (2005) surveyed people working full-time in banking, marketing, manufacturing, medicine, or education, asking them how frequently (never to daily) they had engaged in some form of organizational CWB (e.g., left work early, dragged out work to get overtime) or personal CWB (e.g., played a mean prank on someone, acted rudely). They found that idealism was negatively correlated with both organizational deviance and interpersonal deviance, and relativism was correlated with interpersonal deviance. When Henle and her colleagues classified participants into one of the four ethics positions identified by the theory, their findings suggested the situationists (elevated idealism and relativism scores) were the least likely of all ethics types to report engaging in organizational deviance, particularly in comparison to subjectivists.

Other investigations confirm these associations between idealism, relativism, and ethical behavior in the workplace. Douglas and Wier (2000), for example, recruited a sample of managers who were members of the Institute of Certified Professional Managers. Most were business professionals who held positions that required planning and budgeting. They asked these experts how frequently they engaged in budgetary slacking: accounting practices that obfuscate costs, profits, and debt levels (Daumoser, Hirsch, & Sohn, 2018). Such methods, although considered deceptive, are not necessarily prohibited, and are used to create flexibility when preparing materials needed for regulatory and advisory purposes, including taxation and annual reporting (shifting assets from one account or corporate unit to another to avoid budget limits or hide profits and losses, understating forecasted revenues and projected costs, etc.). Their analysis indicated that the greater the pressure put on these managers by senior-level leaders in the company to demonstrate profits and to meet projected goals, the more likely these managers were to use these strategies. Levels of idealism and relativism, however, were also implicated as causes of managers accounting strategies: Idealism was negatively related to questionable budgetary practices, but relativism was positively correlated with such practices (see, too, Douglas & Wier, 2005; Greenfield, Norman, & Wier, 2008; Harvey, 2015).

Not every study of questionable business practices has confirmed the link between those behaviors and ethics positions (e.g., Eastman, Eastman, & Tolson, 2001; Kott, 2012; Rawwas, Hammoud, & Iyer, 2019). Also, in some cases only one of the theory's constructs, and not their combination, emerges as a significant predictor of lapses in either anticipated or reported ethical misconduct. For example, Al-Khatib and his colleagues (2011) investigated the relationship between opportunism—the tendency to pursue personal interests using expedient, ethically questionable methods—and relativism. They asked marketing managers or senior marketing executives in the U.S. and Belgium to "reflect on a major contract they negotiated within the past year" (p. 139). They then completed the SINS: the Self-reported Inappropriate Negotiation Strategies scale (Robinson, Lewicki, & Donahue, 2000). This survey asks respondents to rate a variety of questionable, but common, strategies that a person might use when trying to close a deal. It includes, for example, pretending to like the other party, attempting to get the other party fired to deal with a new negotiator, bribing, offering future concessions that you will not actually honor, and so on. These researchers discovered that relativism predicted these negotiators level of opportunism and that opportunism predicted their use of these inappropriate negotiation strategies.

In many cases, too, the relationships among idealism and relativism wax and wane depending on the organizational context. As a multilevel approach suggests, unethical behavior is not only determined by such individualistic qualities as employees' sense of equity, loyalty to the company, or their moral positions, but also such organizational-level variables as size of the work unit, its cohesion, and ethical climate. Fernando, Dharmage, and Almeida (2008), for example, questioned senior managers working in publicly traded companies in Australia about their firm's tolerance of moral missteps. To assess ethical culture, they asked the respondents if the organizations' executive officers had made it clear to others that unethical behavior will not be tolerated. They discovered that relativism, but not idealism, was related to these executives' descriptions of their corporate moral culture. Individuals who were more relativistic believed that actions that were unethical would be tolerated in their organization.

Hastings and Finegan (2011) also confirmed the importance of considering both person-level and situation-level variables in their study of organizational justice and unethical behavior. They distinguish between three forms of organizational justice: procedural, distributive, and interactional (also called interpersonal). Procedural justice results when the methods used to make decisions about the allocation of resources seem to be fair ones, and is measured by responses to such items as "Procedures are designed to collect accurate information necessary for making decisions" (Hastings & Finegan, 2011, p. 694). Distributive justice concerns how rewards and costs are shared (distributed) within the organization and asks if people feel they are "fairly rewarded for the work they have done well" (p. 694). Interactional justice pertains to organizational civility. In workplaces that are interactionally fair people respect each other, refrain from incivility, and communicate openly about workplace issues.

Hastings and Finegan examined the interrelations among justice and ethics by recruiting young men and women who were currently employed in the food, sales, and service industries, and asked them—under conditions that guaranteed their anonymity—how frequently the engaged in organizational deviance (e.g., left work early, dragged out work to get overtime), personal deviance (e.g., played a mean prank on someone, acted rudely), or constructive organizational behavior (e.g., changing "what is wrong with the situation to make it better," p. 695). As they predicted, idealism was negatively associated with self-reported deviance, but positively associated with constructive behaviors. In some cases, however, idealism interacted with both relativism and justice to predict who would act ethically and unethically. Situationists who worked in places rife with interactional injustice responded pro-socially: They engaged in constructive organizational behaviors to reduce tension and incivility. Subjectivists, in contrast, leaned in a different direction. They were more likely than all other ethics types to engage in various forms of organizational deviance when they believed that their workplace's decisional procedures were unfair ones (low procedural justice).

Prosocial Behavior: Whistle-Blowing

Consider this quandary. Pat has been working at United Chemicals for over 20 years. She takes her work in the petrochemicals division very seriously, so when she learns that some plant personnel are not following proper chemical handling procedures, she reports the violation to management. But management explains that United Chemicals has been using the same handling procedures for 30 years and no one has been injured yet. But Pat disagrees, for she feels that safety should come first. So Pat engages in whistle-blowing: "the disclosure by organization members (former or current) of illegal, immoral, or illegitimate practices under the control of their employers, to persons or organizations that may be able to effect action" (Near & Miceli, 1985, p. 4). She reports the violations to authorities, and the company must make extensive and costly changes to improve the safety of the work environment.

Some people would consider Pat to be a hero for following her moral compass, but others may challenge her choice. Idealists, including absolutists and situationists, would share Pat's desire to minimize the possibility of harm: Workplace safety should not be sacrificed in the name of convenience or profit. But those who are not so idealistic, in contrast, may point out that United Chemicals safety record was unblemished, so why make changes to a system that is already working well? This reaction, however, may be tempered for those who endorse a more relativistic moral position. Situationists and subjectivists may be reluctant to challenge Pat's choice, since "what one person considers to be moral may be judged to be immoral by another person." Less relativistic individuals, in contrast, may base their judgments on two, somewhat conflicting, considerations. Pat's choice is justified by the standards that regulate workplace safety, but she also disobeyed the orders of her direct superiors in the organization. Absolutists, who are sensitive to harm and standards, may consider Pat's actions to be laudable, but exceptionists may be less sympathetic when evaluating those who make public their organization's failures.

We investigated these possibilities by asking individuals who varied in ethics positions to judge the morality of Pat's decision to blow the whistle on United Chemical (Forsyth & O'Boyle, 2006). As predicted, people generally judged Pat very favorably; the average rating was an eight on a nine-point scale, where higher numbers corresponded to more positive moral judgments. But idealism boosted those evaluations even further, with nearly half (49%) of the idealists rating Pat as "completely moral"—a nine on the nine-point scale—whereas less than a quarter (22.6%) of the low idealists rated Pat so positively. But these differences between idealists were particularly pronounced among those who were lower in their level of relativism. The mean rating of Pat's morality was 8.5 for absolutists, but only 7.3 for exceptionists. Two thirds (67.7%) of the absolutists rated Pat as completely moral, compared to a meager 16.7% of the exceptionists. Exceptionists, one must conclude, are not as admiring as others when considering the heroism of the whistleblower.

Absolutists' positive evaluations of whistle-blower Pat, however, should not be taken as evidence that absolutists will, themselves, report the corporate misdeeds they encounter. When researchers asked the managers they surveyed about their willingness to report wrongdoing committed in the organization to someone either inside or outside of that organization, they discovered that idealism was negatively associated with both forms of whistle-blowing (Nayir & Herzig, 2012). Chui and Stembridge (2001), however, in their study of managers working in corporations in the U.S., report a different result. They found that idealism, but not relativism, was associated with respondents' behavioral intentions to make a report if they themselves were ever in such a situation. Given these conflicting findings, additional research is needed to clarify the relationship between ethics positions and likelihood of whistle-blowing.

Leadership

A CEO bankrupts the company she is supposed to be leading. A politician uses government funds to pay for his personal expenses. A boss blatantly favors the men in the office in terms of pay and promotions. A company's executive leadership decides to relocate a factory overseas, causing economic ruin for the local residents. A supervisor never reviews subordinates' work, and the quality of the company's products decline.

Probably for as long as human societies have asked individuals to take responsibility for coordinating the actions and outcomes of others, people have questioned their leaders' motivations, fairness, and integrity. Leadership is an adaptive, goal-seeking process, for it organizes and motivates group members' attempts to attain personal and group goals. Unfortunately, not all leaders are effective, or even ethical. Leaders sometimes take their group in directions it should not go. They act to promote their own personal outcomes and overlook the good of the group. Leaders manipulate followers, persuading them to make sacrifices, while the leaders enjoy the rewards of their power and influence. They push their agendas too hard, their groups obey their demands, and only later do all realize their mistakes. Such leaders are influential—but in a negative way (Ciulla & Forsyth, 2011).

A Leader's Ethics

Contemporary analyses trace leaders' ethical integrity to their capacity to remain true to their chosen goals, procedures, and values, even in the face of strong social and personal pressures. Theories of authentic leadership, for example, suggest that most effective, and most ethical, leaders have a strong and relatively stable core of moral beliefs and practical values that significantly determine the way they conduct themselves as leaders. Their self-awareness extends to their emotions and motivations, so they are more likely to control their feelings in situations that might provoke others to display hostile, threatening, or contentious emotions, and they help others moderate their affective reactions as well (Ilies, Morgeson, & Nahrgang, 2005). But leaders also face more temptations than most people because of their power, privilege, and position. When leaders believe that they "live by a different set of moral requirements," that their followers have given them permission to "break the rules," or that they are seeking a "greater good," then they are likely to do things that others might question (Price, 2010, p. 399).

A leader's level of idealism and relativism, however, may moderate the influence of situational pressures. Waldman, Wang, Hannah, and Balthazard (2017), in their analysis of the ethics of leadership, suggest that relativism—although an advantage in some circumstances—may be a liability for leaders. Leaders set the standards for their organizations, and followers expect their leaders to model those standards. In many of the recent cases of failed ethical leadership, such as CEOs of large organizations that acted to promote their personal interests, their fundamental failing was a lack of constancy in their moral values. As for idealism, a concern for others' welfare is consistent with many forms of ethical leadership (Brown & Treviño, 2006). However, as Waldman and his colleagues (2017) note, leaders must also be fair, so in many cases they must make choices that maximize the well-being of the collective at the expense of specific individuals. Such choices "necessitate harming some individuals at times (e.g., punishing a follower for an ethical transgression), or at least not serving the personal needs or welfare of all individuals" (p. 1292). They therefore conclude that subjectivists would be less likely to earn high marks as moral leaders, whereas exceptionists—with their lower levels of relativism and idealism—are more likely to hold the higher moral ground.

Waldman and his colleagues tested their hypotheses about the ethics of leadership by recruiting 67 men and 40 women who held leadership positions in the U.S. Army, not-for-profit organizations, or private-sector banking, health care, and marketing companies. To determine if these individuals lead others in ways that were ethical, they asked these leaders' peers and subordinates to rate them on the Ethical Leadership Scale developed by Brown, Treviño, and Harrison (2005). This scale includes such items as "Conducts his or her personal life in an ethical manner," "Disciplines employees who violate ethical standards," and "When making decisions, asks 'what is the right thing to do?'." These ratings, as they expected, were significantly associated with the leaders' levels of idealism and relativism: Those with higher levels of idealism were thought to be more ethical leaders ($r = +0.10$), whereas those who were more relativistic were viewed as less ethical ($r = -0.30$). Their analyses also indicated, however, that these relations were sustained primarily by the low levels of ethical leadership exhibited by the subjectivists and the elevated scores of the exceptionists. They concluded that leaders who are relativistic are more likely to be rated as less ethical by their followers, particularly if they are also low in idealism.

But Waldman and his colleagues did more than just survey leaders and their subordinates about ethical leadership, idealism, and relativism. They also used a brain-scanning procedure, low-resolution brain electromagnetic tomography, to record the neuronal activity in certain areas of each leader's brain. Drawing on prior studies of the neuronal bases of self-related information processes, they indexed the degree of coherence (connectivity) in the default mode network, or DMN, of the right hemisphere. This portion of the brain is more active when people are *not* engaged in goal-directed behavior, and is thought to be responsible for self-reflective thought, including self-awareness and self-regulation. Reasoning that leaders who use more ethical methods when working with others are more self-reflective, Waldman and his colleagues predicted higher levels of connectivity in the DMN of the right hemisphere would be correlated with a leader's scores on the Ethical Leadership scale —and their results supported that prediction. They also discovered, however, that DMN activity was also associated with a leader's level of relativism—as a leader's levels of relativism decreased, degree of coherences in the default mode network increased. Their findings suggest that individuals who are more self-reflective are more likely to rely on moral standards to guide their interventions, and the result is a more ethically commendable approach to leadership.

A Leader's Style

Researchers have identified a number of different styles of leadership—task-focused, relationship-oriented, autocratic, democratic, laissez-faire, transformational, and so on. Some leaders, for example, are task-oriented and directive; they focus their attention on goals and the best ways of reaching those goals. Others, such as the relationship-oriented leaders, are more concerned with the satisfaction and well-being of their followers. Democratic leaders seek input from the people they work with, whereas autocratic types are directive rather than receptive. But most people expect that their leaders, no matter what their style, will be ethical.

Do individuals who differ in their ethics positions also differ in their approach to leadership? Waldman and his research team (2017) examined this question in their study of the neurological bases of leadership. They focused on transformational leadership. This inspirational method of leading others involves elevating one's followers' motivation, confidence, and satisfaction by uniting them in the pursuit of shared, challenging goals and changing their beliefs, values, and needs. Consistent with previous research, leaders who exhibited more of the qualities associated with transformational leaders were rated as more ethical by their subordinates. Transformational leadership was not, however, associated with leaders' neural networks or their levels of idealism and relativism.

Kefenie (2015), too, did not find that the leaders he studied adopted different styles of leadership if they were relativistic or idealistic, with one exception. He asked the leaders he recruited for his research to describe their leadership styles, and to also complete the EPQ. The different ethics types varied in their leadership approaches, but Kefenie identified only one consistent tendency: Subjectivists where more likely than other types to display the characteristics of self-protective leaders. Self-protective leaders tend to be self-centered, status-conscious, concerned with maintaining a positive social image, and comfortable with conflict (Dorfman, Hanges, & Brodbeck, 2004).

VanMeter, Grisaffe, Chonko, and Roberts (2013), however, found that idealism predicted a person's tendency to display qualities consistent with a particularly ethically commendable style of leadership: servant leadership. This style of leadership, as described by Greenleaf (1977), requires leaders serve others rather than themselves. Selfless, supportive, respectful, and ethical, servant leaders do not seek personal gain, but instead act to promote the best interests of their followers. They empower others, help them develop in healthy, adaptive ways, and remain ready to provide them with support and guidance in their endeavors. For Greenleaf, a true servant leader must pass this test: "Do those served grow as persons? Do they, while being served, become healthier, wiser, freer, more autonomous, more likely themselves to become servants?" (pp. 13–14). Greenleaf also adds that a servant leader would never knowingly harm any others, directly or indirectly (Greenleaf, 1996).

Are people with the qualities needed to be a servant leader, as defined by Greenleaf (1996), idealistic, relativistic, or a mix of these two ethics orientations? VanMeter and her colleagues (2013) examined this question directly in a study of 1,128 young adults who completed both the EPQ and a survey that measured the kinds of qualities that typify servant leaders, including genuinely caring for people, respecting people, modeling integrity, leading by example, and showing concern "for the welfare of others" (paraphrased from VanMeter et al., p. 107). As predicted, the idealistic ethics positions, absolutists and situationists, had significantly higher scores on the measure of servant leadership in comparison to the two low idealism groups, exceptionists and subjectivists. Relativism was not a predictor of servant leadership.

Leaders and Their Followers

People do not always have the opportunity to pick their leaders, but when they do, they usually prefer an ethical one rather than an unethical one. History is marked by many exceptions to this tendency, when people follow a Gadhafi, Mugabe, or a Saloth Sars (Pol Pot) rather than a Lincoln, Gandhi, or Mohammed. But when researchers asked individuals in 62 countries to describe the desirable and undesirable qualities of an outstanding leader of an organization, across nearly all cultures' respondents expressed a desire for highly ethical leaders who would hold true to the moral values of the community (Dorfman et al., 2004).

Who, then, would leaders prefer if given the choice between an exceptionist, subjectivist, absolutist, or situationist leader? In a preliminary study of this question, we asked a sample of college students who were completing an advanced course of study of leadership to read a brief description of four leaders who matched the four moral philosophies described in ethics position theory:

- *Absolutist leader*: someone who seeks the best possible outcomes for all concerned, but does so by acting in ways that are consistent with standards of ethics (the principled leader).
- *Situationist leader*: someone who believes ethics are relative and situationally specific, and that what matters most is seeking the best possible outcomes for all concerned (the situational leader).
- *Subjectivist leader*: someone who bases actions on personal values and perspectives, rather than standards of ethics or a desire to achieve positive outcomes for others (the personal leader).

- *Exceptionist leader*: someone who acts in ways that are consistent with standards of ethics, and is not so concerned with achieving positive outcomes for others (the practical leader).

These followers rated the two idealistic leaders, absolutists and situationists, more positively than the less idealistic leaders (subjectivists and exceptionists). Their preferences, however, also varied depending on their own ethics positions. Followers who were absolutists rated the absolutist leader significantly more positively than did subjectivists and exceptionists (with situationist followers falling intermediate to, and not differing from the absolutists and subjectivists). Exceptionists were somewhat more tepid in their enthusiasm for situationist leaders, relative to other followers. The subjectivist leader was preferred only by highly relativistic followers—both the situationists and the subjectivists. And the exceptionist leader, whose description was not as positive as the descriptions of other leaders, was rated more positively only by followers who had elevated idealism scores.

Educational Settings

Educational institutions, like all complicated social systems, are governed by norms that regulate the actions of the individuals in that system. Some of these norms are common to most settings (e.g., do not lie, damage other's property, injure other people, etc.), but schools, colleges, and universities have an additional set of standards that guard against students (a) being credited for learning they did not achieve and (b) gaining advantages or privileges that they do not deserve. Every university or college likely has a list of the specific actions that violate these two principles, but most such lists include cheating.

Cheating and Ethics Positions

Most students know that cheating, in all its various forms, is a serious academic and ethical offense, yet surveys of college students indicate that cheating is no rarity. Three in four students report having engaged in a relatively serious form of academic dishonesty, such as using crib notes, copying off of someone else's examination, working with others on projects that were supposed be done by individuals only, and plagiarizing (e.g., McCabe, Butterfield, & Treviño, 2012). When asked if they cheated in a particular class or during a given semester, between 20% and 30% of the students surveyed reported committing an infraction, and some students reported having cheated repeatedly in the same class throughout the term (Stearns, 2001).

Who is more likely to cheat? Men are slightly more likely to cheat than women, as are students whose time is more limited—say by a job or by participation in extracurricular events—and students who are younger (Whitley, 1998). Students who are members of sororities and fraternities cheat more frequently than other students, as do student athletes (McCabe et al., 2012). Cheating may also be associated with differences in students' ethics positions. Relativists are, in general, skeptical about moral absolutes, and so they may be less likely to accept honor codes as their personal codes. In consequence, they may consider academic misconduct to be allowable in some circumstances. Idealists, in contrast, tend to be harsher when judging those who act immorally, so they may be less likely to act in ways that may bring about moral censure.

VanMeter and her colleagues (2013) investigated these predictions by asking over a thousand college students to evaluate nineteen ways to cheat in school. Some of these methods, such as taking a picture of an exam with a cell phone, copying another person's test, and using crib notes, were individualistic (or unilateral) ones. Others, such as finding out the test questions from students who have already taken the test and sharing work on projects that are supposed to be done individually, were collaborative. The researchers discovered that these students considered the individualistic cheating methods to be much more unethical than the collaborative ones. Overall, however, students who were more idealistic were also more negative in their judgments of both types of cheating, but those who were more relativistic were more lenient. These tendencies resulted in substantial differences between absolutists and subjectivists. Absolutists were the least tolerant of ethical violations, subjectivists were the most tolerant, and the situationists and exceptionists fell intermediate to these two types and did not differ from them. Further research is needed, however, to determine if these judgments translate into differences in actual behavior.

Academic Whistle-blowing

Most schools, colleges, and universities have an academic integrity policy that describes the kinds of activities that are considered inappropriate, immoral, or punishable (e.g., plagiarism, cheating, destruction of materials). Only some of these codes, however, include a non-tolerance clause: the requirement to not only refrain from actions that are identified as unethical, but to also inform school authorities if you observe anyone else violating these standards. Students therefore must not lie, cheat, steal, and so on, but they also must not tolerate other students who do. These ethical mandates are often termed "rat clauses."

Non-tolerance is a form of whistle-blowing and has all its interpersonal and organizational complexities. Students know they should act honorably, but they do not necessarily feel that they are duty-bound to report others' ethical indiscretions. Idealists, being sensitive to harm done to others, may be unwilling to cause another person to suffer the disgrace of a charge of cheating. Relativism, too, may be related to non-tolerance, as individuals who are highly relativistic may be reluctant to insist that everyone abide by the school's code of academic ethics.

Barnett, Bass, and Brown (1996) investigated these possibilities in their study of students' judgments of a person who does not themselves cheat, but instead turns in a student who does. They asked college students to consider the actions of Pat, a student who accidentally witnesses another student cheating on the final examination in the course. The course grades are criterion referenced rather than normed, and so one student's success does not influence other students' grades. But, while working on her own test, "Pat looks up for a moment to ponder a question and sees a student copying answers from another student's exam. . . . After giving it some thought, Pat tells the professor about the cheating as soon as the exam is over" (Barnett et al., 1996, p. 1171).

In this study, idealism and relativism both predicted students' judgments of Pat—increases in idealism were associated with more positive evaluations of Pat turning in the cheater, whereas increases in relativism were associated with more negative evaluations. These moral judgments, too, were correlated with students' predictions about how they would act if they found themselves in a similar situation. Those who thought that Pat was moral were more likely to claim that they would also report cheating to the class instructor. In this study, however, only relativism was significantly correlated with students' intention to report cheating; idealism was correlated with judgments, but not with behavioral intentions. Other studies, however, suggest that idealism, too, may predict who is more likely to report honors violations to school authorities (e.g., Smith & Shen, 2013).

Educational Experiences and Ethics

Most fields and disciplines require their students, practitioners, and professionals adhere to a code of ethics. Physicians are required to act with benevolence toward their patients, lawyers must not only serve their clients but also never act unlawfully, researchers must not falsify data, and journalists must verify their information and protect their sources. In addition to their codes of ethics, they may require individuals who are joining their fields to undergo an educational experience designed to teach them about ethics, in general, and the ethical standards of their field, in particular.

These educational experiences, however, do not always result in a finely calibrated moral compass. Meta-analytic reviews of the effectiveness of these courses, across a number of disciplines, suggest that they have very little impact on students' sensitivity to moral issues, their judgments about morally questionable practices, or moral integrity (Antes et al., 2009; Waples, Antes, Murphy, Connelly, & Mumford, 2009). Wang and Calvano (2015), for example, used a quasi-experimental design to examine the effect of taking a class on business ethics. All students completed a measure of moral choice in which one decision was clearly more ethically sound—returning lost money to its owner or correcting a billing error—than another. Approximately half of the students completed these assessments at the end of the semester, and the others before enrolling in the course. Unexpectedly, the researchers found that a course in ethics only increased the ethical integrity of the male students, but not the female students. This difference, however, was caused by differences between men and women before taking the course. Women, without studying business ethics, were already significantly more moral then men—and the course did not change that. Thus, the course helped the men to catch up, but it did not help the women advance any further in terms of moral growth.

Wang and Calvano identified one possible source of this moratorium in moral development for the women: relativism. They administered the EPQ in their study, and they found that female students who had taken the course in ethics were more relativistic than female students who had not taken the course. Given that relativism, particularly if not combined with a high level of idealism, is an indicator of reduced moral integrity, their findings call into question the effectiveness of using a structured class on ethics to change students' moral integrity (see Godos-Díez, Fernández-Gago, & Cabeza-García, 2015).

These findings are consistent with research that has tested the impact of another common educational program on students' morality: studying abroad. These programs are generally lauded as effective means of reducing cultural biases and stimulating creativity, but Lu and his colleagues (2017) have identified a potential downside to these programs: a decline in moral integrity. These investigators compared the moral behaviors of students before, during, and after their study abroad program by giving them the opportunity to cheat when completing various tasks. For example, to measure morality students completed a series of anagrams which they self-scored, and without their knowledge any misrepresentation of their true scores could be tracked. Across six different studies, students with experiences in other countries cheated more than students who had not spent time living in other cultures. Moreover, the relationship between foreign experience and morality was mediated by changes in students' relativism. Using the EPQ they confirmed that living in another country increased students' level of relativism, which in turn increased their tendency to act immorally. Their findings are consistent with other work that suggests that exposure to moral relativism increases immoral behavior (Rai & Holyoak, 2013).

Research Ethics

Social scientists, as members of the scientific community, strive to expand our knowledge of human behavior and apply that understanding for the enrichment of society and its members. Their work seeks goals that few would considerable undesirable, for the pursuit of knowledge is valued by most. Their methods, however, sometimes raise fundamental questions about the rights of individuals and the ethical responsibilities of investigators. Society condemns those who use others for their own purposes, who deceive others by giving them false information, and who subject others to stressful experiences, and researchers are not exempted from compliance with these norms. Yet researchers, in the name of science, sometimes do all these things, and the result is predictable—at least predictable based on ethics position theory. Some people object, strenuously, when researchers mislead or manipulate people who are taking part in their studies, but others do not (Forsyth, 1981b).

On the Ethics of Psychological Research

This selective sampling of the practical implications of ethics position theory ends by returning to the question that initially generated the search for the source of individual variations in moral judgments: the ethics of scientific research. In scientific research that involves human participants, researchers sometimes deceive participants by misleading them about the nature and purpose of the situation. Research studies can also be stressful experiences, and often the people who take part do not freely agree to do so. They might be lured into the study by the promise of payment, extra credit, or some elaborate subterfuge. Researchers do not always ask the people they study to give their consent to participate. People's right to privacy can be violated if they are studied by researchers without their awareness (Ascheman, 2013).

People vary in their appraisals of the ethics of research with human participants. As Reynolds (1979), in his book *Ethical Dilemmas and Social Science Research*, notes: "Discussions of moral or ethical dilemmas in the social science literature seem to have several dominant features. Foremost is the wide range of positions and judgments expressed by social scientists" (p. 3). Consider, for example, the ethical controversy that arose following the publication of Milgram's (1963) studies of obedience. Milgram defended his research on scientific grounds, but others condemned him for using methods that required deceiving and stressing the participants (e.g., Baumrind, 1964). The federal government, acting partly in response to criticisms of the ethics of Milgram's research, developed a code of standards that all researchers must follow to protect human subjects from harm (Schrag, 2010).

That people disagreed about the ethics of Milgram's research is not surprising: Diversity in moral reactions is commonplace. Nor is it surprising that these variations can be explained, in part, by people's ethics positions. As Chapter 2 explained, it was this case that sparked our initial investigations of the source of variability in moral reactions (Schlenker & Forsyth, 1977). When we asked people to evaluate Milgram's research, we found that exceptionists were willing to make exceptions to the general rule that prohibits lying if the study yielded valuable scientific data. Their moral judgments correlated with the benefits of the research—amount learned, scientific value, and contribution to science—but they were less influenced by such costs as threat to participants, harm, or the foreseeability of harm. The reverse, however, held true for absolutists, for cost factors correlated significantly with moral judgments, but the benefit factors did not. Relativists' moral judgments most completely covaried with both benefits and costs, especially if they were also idealistic (situationists).

These patterns also emerged in a second study—one that examined people's evaluations of the morality of fifteen different research projects, including field, laboratory, deception, unobtrusive, and scenario research (Forsyth & Pope, 1984). Some of these studies were relatively benign ones; people giving their impressions of someone who is described as warm or cold (Asch, 1946) or allowing researchers to inventory their household products (Freedman & Fraser, 1966). Others, however, were more fraught, in that they involved invasion of privacy (e.g., Middlemist, Knowles, & Matter, 1976), deception (Festinger & Carlsmith, 1959), or exposure to negative stimuli such as electric shock (Gerard & Mathewson, 1966). We asked volunteers who had previously completed the EPQ to rate the ethical similarity of the 15 stimulus studies via a series of paired-comparison judgments, which we examined using multidimensional scaling (MDS). This inductive scaling process allowed us to identify the dimensions that best accounted for people's perceptions of the 15 studies and label them by examining (a) the location of the experiments in the spatial configuration and (b) the relation between the obtained dimensions and a series of subject-supplied ratings of the experiments.

Our analysis indicated respondents, as they considered the ethics of these studies, took notice of the potential harm to participants, the use of manipulative procedures that were inconsistent with traditional moral practices (e.g., deception, elaborate pretense), implementing safeguards that protected participants rights and well-being (e.g., informed consent), and the ratio between benefits and risks. However, the specifics of each of these dimensions differed for each ethics position, and so a separate scaling solution was required for each group. Moreover, these dimensions influenced moral judgments differently for each ethical type. For example, all the participants took note of the potential harm that the study could cause participants, but some weighed this factor more heavily than others both when comparing the studies and when formulating their moral appraisals.

Exceptionists' ratings were organized around four themes: manipulativeness, harm, deception, and the ratio of risks to benefits. Consistent with their commitment to moral standards, they differentiated between studies that used substantial amounts of deception and those that did not. Like all judges, they were also sensitive to the possibility of harm to participants, and the study's potential for causing harm was most closely associated with their judgments of a study's ethical acceptability. Exceptionists, however, also considered the scientific legitimacy of the study, which they balanced against the study's more ethically questionable procedures. Provided potential scientific benefits were substantial and the risks were minimized through the use of appropriate procedures or safeguards, exceptionists considered the study to be acceptable.

For subjectivists, what mattered most was the invasiveness of the project, the potential for harm, and the study's positive features (use of consent, contribution to knowledge) that justified the study's methods. Like exceptionists, high scientific legitimacy was a positive factor that partially mitigated the negative aspects of the research, but subjectivists did not balance risks against benefits. Instead, dimensions corresponding to negative and positive aspects of the research were weighed independently. Also, unlike individuals who endorsed other ethics positions, subjectivists were more negative toward studies that violated people's expectations for privacy.

Absolutists, as their idealistic sensitivity to harm would suggest, distinguished primarily between studies that could cause harm and those that posed less risk to participants. Their ratings of the various studies were organized around three dimensions that corresponded to potential for harm and upset, invasion of privacy resulting in psychological harm, and the use of procedures that reduced the risk of harm for the participants. Given their emphasis on harm, absolutists' judgments of the studies were more negative than the judgments offered by individuals who endorsed the other ethics positions: far more of the fifteen experiments clustered at the unethical end of the absolutists' moral judgment continuum.

Situationists based their ethical evaluations of the studies on only two criteria: the balance between the risks (e.g., use of deception, potential for harm) and benefits (e.g., scientific contribution) and the degree to which those who took part in the study could have been upset when they discovered the study's actual purposes. Their moral judgments, however, were determined more by their perceptions of the risks/benefits ratio in the study ($r = -0.84$) than by how upsetting the study might be for participants ($r = +0.49$). Situationists were unique, however, in that they also distinguished between studies that could have caused psychological and physical harm and those that failed to give subjects the opportunity to consent (informed consent), but these two dimensions were not related to their judgments of the ethics of the studies.

Consensus on Harm

Because social scientists study people rather than rocks, plants, atomic particles, or planets, they run up against challenges and problems that other scientists never encounter. Social scientists must not only design studies that are scientifically sound, but they must also make certain their work does not violate moral standards. Such judgments, however, are rarely unanimous ones, for disagreement and conflict are the rule, rather than the exception, in discussions of research ethics. But even though variance may be unavoidable when judging the ethics of research, most agree—in principle—with the standards set forth in the *Belmont Report* developed by the National Commission for the Protection of Human Subjects of Biomedical and Behavioral Research (1979). That report, which formed the basis for the standards and regulatory requirements mandated by the U.S. government's Common Rule for evaluating research, stressed the requirements that all researchers protect participants from harm.

This requirement, too, was manifested in the responses of participants in our studies of ethical judgments of psychological research. Although individuals who endorsed certain moral positions—the absolutists in particular—weighed the potential for harm more than others, all those who took part in our research considered the potential for harm to be the first principle in evaluating research.

Variations in Moral Judgment

Why do some people work to the best of their ability at their jobs, whereas others loaf, disrupt, and undermine? Why do some leaders believe that any action that benefits them personally is allowable, whereas others put honor before self-adulation? Why do most students abide by the school's honor code, but others think cheating is morally allowable? Why do some researchers conduct studies that irritate, upset, annoy, and harm participants but others argue that the scientific ends never justify the means?

This variance in moral thoughts, emotions, and behavior is the cause of considerable conflict, consternation, and general mayhem, but ethics position theory suggests that these differences between people are to be expected. The exceptionist cannot tolerate the easygoing appraisals of the relativist. The relativist cannot understand the rigidity of the absolutist. The absolutist questions the moral inconsistencies of the subjectivist. The situationist demands to know the specifics of any particular context before forming an appraisal. The subjectivist wonders what all the fuss is about. But these variations are not arbitrary ones, formed by some accident of history, happenstance of upbringing, or the random intermingling of genetic material. They are rooted, instead, in variations in people's construal of harmful outcomes and actions that are inconsistent with standards.

Recognizing these two critical aspects of morality, and their consistent influence across people and contexts, offers no solution to moral conflict, but it does offer a promise of understanding—and with understanding may come resolution. In terms of self-knowledge, the rational moral decision maker should remain ever mindful of the influence of these two considerations on their choices. Our moral judgments, says the theory, are informed by our intuitive estimates of potential harm and by the compatibility of the action with moral standards, so any factor that biases those two estimates will also bias our judgments. But moral uncertainty, too, can be remedied by revisiting those estimates and asking two questions: "What harm will result?" and "What are my community's values?"

Nor must moral disagreements become conflicts rather than discussions. Moral outliers—those who consider neither harm nor standards when making moral choices—resist influence, but for most people moral disagreements are a matter of degree rather than kind. Rare is the person who is oblivious to the harm that may result from an action, but people do vary in their willingness to accept some harm in the pursuit of a greater good. Rare is the person who acts without considering society's moral standards, but not everyone insists on perfect conformity to those standards. At the center of any moral controversy is the middle ground that offers an acceptable compromise to all. Ethics position theory enjoins us to avoid ridiculing and rejecting another person's moral stance, but to instead consider the source of our differences. Our studies of individual differences in people's ethical beliefs suggest that we will likely never reach complete agreement on all moral issues, but at least we can aim for a fuller understanding of why we disagree.

APPENDIX

The Ethics Position Questionnaire (EPQ-5)

You will find a series of general statements listed below. Each represents a commonly held opinion and there are no right or wrong answers. You will probably disagree with some items and agree with others. We are interested in the extent to which you agree or disagree with such matters of opinion.

Please read each statement carefully. Then indicate the extent to which you agree or disagree where:

1 = Strongly disagree   3 = Neutral   4 = Agree

2 = Disagree   5 = Strongly Agree

1 2 3 4 5   1. A person should make certain that their actions never intentionally harm another even to a small degree.

1 2 3 4 5   2. The existence of potential harm to others is always wrong, irrespective of the benefits to be gained.

1 2 3 4 5   3. One should never psychologically or physically harm another person.

1 2 3 4 5   4. One should not perform an action which might in any way threaten the dignity and welfare of another individual.

1 2 3 4 5   5. If an action could harm an innocent other, then it should not be done.

_____ Sum of items 1 to 5 divided by 5.

1 2 3 4 5   6. What is ethical varies from one situation and society to another.

1 2 3 4 5   7.   Moral standards should be seen as being individualistic; what one person considers to be moral may be judged to be immoral by another person.

1 2 3 4 5   8.   Questions of what is ethical for everyone can never be resolved since what is moral or immoral is up to the individual.

1 2 3 4 5   9.   Moral standards are simply personal rules that indicate how a person should behave, and are not to be applied in making judgments of others.

1 2 3 4 5   10.   Ethical considerations in interpersonal relations are so complex that individuals should be allowed to formulate their own individual codes.

_____ Sum of items 6 to 10 divided by 5.

REFERENCES

Abeng, T. (1997). Business ethics in Islamic context: Perspectives of a Muslim business leader. *Business Ethics Quarterly*, 7, 47–54.

Abou Hashish, E. A., & Ali Awad, N. H. (2017). Relationship between ethical ideology and moral judgment: Academic nurse educators' perception. *Nursing Ethics*, 1–14. doi.org/10.1177/0969733017722825

Adorno, T. W., Frenkel-Brunswick, E., Levinson, D., & Sanford, N. (1950). *The authoritarian personality*. New York: Harper & Row.

Alas, R., Gao, J., & Carneiro, J. (2010). Connections between ethics and cultural dimensions. *Engineering Economics*, 21(3), 255–262.

Alicke, M. D. (2012). Self-injuries, harmless wrongdoing, and morality. *Psychological Inquiry*, 23, 125–128.

Alicke, M. D., Mandel, D. R., Hilton, D. J., Gerstenberg, T., & Lagnado, D. A. (2015). Causal conceptions in social explanation and moral evaluation: A historical tour. *Perspectives on Psychological Science*, 10(6), 790–812.

Alicke, M. D., Rose, D., & Bloom, D. (2011). Causation, norm violation, and culpable control. *The Journal of Philosophy*, 108(12), 670–696.

Al-Khatib, J. A., Dobie, K., & Vitell, S. J. (1995). Consumer ethics in developing countries: An empirical investigation. *Journal of European Marketing*, 4, 87–109.

Al-Khatib, J. A., Malshe, A., Sailors, J. J., & Clark, I. (2011). The impact of deceitful tendencies, relativism and opportunism on negotiation tactics: A comparative study of US and Belgian managers. *European Journal of Marketing*, 45(1/2), 133–152.

Al-Khatib, J. A., Rawwas, M. Y., Swaidan, Z., & Rexeisen, R. J. (2005). The ethical challenges of global business-to-business negotiations: An empirical investigation of developing countries' marketing managers. *Journal of Marketing Theory and Practice*, 13(4), 46–60.

Al-Khatib, J. A., Robertson, C. J., & Lascu, D. (2004). Post-communist consumer ethics: The case of Romania. *Journal of Business Ethics*, 54, 81–96.

Al-Khatib, J. A., Stanton, A. D., & Rawwas, M. Y. A. (2005). Ethical segmentation of consumers in developing countries: A comparative analysis. *International Marketing Review*, 22, 225–246.

Allport, G. W. (1937). *Personality: A psychological interpretation*. New York: Holt, Rinehart & Winston.

Altemeyer, B. (1988). *Enemies of freedom: Understanding right-wing authoritarianism*. San Francisco, CA: Jossey-Bass.

American Psychological Association. (1973). *Ethical principles in the conduct of research with human participants*. Washington, DC: American Psychological Association.

Anderson, N. H. (1968). Likableness ratings of 555 personality-trait words. *Journal of Personality and Social Psychology, 9*(3), 272–279.

Anderson, N. H. (2008). *Unified social cognition*. New York: Psychology Press.

Anscombe, G. E. M. (1957). *Intention*. Oxford: Basil Blackwell.

Antes, A. L., Murphy, S. T., Waples, E. P., Mumford, M. D., Brown, R. P., Connelly, S., & Devenport, L. D. (2009). A meta-analysis of ethics instruction effectiveness in the sciences. *Ethics & Behavior, 19*(5), 379–402.

Aquino, K., Freeman, D., Reed, I. I., Lim, V. K., & Felps, W. (2009). Testing a social-cognitive model of moral behavior: The interactive influence of situations and moral identity centrality. *Journal of Personality and Social Psychology, 97*(1), 123–141.

Aquino, K., & Kay, A. (2018). A social cognitive model of moral identity. In K. Gray & J. Graham (Eds.), *The atlas of moral psychology* (pp. 133–140). New York: Guilford Press.

Aquino, K., & Reed, I. I. (2002). The self-importance of moral identity. *Journal of Personality and Social Psychology, 83*(6), 1423–1440.

Aristotle. (1935). *Aristotle* (P. Wheelwright, Trans.). Indianapolis, IN: Bobbs-Merrill. (Original work published 350 BCE).

Arli, D., & Leo, C. (2017). Why do good people do bad things? The effect of ethical ideology, guilt proneness, and self-control on consumer ethics. *Asia Pacific Journal of Marketing and Logistics, 29*(5), 1055–1078.

Asch, S. E. (1946). Forming impressions of personality. *Journal of Abnormal and Social Psychology, 41*, 258–290.

Ascheman, P. L. (2013). *Ethical judgments of deception in psychological research*. Unpublished doctoral dissertation, Iowa State University, Ames, IA. Retrieved from ISU Digital Repository lib.dr.iastate.edu

Atkins, D. C., Baucom, D. H., & Jacobson, N. S. (2001). Understanding infidelity: Correlates in a national random sample. *Journal of Family Psychology, 15*(4), 735–749.

Austin, J. L. (1962). *How to do things with words* (J. O. Urmson & M. Sbisá, Eds.). Cambridge, MA: Harvard University Press.

Axinn, C., Blair, M., & Thach, A. (2004). Comparing ethical ideologies across cultures. *Journal of Business Ethics, 54*(2), 103–120.

Banai, M., Stefanidis, A., Shetach, A., & Özbek, M. F. (2014). Attitudes toward ethically questionable negotiation tactics: A two-country study. *Journal of Business Ethics, 123*(4), 669–685.

Barnett, T., Bass, K., & Brown, G. (1994). Ethical ideology and ethical judgment regarding ethical issues in business. *Journal of Business Ethics, 13*(6), 469–480.

Barnett, T., Bass, K., & Brown, G. (1996). Religiosity, ethical ideology, and intentions to report a peer's wrongdoing. *Journal of Business Ethics, 15*(11), 1161–1174.

Barnett, T., Bass, K., Brown, G., & Hebert, F. J. (1998). Ethical ideology and the ethical judgments of marketing professionals. *Journal of Business Ethics, 17*(7), 715–723.

Bartels, D. M. (2008). Principled moral sentiment and the flexibility of moral judgment and decision making. *Cognition, 108*(2), 381–417.

Batson, C. D. (2011). Empathy-induced altruism: Friend or foe of the common good. In D. R. Forsyth & C. Hoyt (Eds.), *For the greater good of all: Perspectives on individualism, society, and leadership* (pp. 29–47). New York: Palgrave Macmillan.

Baughn, C., Bodie, N. L., Buchanan, M. A., & Bixby, M. B. (2010). Bribery in international business transactions. *Journal of Business Ethics, 92*(1), 15–32.

Baumeister, R. F., & Leary, M. R. (1995). The need to belong: Desire for interpersonal attachments as a fundamental human motivation. *Psychological Bulletin, 117*, 497–529.

Baumrind, D. (1964). Some thoughts on ethics of research: After reading Milgram's "behavioral study of obedience". *American Psychologist, 26*, 887–896.

Beebe, N. L., & Guynes, J. (2006). A model for predicting hacker behavior. *AMCIS Proceedings*, 409. Retrieved from http://aisel.aisnet.org/amcis2006/409

Bennett, R. J., & Robinson, S. L. (2000). Development of a measure of workplace deviance. *Journal of Applied Psychology, 85*(3), 349–360.

Bentham, J. (1834). *Deontology: The science of morality* (J. Bowring, Ed.). London: Longman, Bees, Orme, Browne, Green, and Longman. Retrieved from https://archive.org/details/deontologyorthes01bentuoft/

Bentham, J. (1948). *An introduction to the principles of morals and legislation*. New York: Hafner. (Original work published 1789).

Berkowitz, L., & Walker, N. (1967). Laws and moral judgments. *Sociometry, 30*(4), 410–422.

Bhattacharya, S., Neelam, N., & Murthy, V. (2018). Ethical value positioning of management students of India and Germany. *Journal of Academic Ethics, 16*, 257. doi.org/10.1007/s1080

Birnbaum, M. H. (1972). Morality judgments: Tests of an averaging model. *Journal of Experimental Psychology, 93*, 35–42.

Boaz, F. (1911). *The mind of primitive man*. New York: Palgrave Macmillan.

Bobowik, M., Basabe, N., Páez, D., Jiménez, A., & Bilbao, M. A. (2011). Personal values and well-being among Europeans, Spanish natives and immigrants to Spain: Does the culture matter? *Journal of Happiness Studies, 12*(3), 401–419.

Bond, M. H., & Hwang, K. K. (1986). *The social psychology of Chinese people*. Oxford: Oxford University Press.

Bornstein, R. F., Denckla, C. A., & Chung, W.-J. (2013). Psychodynamic models of personality. In I. B. Weiner (Ed. in-chief), *Handbook of psychology* (Vol. 5, H. Tennen & J. Suls, Eds., pp. 43–64). New York: Wiley.

Bowes-Sperry, L., & Powell, G. N. (1999). Observers' reactions to social-sexual behavior at work: An ethical decision making perspective. *Journal of Management, 25*(6), 779–802.

Bowman, K., & Marisco, J. (2014, January 22). Opinions about abortion haven't changed much since: Roe v. Wade. *The Atlantic*. Retrieved from www.theatlantic.com/politics/archive/2014/01/opinions-about-abortion-havent-changed-since-em-roe-v-wade-em/283226/

Boyce, W. D., & Jensen, L. C. (1978). *Moral reasoning: A psychological-philosophical integration*. Lincoln, NE: University of Nebraska Press.

Brandt, R. B. (1959). Review of good will and ill will by Frank Chapman Sharp. *The Philosophical Review, 60*(3), 400–402. doi:10.2307/2181880

Brooks, A. C. (2006). *Who really cares: America's charity divide-who gives, who doesn't, and why it matters*. New York: Basic Books.

Brosnan, S. F. (2011). What do capuchin monkeys tell us about cooperation? In D. R. Forsyth & C. Hoyt (Eds.), *For the greater good of all: Perspectives on individualism, society, and leadership* (pp. 11–27). New York: Palgrave Macmillan.

Brown, D. E. (1991). *Human universals*. New York: McGraw-Hill.

Brown, M. E., & Treviño, L. K. (2006). Ethical leadership: A review and future directions. *The Leadership Quarterly, 17*(6), 595–616.

Brown, M. E., Treviño, L. K., & Harrison, D. A. (2005). Ethical leadership: A social learning perspective for construct development and testing. *Organizational Behavior and Human Decision Processes, 97*(2), 117–134.

Burnett, E. A. (2017). *Bad behavior with good intentions: The role of organizational climate in unethical pro-organizational behavior.* Unpublished master's thesis, Clemson University, Clemson, SC.

Buss, A. R., & Poley, W. (1976). *Individual differences: Traits and factors.* New York: Halsted Press.

Butterfield, K. D., Treviño, L. K., & Weaver, G. R. (2000). Moral awareness in business organizations: Influences of issue-related and social context factors. *Human Relations, 53*(7), 981–1018.

Candee, D., & Kohlberg, L. (1987). Moral judgment and moral action: A reanalysis of Haan, Smith, and Block's (1968) free speech movement data. *Journal of Personality and Social Psychology, 52*, 554–564.

Carr, A. (1968). Is business bluffing ethical? *Harvard Business Review, 46*(1), 143–153.

Chagnon, N. A. (2013). *Noble savages: My life among two dangerous tribes.* New York: Simon & Schuster.

Chakroff, A., Russell, P. S., Piazza, J., & Young, L. (2017). From impure to harmful: Asymmetric expectations about immoral agents. *Journal of Experimental Social Psychology, 69*, 201–209.

Chaudhry, P. E., & Stumpf, S. A. (2011). Consumer complicity with counterfeit products. *Journal of Consumer Marketing, 28*(2), 139–151.

Chen, S. Y., & Liu, C. C. (2009). Relationships between personal religious orientation and ethical ideologies. *Social Behavior and Personality: An International Journal, 37*(3), 313–320.

Christie, R. (1970). Scale construction. In R. Christie & F. L. Geis (Eds.), *Studies in Machiavellianism* (pp. 10–34). New York: Academic Press.

Chui, R. K., & Stembridge, A. F. (2001). How managers judge whether or not they want to report a peer's unethical behavior. *InFo, 4*(1), 5–16.

Cialdini, R. B. (2009). *Influence: Science and practice* (6th ed.). Boston: Allyn and Bacon.

Ciulla, J. B., & Forsyth, D. R. (2011). Leadership ethics. In A. Bryman, D. Collinson, K. Grint, B. Jackson, & M. Uhl-Bien (Eds.), *Handbook of leadership* (pp. 229–241). London: Sage.

Clouse, M., Giacalone, R. A., Olsen, T. D., & Patelli, L. (2017). Individual ethical orientations and the perceived acceptability of questionable finance ethics decisions. *Journal of Business Ethics, 144*(3), 549–558.

Cohen, D. J., & Ahn, M. (2016). A subjective utilitarian theory of moral judgment. *Journal of Experimental Psychology: General, 145*(10), 1359–1381.

Cohen, T. R., Panter, A. T., Turan, N., Morse, L., & Kim, Y. (2014). Moral character in the workplace. *Journal of Personality and Social Psychology, 107*(5), 943–963.

Cohen, T. R., Wolf, S. T., Panter, A. T., & Insko, C. A. (2011). Introducing the GASP scale: A new measure of guilt and shame proneness. *Journal of Personality and Social Psychology, 100*(5), 947–966.

Colby, A., & Kohlberg, L. (1987). *The measurement of moral judgment: Vol. 1. Theoretical foundations and research validation.* New York: Cambridge University Press.

Colby, A., Kohlberg, L., Speicher, B., Candee, D., Hewer, A., Gibbs, J., & Power, C. (1987). *The measurement of moral judgement: Standard issue scoring manual* (Vol. 2). Cambridge, UK: Cambridge University Press.

Cornwell, B., Chi Cui, C., Mitchell, V., Schlegelmilch, B., Dzulkiflee, A., & Chan, J. (2005). A cross-cultural study of the role of religion in consumers' ethical positions. *International Marketing Review, 22*(5), 531–546.

Costa, P. T., Jr., & McCrae, R. R. (1992). Four ways five factors are basic. *Personality and Individual Differences, 13*(6), 653–665.

Costa, P. T., Jr., & McCrae, R. R. (2013). *Personality in adulthood: A five-factor theory perspective.* New York: Routledge.

Crockett, M. J., Clark, L., Hauser, M. D., & Robbins, T. W. (2010). Serotonin selectively influences moral judgment and behavior through effects on harm aversion. *Proceedings of the National Academy of Sciences, 107*(40), 17433–17438.

Cui, C. C., Mitchell, V., Schlegelmilch, B. B., & Cornwell, B. (2005). Measuring consumers' ethical position in Austria, Britain, Brunei, Hong Kong, and USA. *Journal of Business Ethics, 62*(1), 57–71.

Cummisky, D. (1996). *Kantian consequentialism.* New York: Oxford University Press.

Curry, O. S., Chesters, M. J., & Van Lissa, C. J. (2019). Mapping morality with a compass: Testing the theory of "morality as cooperation" with a new questionnaire. *Journal of Research in Personality, 78*(1), 106–124.

Cushman, F., Young, L., & Hauser, M. (2006). The role of conscious reasoning and intuition in moral judgment: Testing three principles of harm. *Psychological Science, 17*(12), 1082–1089.

Dahlsgaard, K., Peterson, C., & Seligman, M. E. (2005). Shared virtue: The convergence of valued human strengths across culture and history. *Review of General Psychology, 9*(3), 203–213.

Dalal, R. S. (2005). A meta-analysis of the relationship between organizational citizenship behavior and counterproductive work behavior. *Journal of Applied Psychology, 90*(6), 1241–1255.

D'Arcy, E. (1963). *Human acts: An essay in their moral evaluation.* Oxford: Clarendon Press.

Daumoser, C., Hirsch, B., & Sohn, M. (2018). Honesty in budgeting: A review of morality and control aspects in the budgetary slack literature. *Journal of Management Control, 29*(2), 115–159.

Davis, M. A., Andersen, M. G., & Curtis, M. B. (2001). Measuring ethical ideology in business ethics: A critical analysis of the Ethics Position Questionnaire. *Journal of Business Ethics, 32*(1), 35–53.

Davis, M. A., Johnson, N. B., & Ohmer, D. G. (1998). Issue-contingent effects on ethical decision making: A cross-cultural comparison. *Journal of Business Ethics, 17,* 373–389.

Davis, M. H. (1983). Measuring individual differences in empathy: Evidence for a multidimensional approach. *Journal of Personality and Social Psychology, 44*(1), 113–126.

Decety, J., & Cowell, J. M. (2014). The complex relation between morality and empathy. *Trends in Cognitive Sciences, 18*(7), 337–339.

Deering, T. E. (1998). The ethical perspective of British and American pre-service teachers. *Educational Research, 40,* 353–258.

DeLeeuw, K. E., & Mayer, R. E. (2008). A comparison of three measures of cognitive load: Evidence for separable measures of intrinsic, extraneous, and germane load. *Journal of Educational Psychology, 100*(1), 223–234.

DePaulo, B. M. (2004). The many faces of lies. In A. G. Miller (Ed.), *The social psychology of good and evil* (pp. 303–326). New York: Guilford Press.

Dewey, J. (1900). Psychology and social practice. *Psychological Review,* 7(2), 105–124. doi.org/10.1037/h0066152

Dewey, J. (1922). *Human nature and conduct: An introduction to social psychology.* New York: Henry Holt.

Dewey, J., & Tufts, J. H. (1909). *Ethics.* New York: Henry Holt.

Diener, E. D., Emmons, R. A., Larsen, R. J., & Griffin, S. (1985). The satisfaction with life scale. *Journal of Personality Assessment, 49*(1), 71–75.

Di Norcia, V., & Larkins, J. T. (2000). Mixed motives and ethical decisions in business. *Journal of Business Ethics, 25*(1), 1–13.

Ditto, P. H., & Liu, B. (2012). Deontological dissonance and the consequentialist crutch. In M. Mikulincer & P. R. Shaver (Eds.), *The social psychology of morality: Exploring the causes of good and evil* (pp. 51–70). Washington, DC: American Psychological Association.

Donoho, C., Heinze, T., & Kondo, C. (2012). Gender differences in personal selling ethics evaluations: Do they exist and what does their existence mean for teaching sales ethics? *Journal of Marketing Education, 34*(1), 55–66.

Dorfman, P. W., Hanges, P. J., & Brodbeck, F. C. (2004). Leadership and cultural variation: The identification of culturally endorsed leadership profiles. In R. J. House, P. J. Hanges, M. Javidan, P. W. Dorfman, & V. Gupta (Eds.), *Culture, leadership, and organizations: The GLOBE study of 62 societies* (pp. 669–719). Thousand Oaks, CA: Sage.

Douglas, P. C., & Wier, B. (2000). Integrating ethical dimensions into a model of budgetary slack creation. *Journal of Business Ethics, 28*(3), 267–277.

Douglas, P. C., & Wier, B. (2005). Cultural and ethical effects in budgeting systems: A comparison of US and Chinese managers. *Journal of Business Ethics, 60*(2), 159–174.

Duckitt, J. (2009). Authoritarianism and dogmatism. In M. R. Leary & R. H. Hoyle (Eds.), *Handbook of individual differences in social behavior* (pp. 298–317). New York: Guilford Press.

Dunning, D. (2016). False moral superiority. In A. G. Miller (Ed.), *The social psychology of good and evil* (2nd ed., pp. 249–269). New York: Guilford Press.

Durkheim, É. (1951). *Suicide* (J. A. Spaulding & G. Simpson, Trans.). New York: Free Press.

Eastman, J. K., Eastman, K. L., & Tolson, M. A. (2001). The relationship between ethical ideology and ethical behavior intentions: An exploratory look at physicians' responses to managed care dilemmas. *Journal of Business Ethics, 31*(3), 209–224.

Elias, R. Z. (2002). Determinants of earnings management ethics among accountants. *Journal of Business Ethics, 40*(1), 33–45.

Ellemers, N. (2017). *Morality and the regulation of social behavior: Groups as moral anchors.* New York: Routledge.

Endler, N. S. (1975). The case for person-situation interactions. *Canadian Psychological Review, 16*(1), 12–21.

Erffmeyer, R. C., Keillor, B. D., & LeClair, D. T. (1999). An empirical investigation of Japanese consumer ethics. *Journal of Business Ethics, 18*, 35–50.

Ethics. (2018). *Oxford English dictionary.* New York: Oxford University Press. Retrieved from www.oed.com/view/Entry/355823

Etter, S., Cramer, J. J., & Finn, S. (2006). Origins of academic dishonesty: Ethical orientations and personality factors associated with attitudes about cheating with information technology. *Journal of Research on Technology in Education, 39*(2), 133–155.

EWVS: European Values Study Group and World Values Survey. (2006). European and World Values Surveys four-wave integrated data file, 1981–2004, v.20060423 [Data file]. Retrieved from www.wvsevsdb.com/wvs/WVSData.jsp

Fatoki, O. (2014). The ethical ideology of university students in South Africa. *Journal of Social Sciences, 40*(2), 177–183.

Fernando, M., Dharmage, S., & Almeida, S. (2008). Ethical ideologies of senior Australian managers: An empirical study. *Journal of Business Ethics, 82*(1), 145–155.

Ferrell, O., Gresham, L. G., & Fraedrich, J. (1989). A synthesis of ethical decision models for marketing. *Journal of Macromarketing, 9*(2), 55–64.

Festinger, L., & Carlsmith, J. M. (1959). Cognitive consequences of forced compliance. *Journal of Abnormal and Social Psychology, 58*, 203–210.

Feygina, I., & Henry, P. J. (2015). Culture and prosocial behavior. In D. A. Schroeder & W. G. Graziano (Eds.), *The Oxford handbook of prosocial behavior* (pp. 188–208). New York: Oxford University Press.

Finkelhor, D., Hotaling, G., Lewis, I. A., & Smith, C. (1990). Sexual abuse in a national survey of adult men and women: Prevalence, characteristics and risk factors. *Child Abuse & Neglect, 14*(1), 19–28.

Flanagan, O. (1991). *Varieties of moral personality: Ethics and psychological realism.* Cambridge, MA: Harvard University Press.

Flanagan, O. (2017). *The geography of morals.* New York: Oxford University Press.

Fleeson, W. (2004). Moving personality beyond the person-situation debate: The challenge and the opportunity of within-person variability. *Current Directions in Psychological Science, 13*(2), 83–87.

Fleischhut, N., Meder, B., & Gigerenzer, G. (2017). Moral hindsight. *Experimental Psychology, 64*, 110–123. doi.org/10.1027/1618-3169/a000353

Fletcher, J. (1966). *Situation ethics.* Philadelphia: Westminster Press.

Forsyth, D. R. (1978). *Moral attribution and the evaluation of action.* Unpublished doctoral dissertation, University of Florida, Gainesville, FL. Retrieved from http://ufdc.ufl.edu/AA00003906/00001

Forsyth, D. R. (1980). A taxonomy of ethical ideologies. *Journal of Personality and Social Psychology, 39*(1), 175–184.

Forsyth, D. R. (1981a). Moral judgment: The influence of ethical ideology. *Personality and Social Psychology Bulletin, 7*, 218–223.

Forsyth, D. R. (1981b). A psychological perspective on ethical uncertainties in behavioral research. In A. J. Kimmel (Ed.), *New directions for methodology of social and behavioral science: Ethics of human subject research*, No. 10. San Francisco, CA: Jossey-Bass.

Forsyth, D. R. (1985). Individual differences in information integration during moral judgment. *Journal of Personality and Social Psychology, 49*, 264–272.

Forsyth, D. R. (1992). Judging the morality of business practices: The influence of personal moral philosophies. *Journal of Business Ethics, 11*, 461–470.

Forsyth, D. R. (1994). Honorable intentions versus praiseworthy accomplishments: The impact of motives and outcomes on the moral self. *Current Psychology: Developmental, Learning, Personality, Social, 12*, 296–311.

Forsyth, D. R. (2001). Breaking standards of morality when studying morality: Case commentaries. *Ethics & Behavior, 11*, 357–360.

Forsyth, D. R. (2008). Ethics in experimentation. In W. A. Darity (Ed.), *International encyclopedia of the social sciences* (Vol. 2, 2nd ed., pp. 635–637). New York: Palgrave Macmillan.

Forsyth, D. R., & Berger, R. E. (1982). The effects of ethical ideology on moral behavior. *Journal of Social Psychology, 117*(1), 53–56.

Forsyth, D. R., Iyer, R., & Haidt, J. (2012). Idealism, relativism, and ethics: The moral foundations of individual differences in political orientation. Presented at the Annual Meetings of the Society for Personality and Social Psychology, San Diego, CA.

Forsyth, D. R., & Nye, J. L. (1990). Personal moral philosophies and moral choice. *Journal of Research in Personality, 24*(4), 398–414.

Forsyth, D. R., Nye, J. L., & Kelley, K. (1988). Idealism, relativism, and the ethic of caring. *Journal of Psychology, 122,* 243–248.

Forsyth, D. R., & O'Boyle, E. H., Jr. (2006, November). The psychology of leadership ethics. Paper presented at the Annual Meetings of the International Leadership Association, Chicago.

Forsyth, D. R., & O'Boyle, E. H., Jr. (2011). Rules, standards, and ethics: Relativism predicts cross-national differences in the codification of moral standards. *International Business Review, 20,* 353–361.

Forsyth, D. R., & O'Boyle, E. H., Jr. (2012). Ethics position theory and unethical work behavior. In R. A. Giacalone & M. D. Promislo (Eds.), *Handbook of unethical work behavior: Implications for individual well-being* (pp. 221–236). New York: M.E. Sharpe.

Forsyth, D. R., O'Boyle, E. H., Jr., & McDaniel, M. A. (2008). East meets west: A meta-analytic investigation of cultural variations in idealism and relativism. *Journal of Business Ethics, 83*(4), 813–833.

Forsyth, D. R., & Pope, W. R. (1984). Ethical ideology and judgments of social psychological research. *Journal of Personality and Social Psychology, 46,* 1365–1375.

Forsyth, D. R., Pope, W. R., & McMillan, J. H. (1985). Students' reactions after cheating: An attributional analysis. *Contemporary Educational Psychology, 10*(1), 72–82.

Forsyth, D. R., & Scott, W. L. (1984). Attributions and moral judgments: Kohlberg's stage theory as a taxonomy of moral attributions. *Bulletin of the Psychonomic Society, 22*(4), 321–323.

Foucault, M. (1990). *The history of sexuality: The use of pleasure* (Vol. 2). New York: Knopf.

Frankena, W. (1973). *Ethics* (2nd ed.). Englewood Cliffs, NJ: Prentice-Hall. Retrieved from www.ditext.com/frankena/ethics.html

Freedman, J. L., & Fraser, S. (1966). Compliance without pressure: The foot-in-the-door technique. *Journal of Personality and Social Psychology, 4,* 195–202.

Freud, S. (1920). *A general introduction to psychoanalysis.* New York: Boni & Liveright.

Friesdorf, R., Conway, P., & Gawronski, B. (2015). Gender differences in responses to moral dilemmas: A process dissociation analysis. *Personality and Social Psychology Bulletin, 41*(5), 696–713.

Fry, D. P. (2007). *Beyond war: The human potential for peace.* New York: Oxford University Press.

Gallup Organization. (2018, May). *Gallup Poll* [survey question]. 31115023.00025. Gallup Organization [producer]. Cornell University, Ithaca, NY: Roper Center for Public Opinion Research, iPOLL [distributor]. Retrieved August 18, 2018.

Gawronski, B., Armstrong, J., Conway, P., Friesdorf, R., & Hütter, M. (2017). Consequences, norms, and generalized inaction in moral dilemmas: The CNI model of moral decision-making. *Journal of Personality and Social Psychology, 113*(3), 343–376.

Gelernter, D. (1998). What do murderers deserve? *Commentary.* Retrieved from www.commentarymagazine.com/articles/what-do-murderers-deserve/

Gelfand, M. J., Nishii, L. H., & Raver, J. L. (2006). On the nature and importance of cultural tightness-looseness. *Journal of Applied Psychology, 91*(6), 1225–1244.

Gerard, H. B., & Mathewson, G. (1966). The effects of severity of initiation on liking for a group: A replication. *Journal of Experimental Social Psychology, 2*, 278–287.

Gerlach, P., Teodorescu, K., & Hertwig, R. (2019). The truth about lies: A meta-analysis on dishonest behavior. *Psychological Bulletin, 145*(1), 1–44.

Giacalone, R. A., Fricker, S., & Beard, J. W. (1995). The impact of ethical ideology on modifiers of ethical decisions and suggested punishment for ethical infractions. *Journal of Business Ethics, 14*(7), 497–510.

Giacalone, R. A., Jurkiewicz, C. L., & Promislo, M. (2016). Ethics and well-being: The paradoxical implications of individual differences in ethical orientation. *Journal of Business Ethics, 137*(3), 491–506.

Giammarco, E. A. (2016). The measurement of individual differences in morality. *Personality and Individual Differences, 88*, 26–34.

Gilligan, C. (1982). *In a different voice.* Cambridge, MA: Harvard University Press.

Gilligan, C. (2014). Moral injury and ethic of care: Reframing the conversation about differences. *Journal of Social Philosophy, 45*(1), 89–106.

Gino, F., Schweitzer, M. E., Mead, N. L., & Ariely, D. (2011). Unable to resist temptation: How self-control depletion promotes unethical behavior. *Organizational Behavior and Human Decision Processes, 115*(2), 191–203.

Glenn, A. L., Koleva, S., Iyer, R., Graham, J., & Ditto, P. H. (2010). Moral identity in psychopathy. *Judgment and Decision Making, 5*(7), 497–505.

Godos-Díez, J. L., Fernández-Gago, R., & Cabeza-García, L. (2015). Business education and idealism as determinants of stakeholder orientation. *Journal of Business Ethics, 131*(2), 439–452.

Goldberg, L. R. (1990). An alternative description of personality: The big-five factor structure. *Journal of Personality and Social Psychology, 59*(6), 1216–1229.

Goodwin, G. P., Piazza, J., & Rozin, P. (2014). Moral character predominates in person perception and evaluation. *Journal of Personality and Social Psychology, 106*(1), 148–168.

Gore, J. S., & Cross, S. E. (2006). Pursuing goals for us: Relationally autonomous reasons in long-term goal pursuit. *Journal of Personality and Social Psychology, 90*, 848–861.

Graham, J., Haidt, J., Koleva, S., Motyl, M., Iyer, R., Wojcik, S. P., & Ditto, P. H. (2013). Moral foundations theory: The pragmatic validity of moral pluralism. *Advances in Experimental Social Psychology, 47*, 55–130.

Graham, J., Haidt, J., & Nosek, B. A. (2009). Liberals and conservatives rely on different sets of moral foundations. *Journal of Personality and Social Psychology, 96*(5), 1029–1046.

Graham, J., Nosek, B. A., Haidt, J., Iyer, R., Koleva, S., & Ditto, P. H. (2011). Mapping the moral domain. *Journal of Personality and Social Psychology, 101*(2), 366–385.

Gray, K., & Schein, C. (2016). No absolutism here: Harm predicts moral judgment 30× better than disgust: Commentary on Scott, Inbar, & Rozin (2016). *Perspectives on Psychological Science, 11*(3), 325–329.

Gray, K., Young, L., & Waytz, A. (2012). Mind perception is the essence of morality. *Psychological Inquiry, 23*(2), 101–124. doi:10.1080/1047840X.2012.651387

Greenfield, A. C., Norman, C. S., & Wier, B. (2008). The effect of ethical orientation and professional commitment on earnings management behavior. *Journal of Business Ethics, 83*(3), 419–434.

Greenleaf, R. K. (1977). *Servant leadership: A journey into the nature of legitimate power and greatness*. Mahwah, NJ: Paulist Press.

Greenleaf, R. K. (1996). *On becoming a servant leader: The private writings of Robert K. Greenleaf*. San Francisco, CA: Jossey-Bass.

Grieve, R., & McSwiggan, C. (2014). Predicting intentions to fake in psychological testing: Which normative beliefs are important? *Revista de Psicología del Trabajo y de las Organizaciones, 30*(1), 23–28.

Güğerçin, U., & Ay, Ü. (2017). Factor analytic structure of Ethics Position Questionnaire: A study on the bank employees. *Journal of Economics and Administrative Sciences, 35*(4), 53–78.

Guglielmo, S. (2015). Moral judgment as information processing: An integrative review. *Frontiers in Psychology, 6*, 1637. doi:10.3389/fpsyg.2015.01637

Haan, N. (1978). Two moralities in action contexts. *Journal of Personality and Social Psychology, 36*, 286–305.

Haan, N. (1986). Systematic variability in the quality of moral action, as defined in two formulations. *Journal of Personality and Social Psychology, 50*(6), 1271–1284.

Haan, N., Aerts, E., & Cooper, B. A. B. (1985). *On moral grounds: The search for practical morality*. New York: New York University Press.

Hadjistavropoulos, T., Malloy, D. C., Sharpe, D., & Fuchs-Lacelle, S. (2003). The ethical ideologies of psychologists and physicians: A preliminary comparison. *Ethics & Behavior, 13*(1), 97–104.

Haidt, J. (2001). The emotional dog and its rational tail: A social intuitionist approach to moral judgment. *Psychological Review, 108*(4), 814–834.

Haidt, J. (2012). *The righteous mind: Why good people are divided by politics and religion*. New York: Pantheon.

Haidt, J., & Graham, J. (2007). When morality opposes justice: Conservatives have moral intuitions that liberals may not recognize. *Social Justice Research, 20*(1), 98–116.

Haidt, J., & Joseph, C. (2004). Intuitive ethics: How innately prepared intuitions generate culturally variable virtues. *Daedalus, 133*(4), 55–66.

Haidt, J., Koller, S. H., & Dias, M. G. (1993). Affect, culture, and morality, or is it wrong to eat your dog? *Journal of Personality and Social Psychology, 65*(4), 613–628.

Hall, J. A. (2011). Sex differences in friendship expectations: A meta-analysis. *Journal of Social and Personal Relationships, 28*(6), 723–747.

Hare, R. D., & Neumann, C. S. (2009). Psychopathy: Assessment and forensic implications. *The Canadian Journal of Psychiatry, 54*(12), 791–802.

Hare, R. M. (1981). *Moral thinking: Its levels, method, and point*. New York: Oxford University Press.

Hart, H. L. A. (1968). *Punishment and responsibility: Essays in the philosophy of law*. Oxford: Clarendon Press.

Hartshorne, H., & May, M. A. (1928). *Studies in deceit, Book I: General methods and results, Book II: Statistical methods and results*. New York: Palgrave Macmillan.

Harvey, M. E. (2015). The effect of employee ethical ideology on organizational budget slack: An empirical examination and practical discussion. *Journal of Business & Economics Research (Online), 13*(1), 83. doi.org/10.19030/jber.v13i1.9084

Haslam, S. A., Reicher, S. D., & Birney, M. E. (2014). Nothing by mere authority: Evidence that in an experimental analogue of the Milgram paradigm participants are motivated not by orders but by appeals to science. *Journal of Social Issues, 70*(3), 473–488.

Hastings, S. E., & Finegan, J. E. (2011). The role of ethical ideology in reactions to injustice. *Journal of Business Ethics, 100*(4), 689–703.

Heider, F. (1958). *The psychology of interpersonal relations*. New York: Wiley.

Henle, C. A., Giacalone, R. A., & Jurkiewicz, C. L. (2005). The role of ethical ideology in workplace deviance. *Journal of Business Ethics, 56*, 219–230.

Henrich, J., Heine, S. J., & Norenzayan, A. (2010). The weirdest people in the world? *Behavioral and Brain Sciences, 33*(2–3), 61–83.

Higgins, E. T. (1990). Personality, social psychology, and person-situation relations: Standards and knowledge activation as a common language. In L. A. Pervin (Ed.), *Handbook of personality* (pp. 301–338). New York: Guilford Press.

Ho, F. N., Vitell, S. J., Barnes, J. H., & Desborde, R. (1997). Ethical correlates of role conflict and ambiguity in marketing: The mediating role of cognitive moral development. *Journal of the Academy of Marketing Science, 25*(2), 117. doi.org/10.1007/BF02894347

Hobbes, T. (1839). *The English works of Thomas Hobbes of Malmesbury* (W. Molesworth, Ed.). London: John Bohn.

Hofmann, W., Wisneski, D. C., Brandt, M. J., & Skitka, L. J. (2014). Morality in everyday life. *Science, 345*(6202), 1340–1343.

Hofstede, G. (1980). *Culture's consequences: International differences in work-related values*. Newbury Park, CA: Sage.

Hofstede, G., Hofstede, G. J., & Minkov, M. (2010). *Cultures and organizations: Software of the mind* (3rd ed.). New York: McGraw-Hill.

Hogan, R. (1973). Moral conduct and moral character: A psychological perspective. *Psychological Bulletin, 79*, 217–232.

Holton, G. A. (2004). Defining risk. *Financial Analysts Journal, 60*(6), 19–25.

Holyoak, K. J., & Powell, D. (2016). Deontological coherence: A framework for commonsense moral reasoning. *Psychological Bulletin, 142*(11), 1179–1203.

Horne, Z., Powell, D., & Hummel, J. (2015). A single counterexample leads to moral belief revision. *Cognitive Science, 39*(8), 1950–1964.

House, R. J., & Javidan, M. (2004). Overview of GLOBE. In R. J. House, P. J. Hanges, M. Javidan, P. W. Dorfman, & V. Gupta (Eds.), *Culture, leadership, and organizations: The GLOBE study of 62 societies* (pp. 9–28). Thousand Oaks, CA: Sage.

Hume, D. (2007). *A dissertation on the passions and the natural history of religion* (T. L. Beauchamp, Ed.). Oxford: Clarendon Press. (Originally work published 1755).

Husted, B. W., & Allen, D. B. (2008). Toward a model of cross-cultural business ethics: The impact of individualism and collectivism on the ethical decision-making process. *Journal of Business Ethics, 82*(2), 293–305.

Ilies, R., Morgeson, F. P., & Nahrgang, J. D. (2005). Authentic leadership and eudaemonic well-being: Understanding leader-follower outcomes. *The Leadership Quarterly, 16*(3), 373–394.

Inglehart, R. (1997). *Modernization and postmodernization: Cultural, economic, and political change in 43 societies*. Princeton, NJ: Princeton University Press.

Inglehart, R., & Baker, W. E. (2000). Modernization, cultural change, and the persistence of traditional values. *American Sociological Review, 65*, 19–51.

Irwin, E. (1995). *Plato's ethics*. New York: Oxford University Press.

Ishida, C. (2006). How do scores of DIT and MJT differ? A critical assessment of the use of alternative moral development scales in studies of business ethics. *Journal of Business Ethics, 67*(1), 63–74.

Iyer, R., Koleva, S., Graham, J., Ditto, P., & Haidt, J. (2012). Understanding libertarian morality: The psychological dispositions of self-identified libertarians. *PloS One*, 7(8), e42366.

Jaffee, S., & Hyde, J. S. (2000). Gender differences in moral orientation: A meta-analysis. *Psychological Bulletin*, 126(5), 703–726.

James, W. (1973). The moral philosopher and the moral life. In P. E. Davis (Ed.), *Introduction to moral philosophy* (pp. 145–158). Columbus, OH: C. E. Merrill. (Original work published 1891).

James, W. (1979). *The will to believe and other essays in popular philosophy.* Cambridge, MA: Harvard University Press. (Original work published 1897).

Janoff-Bulman, R., & Carnes, N. C. (2013). Surveying the moral landscape: Moral motives and group-based moralities. *Personality and Social Psychology Review*, 17(3), 219–236.

Johari, R. J., Sanusi, Z. M., & Ismail, A. H. (2012). Exploratory factor analysis of the Ethical Orientation Scale. *Asian Journal of Accounting and Governance*, 3, 1–11. doi:10.17576/ajag-2012-3-6511

Johnson, M. (2014). *Morality for humans: Ethical understanding from the perspective of cognitive science.* Chicago: University of Chicago Press.

Jones, J. C., Spraakman, G., & Sánchez-Rodríguez, C. (2014). What's in it for me? An examination of accounting students' likelihood to report faculty misconduct. *Journal of Business Ethics*, 123(4), 645–667.

Jones, T. M. (1991). Ethical decision making by individuals in organizations: An issue-contingent model. *Academy of Management Review*, 16(2), 366–395.

Jost, J. T., Glaser, J., Kruglanski, A. W., & Sulloway, F. J. (2003). Political conservatism as motivated social cognition. *Psychological Bulletin*, 129(3), 339.

Kant, I. (1973). On a supposed right to tell lies from benevolent motives (T. K. Abbott, Trans.). In P. E. Davis (Ed.), *Introduction to moral philosophy* (pp. 254–258). Columbus, OH: C. E. Merrill. (Original work published 1873).

Kant, I. (2014). *Fundamental principles of the metaphyshics of morals* (T. K. Abbott, Trans.). Adelaide, Australia: The University of Australia Library. Retrieved from https://ebooks.adelaide.edu.au/k/kant/immanuel/k16prm/ (Original work published 1788).

Kant, I. (2018). *Groundwork for the metaphysics of morals* (A. W. Wood, Trans.). New Haven, CT: Yale University Press. (Original work published 1785).

Karande, K., Rao, C. P., & Singhapakdi, A. (2002). Moral philosophies of marketing managers: A comparison of American, Australian, and Malaysian cultures. *European Journal of Marketing*, 36(7/8), 768-791.

Kefenie, L. A. (2015). *The search for good leadership behaviors: A study of the relationship between second-order global leadership dimensions and ethical ideologies.* Unpublished doctoral dissertation, Eastern University, Philadelphia, PA. Retrieved from ProQuest Dissertations & Theses Global. (Order No. 10105458).

Kelley, H. H. (1971). Moral evaluation. *American Psychologist*, 26(3), 293–300.

Kernes, J. L., & Kinnier, R. T. (2005). Psychologists' search for the good life. *Journal of Humanistic Psychology*, 45, 82–105.

Keyton, J., & Rhodes, S. C. (1997). Sexual harassment: A matter of individual ethics, legal definitions, or organizational policy? *Journal of Business Ethics*, 16(2), 129–146.

Khan, T. I., Akbar, A., Jam, F. A., & Saeed, M. M. (2016). A time-lagged study of the relationship between big five personality and ethical ideology. *Ethics & Behavior*, 26(6), 488–506.

Kidwell, J. M., Stevens, R. E., & Bethke, A. L. (1987). Differences in ethical perceptions between male and female managers: Myth or reality? *Journal of Business Ethics*, *6*(6), 489–493.

Kim, Y., & Choi, Y. (2003). Ethical standards appear to change with age and ideology: A survey of practitioners. *Public Relations Review*, *29*(1), 79–89.

Kish-Gephart, J. J., Harrison, D. A., & Treviño, L. K. (2010). Bad apples, bad cases, and bad barrels: Meta-analytic evidence about sources of unethical decisions at work. *Journal of Applied Psychology*, *95*(1), 1–31.

Klass, E. T. (1978). Psychological effects of immoral actions: The experimental evidence. *Psychological Bulletin*, *85*(4), 756–771.

Klein, N., & O'Brien, E. (2016). The tipping point of moral change: When do good and bad acts make good and bad actors? *Social Cognition*, *34*(2), 149–166.

Klein, R. A., Vianello, M., Hasselman, F., Adams, B. G., Adams, R. B., Jr., Alper, S., . . . Nosek, B. (2018). Many Labs 2: Investigating variation in replicability across samples and settings. *Advances in Methods and Practices in Psychological Science*, *1*(4), 443–490.

Kluckhohn, C. (1951). Values and value-orientations in the theory of action: An exploration in definition and classification. In T. Parsons & E. Shils (Eds.), *Toward a general theory of action* (pp. 388–433). Cambridge, MA: Harvard University Press.

Kohlberg, L. (1958). *The development of modes of thinking and choice in years 10 to 16.* Unpublished doctoral dissertation, University of Chicago, Chicago, IL.

Kohlberg, L. (1963). The development of children's orientations toward a moral order, I: Sequence in the development of human thought. *Vita Humana*, *6*(1–2), 11–33.

Kohlberg, L. (1968). The child as moral philosopher. *Psychology Today*, *2*(4), 25–30.

Kohlberg, L. (1969). Stage and sequence: The cognitive development approach to socialization. In D. A. Goslin (Ed.), *Handbook of socialization theory and research* (pp. 325–480). New York: Rand McNally.

Kohlberg, L. (1983). *Essays in moral development* (Vol. 2). New York: Harper & Row.

Koleva, S. P., Graham, J., Iyer, R., Ditto, P. H., & Haidt, J. (2012). Tracing the threads: How five moral concerns (especially Purity) help explain culture war attitudes. *Journal of Research in Personality*, *46*(2), 184–194.

Kott, J. K. (2012). *The role of ethics in employee behavior.* Unpublished doctoral dissertation, University of Tennessee, Knoxville, TN. Retrieved from https://scholar.utc.edu/theses/43

Kour, M. (2017). Ethical ideology of business students in India: An empirical study. *International Journal of Business Ethics in Developing Economies*, *6*(2), 36. Retrieved from www.publishingindia.com

Krebs, D. L., & Denton, K. (2005). Toward a more pragmatic approach to morality: A critical evaluation of Kohlberg's model. *Psychological Review*, *112*(3), 629–649.

Kundu, P., & Cummins, D. D. (2013). Morality and conformity: The Asch paradigm applied to moral decisions. *Social Influence*, *8*(4), 268–279.

Kung, F. H., & Huang, L. C. (2013). Auditors' moral philosophies and ethical beliefs. *Management Decision*, *51*(3), 479–500.

Kurtines, W. M. (1986). Moral behavior as rule governed behavior: Person and situation effects on moral decision making. *Journal of Personality and Social Psychology*, *50*, 784–791.

Lanckneus, M. (2016). *Psychological variables and the impact on ethical consumption in the fashion industry*, Unpublished doctoral dissertation, Ghent University, Ghent, Belgium.

Landy, J. F., & Uhlmann, E. L. (2018). Morality is personal. In K. Gray & J. Graham (Eds.), *The atlas of moral psychology* (pp. 121–132). New York: Guilford Press.

Langlois, C. C., & Schlegelmilch, B. B. (1990). Do corporate codes of ethics reflect national character? Evidence from Europe and the United States. *Journal of International Business Studies, 21*(4), 519–539.

Lawrence, J. E., & Shaub, M. K.(1997). The ethical construction of auditors: An examination of the effects of gender and career level. *Managerial Finance, 23*(12), 52–68.

Leary, M. R., Knight, P. D., & Barnes, B. D. (1986). Ethical ideologies of the Machiavellian. *Personality and Social Psychology Bulletin, 12*(1), 75–80.

Lecky, W. E. H. (1919). *History of European morals: From Augustus to Charlemagne* (Vol. 1, 3rd ed.). New York: Appleton.

Lee, K., & Ashton, M. C. (2012). *The H factor of personality: Why some people are manipulative, self-entitled, materialistic, and exploitive: And why it matters to everyone else.* Waterloo, CA: Wilfrid Laurier University Press.

Leloup, L., Meert, G., & Samson, D. (2018). Moral judgments depend on information presentation: Evidence for recency and transfer effects. *Psychologica Belgica, 58*(1), 256–275.

Levenson, M. R., Kiehl, K. A., & Fitzpatrick, C. M. (1995). Assessing psychopathic attributes in a noninstitutionalized population. *Journal of Personality and Social Psychology, 68*(1), 151–158.

Levine, R. V., Norenzayan, A., & Philbrick, K. (2001). Cross-cultural differences in helping strangers. *Journal of Cross-Cultural Psychology, 32*(5), 543–560.

Lipton, R. (1936). *The study of man.* New York: Appleton-Century-Crofts.

Lu, J. G., Quoidbach, J., Gino, F., Chakroff, A., Maddux, W. W., & Galinsky, A. D. (2017). The dark side of going abroad: How broad foreign experiences increase immoral behavior. *Journal of Personality and Social Psychology, 112*(1), 1–16.

MacIntyre, A. (2003). *A short history of ethics: A history of moral philosophy from the Homeric age to the 20th century.* New York: Routledge.

Machiavelli, N. (1950). *The prince and the discourses* (L. Ricci, Trans., E. R. P. Vincent, Revised). New York: Random House. (Original work published 1532).

MacNab, Y. C., Malloy, D. C., Hadjistavropoulos, T., Sevigny, P. R., McCarthy, E. F., Murakami, M., . . . Liu, P. L. (2011). Idealism and relativism across cultures: A cross-cultural examination of physicians' responses on the Ethics Position Questionnaire (EPQ). *Journal of Cross-Cultural Psychology, 42*(7), 1272–1278.

Mannes, T. (2010, October 24). Shoplifting down around the world. *San Diego Union Tribune.* Retrieved from www.mctinfoservices.com

Marks, N., Abdallah, S., Simms, A., & Thompson, S. (2006). *The happy planet index.* London: New Economics Foundation.

Marques, P. A., & Azevedo-Pereira, J. (2009). Ethical ideology and ethical judgments in the Portuguese accounting profession. *Journal of Business Ethics, 86*(2), 227–242.

Marta, J. K. M., Attia, A., Singhapakdi, A., & Atteya, N. (2003). A comparison of ethical perceptions and moral philosophies of American and Egyptian business students. *Teaching Business Ethics, 7,* 1–20.

Marta, J. K. M., Heiss, C. M., & De Lurgio, S. A. (2008). An exploratory comparison of ethical perceptions of Mexican and US marketers. *Journal of Business Ethics, 82*(3), 539–555.

May, D. R., & Pauli, K. P. (2002). The role of moral intensity in ethical decision making: A review and investigation of moral recognition, evaluation, and intention. *Business & Society, 41*(1), 84–117.

McCabe, D. L., Butterfield, K. D., & Treviño (2012). *Cheating in college: Why students do it and what educators can do about it.* Baltimore, MD: Johns Hopkins University Press.

McHoskey, J. W. (1996). Authoritarianism and ethical ideology. *The Journal of Social Psychology, 136*(6), 709–717.

McHoskey, J. W., Hicks, B., Betris, T., Szyarto, C., Worzel, W., Kelly, K., . . . Suggs, T. (1999). Machiavellianism, adjustment, and ethics. *Psychological Reports, 85*(1), 138–142.

McNair, S., Okan, Y., Hadjichristidis, C., & de Bruin, W. B. (2019). Age differences in moral judgment: Older adults are more deontological than younger adults. *Journal of Behavioral Decision Making, 32*(1), 47–60.

Meindl, P., Johnson, K. M., & Graham, J. (2016). The immoral assumption effect: Moralization drives negative trait attributions. *Personality and Social Psychology Bulletin, 42*(4), 540–553.

Mende-Siedlecki, P., Baron, S. G., & Todorov, A. (2013). Diagnostic value underlies asymmetric updating of impressions in the morality and ability domains. *Journal of Neuroscience, 33*(50), 19406–19415.

Middlemist, R. D., Knowles, E. S., & Matter, C. F. (1976). Personal space invasions in the lavatory: Suggestive evidence of arousal. *Journal of Personality and Social Psychology, 33*, 541–546.

Milgram, S. (1963). Behavioral study of obedience. *Journal of Abnormal and Social Psychology, 67*, 848–852.

Milgram, S. (1964). Issues in the study of obedience: A reply to Baumrind. *American Psychologist, 19*, 848–852.

Milgram, S. (1965). Some conditions of obedience and disobedience to authority. *Human Relations, 18*, 57–76.

Milgram, S. (1974). *Obedience to authority*. New York: Harper & Row.

Mill, J. S. (1863). *Utilitarianism*. London: Longsman, Green. Retrieved from www.utilitarianism.com/mill1.htm

Mill, J. S. (2011). *On liberty*. New York: Walter Scott Publishing. Retrieved from www.gutenberg.org/files/34901/ (Original work published 1859).

Miller, B. L., Agnich, L. E., Posick, C., & Gould, L. A. (2015). Cheating around the world: A cross-national analysis of principal reported cheating. *Journal of Criminal Justice Education, 26*(2), 211–232.

Minkov, M., Bond, M. H., Dutt, P., Schachner, M., Morales, O., Sanchez, C., . . . Mudd, B. (2018). A reconsideration of Hofstede's fifth dimension: New flexibility versus monumentalism data from 54 countries. *Cross-Cultural Research*. https://doi.org/10.1177/1069397117727488

Mischel, W. (1968). *Personality and assessment*. New York: Wiley.

Moll, J., Zahn, R., de Oliveira-Souza, R., Krueger, F., & Grafman, J. (2005). The neural basis of human moral cognition. *Nature Reviews: Neuroscience, 6*(10), 799–809.

Monin, B., & Merritt, A. (2012). Moral hypocrisy, moral inconsistency, and the struggle for moral integrity. In M. Mikulincer & P. R. Shaver (Eds.), *The social psychology of morality* (pp. 167–184). Washington, DC: American Psychological Association.

Moore, G. E. (1903). *Principia ethica*. Cambridge, UK: Cambridge University Press.

Moral. (2018). *Oxford English dictionary*. New York: Oxford University Press. Retrieved from www.oed.com/view/Entry/122093

Moshagen, M., Hilbig, B. E., & Zettler, I. (2018). The dark core of personality. *Psychological Review, 125*(5), 656–688.

Mudrack, P. E., Bloodgood, J. M., & Turnley, W. H. (2012). Some ethical implications of individual competitiveness. *Journal of Business Ethics, 108*(3), 347–359.

Mudrack, P. E., & Mason, E. S. (2013). Ethical judgments: What do we know, where do we go? *Journal of Business Ethics, 115*(3), 575–597.

Murthy, V., & Bhattacharya, S. (2015). Ethical value positioning of management students. *Productivity*, *56*(3), 267–273.

Nasir, N. E. M., Sallem, N. R. M., & Othman, R. (2014). Extent of idealism and relativism in earnings management behavior. *Journal of Applied Environmental and Biological Sciences*, *4*(6S), 23–29.

National Commission for the Protection of Human Subjects of Biomedical and Behavioral Research. (1979). *The Belmont report*. Washington, DC: Department of Health, Education, and Welfare.

Nayir, D. Z., & Herzig, C. (2012). Value orientations as determinants of preference for external and anonymous whistleblowing. *Journal of Business Ethics*, *107*(2), 197–213.

Nayir, D. Z., Rehg, M. T., & Asa, Y. (2018). Influence of ethical position on whistleblowing behaviour: Do preferred channels in private and public sectors differ? *Journal of Business Ethics*, *149*(1), 147–167.

Near, J. P., & Miceli, M. P. (1985). Organizational dissidence: The case of whistleblowing. *Journal of Business Ethics*, *4*(1), 1–16.

Nichols, S. (2018). The wrong and the bad. In K. Gray & J. Graham (Eds.), *Atlas of moral psychology* (pp. 40–45). New York: Guilford Press.

Nicol, A. A. M., & Rounding, K. (2018). Can ethical ideologies predict prejudice? *Ethics & Behavior*, *28*(8), 662–679.

Noddings, N. (1984). *Caring: A feminine approach to ethics and moral education*. Berkeley, CA: University of California Press.

O'Boyle, E. H., Jr., & Forsyth, D. R. (2018). *The effect of cognitive load on moral judgments*, Unpublished research report, University of Indiana, Bloomington, IN.

O'Boyle, E. H., Jr., & Forsyth, D. R. (2019). *Individual differences in ethics positions: The EPQ-5*, Unpublished manuscript, University of Indiana, Bloomington, IN.

O'Boyle, E. H., Jr., Forsyth, D. R., Banks, G. C., & McDaniel, M. A. (2012). A meta-analysis of the Dark Triad and work behavior: A social exchange perspective. *Journal of Applied Psychology*, *97*(3), 557–579.

O'Boyle, E. H., Jr., Forsyth, D. R., Banks, G. C., Story, P. A., & White, C. D. (2015). A meta-analytic test of redundancy and relative importance of the dark triad and five-factor model of personality. *Journal of Personality*, *83*(6), 644–664.

O'Boyle, E. H., Jr., Forsyth, D. R., & O'Boyle, A. S. (2011). Bad apples or bad barrels: An examination of group- and organizational-level effects in the study of counterproductive work behavior. *Group & Organizational Management*, *36*, 39–69.

Oumlil, A. B., & Balloun, J. L. (2009). Ethical decision-making differences between American and Moroccan managers. *Journal of Business Ethics*, *84*(4), 457–478.

Oyserman, D., Coon, H. M., & Kemmelmeier, M. (2002). Rethinking individualism and collectivism: Evaluation of theoretical assumptions and meta-analyses. *Psychological Bulletin*, *128*(1), 3–72.

Paloutzian, R. F. (2017). *Invitation to the psychology of religion* (3rd ed.). New York: Guilford Press.

Pan, Y., & Sparks, J. R. (2012). Predictors, consequence, and measurement of ethical judgments: Review and meta-analysis. *Journal of Business Research*, *65*(1), 84–91.

Pelto, P. (1968). The difference between "tight" and "loose" societies. *Transaction*, *5*, 37–40.

Penny, G., Francis, L. J., & Robbins, M. (2015). Why are women more religious than men? Testing the explanatory power of personality theory among undergraduate students in Wales. *Mental Health, Religion & Culture*, *18*(6), 492–502.

People vs. Williams. (1965). Appellate Court of Illinois, First District, Second Division, 56 Ill. App 2d 159, 205 N.E.2d 749.

Peterson, C., & Seligman, M. E. P. (2004). *Character strengths and virtues: A handbook and classification*. Washington, DC: American Psychological Association.

Piaget, J. (1960). *The moral judgment of the child*. London: Kegan Paul. (Original work published 1932).

Piliavin, J. A., Callero, P. L., & Evans, D. E. (1982). Addiction to altruism? Opponent-process theory and habitual blood donation. *Journal of Personality and Social Psychology, 43*(6), 1200–1213.

Pinker, S. (2011). *The better angels of our nature*. New York: Penguin.

Plato. (1926). *Lesser Hippias* (H. N. Fowler, Trans.). New York: G. P. Putnam's Sons. (Original work published 376 BCE).

Plato. (1973). *The republic and other works* (B. Jowett, Trans.). New York: Anchor. (Original work published 376 BCE).

Plato. (1994). *Crito* (B. Jowett, Trans.). Retrieved from http://classics.mit.edu//Plato/crito.html (Original work published 360 BCE).

Popper, K. R. (1994). *The open society and its enemies*. London: Routledge. (Original work published 1945).

Price, T. L. (2010). The paradoxical role of moral reasoning in ethical failures of leadership. In B. Schyns & T. Hansbrough (Eds.), *When leadership goes wrong: Destructive leadership, mistakes, and ethical failures* (pp. 383–403). Charlotte, NC: Information Age Publishing.

Rai, T. S., & Fiske, A. P. (2011). Moral psychology is relationship regulation: Moral motives for unity, hierarchy, equality, and proportionality. *Psychological Review, 118*(1), 57–75.

Rai, T. S., & Holyoak, K. J. (2013). Exposure to moral relativism compromises moral behavior. *Journal of Experimental Social Psychology, 49*(6), 995–1001.

Ramsey, R. P., Marshall, G. W., Johnston, M. W., & Deeter-Schmelz, D. R. (2007). Ethical ideologies and older consumer perceptions of unethical sales tactics. *Journal of Business Ethics, 70*(2), 191–207.

Rawwas, M. Y. A. (1996). Consumer ethics: An empirical investigation of the ethical beliefs of Austrian consumers. *Journal of Business Ethics, 15*, 1009–1019.

Rawwas, M. Y. A. (2001). Culture, personality and morality: A typology of international consumers' ethical beliefs. *International Marketing Review, 18*(2), 188–211.

Rawwas, M. Y. A., Hammoud, H. A. R., & Iyer, K. N. (2019). Epistemology, moral philosophy and optimism: A comparative analysis between managers and their subordinates. *Business and Society Review, 124*(1), 5–42.

Rawwas, M. Y. A., & Singhapakdi, A. (1998). Do consumers' ethical beliefs vary with age? A substantiation of Kohlberg's typology in marketing. *Journal of Marketing Theory and Practice, 6*(2), 26–38.

Rawwas, M. Y. A., Vitell, S. J., & Al-Khatib, J. A. (1994). Consumer ethics: The possible effects of terrorism and civil unrest on the ethical values of consumers. *Journal of Business Ethics, 13*, 223–231.

Redfern, K., & Crawford, J. (2004). An empirical investigation of the Ethics Position Questionnaire in the People's Republic of China. *Journal of Business Ethics, 50*(3), 199–210.

Rentfrow, P. J., & Jokela, M. (2016). Geographical psychology: The spatial organization of psychological phenomena. *Current Directions in Psychological Science, 25*(6), 393–398.

Rest, J. R. (1979). *Defining issues test*. Minneapolis: University of Minnesota.

Rest, J. R. (1983). Morality. In P. Mussen (Ed.), *Manual of child psychology* (pp. 556–629). New York: Wiley.

Rest, J. R. (1986). *Moral development: Advances in research and theory*. New York: Praeger.

Rest, J. R., Cooper, D., Coder, R., Masanz, J., & Anderson, D. (1974). Judging the important issues in moral dilemmas: An objective measure of development. *Developmental Psychology*, *10*(4), 491–501.

Rest, J. R., Narvaez, D., Bebeau, M., & Thoma, S. (1999). A neo-Kohlbergian approach: The DIT and schema theory. *Educational Psychology Review*, *11*(4), 291–324.

Reynolds, C. J., & Conway, P. (2018). Not just bad actions: Affective concern for bad outcomes contributes to moral condemnation of harm in moral dilemmas. *Emotion*, *18*(7), 1009–1023.

Reynolds, P. D. (1979). *Ethical dilemmas and social science research*. San Francisco, CA: Jossey-Bass.

Reynolds, S. J. (2008). Moral attentiveness: Who pays attention to the moral aspects of life? *Journal of Applied Psychology*, *93*, 1027–1047.

Riskey, D. R., & Birnbaum, M. H. (1974). Compensatory effects in moral judgment: Two rights don't make up for a wrong. *Journal of Experimental Psychology*, *103*(1), 171.

Robinson, R. J., Lewicki, R. J., & Donahue, E. M. (2000). Extending and testing a five factor model of ethical and unethical bargaining tactics: Introducing the SINS scale. *Journal of Organizational Behavior*, *21*(6), 649–664.

Rokeach, M. (1979). *Understanding human values*. New York: Free Press.

Royston, P., Altman, D. G., & Sauerbrei, W. (2006). Dichotomizing continuous predictors in multiple regression: A bad idea. *Statistics in Medicine*, *25*(1), 127–141.

Rozin, P., & Haidt, J. (2013). The domains of disgust and their origins: Contrasting biological and cultural evolutionary accounts. *Trends in Cognitive Sciences*, *17*(8), 367–368.

Schaich Borg, J., Hynes, C., Van Horn, J., Grafton, S., & Sinnott-Armstrong, W. (2006). Consequences, action, and intention as factors in moral judgments: An fMRI investigation. *Journal of Cognitive Neuroscience*, *18*(5), 803–817.

Schein, C., & Gray, K. (2018). The theory of dyadic morality: Reinventing moral judgment by redefining harm. *Personality and Social Psychology Review*, *22*(1), 32–70.

Schlenker, B. R. (2008). Integrity and character: Implications of principled and expedient ethical ideologies. *Journal of Social and Clinical Psychology*, *27*(10), 1078–1125.

Schlenker, B. R., & Forsyth, D. R. (1977). On the ethics of psychological research. *Journal of Experimental Social Psychology*, *13*, 369–396.

Scholtens, B., & Dam, L. (2007). Cultural values and international differences in business ethics. *Journal of Business Ethics*, *75*(3), 273–284.

Schrag, Z. M. (2010). *Ethical imperialism*. Baltimore, MD: Johns Hopkins University Press.

Schwartz, S. H. (1968). Awareness of consequences and the influence of moral norms on interpersonal behavior. *Sociometry*, *31*, 355–369.

Schwartz, S. H. (1992). Universals in the content and structure of values: Theoretical advances and empirical tests in 20 countries. *Advances in Experimental Social Psychology*, *25*, 1–65.

Schwartz, S. H. (2014). Societal value culture: Latent and dynamic. *Journal of Cross-Cultural Psychology*, *45*(1), 42–46.

Schwartz, S. H., & Bilsky, W. (1987). Toward a universal psychological structure of human values. *Journal of Personality and Social Psychology*, *53*(3), 550–562.

Schwartz, S. H., Caprara, G. V., Vecchione, M., Bain, P., Bianchi, G., Caprara, M. G., . . . Mamali, C. (2014). Basic personal values underlie and give coherence to political values: A cross national study in 15 countries. *Political Behavior, 36*(4), 899–930.

Schwartz, S. H., Cieciuch, J., Vecchione, M., Davidov, E., Fischer, R., Beierlein, C., . . . Demirutku, K. (2012). Refining the theory of basic individual values. *Journal of Personality and Social Psychology, 103*(4), 663.

Schwartz, S. H., Cieciuch, J., Vecchione, M., Torres, C., Dirilen-Gumus, O., & Butenko, T. (2017). Value tradeoffs propel and inhibit behavior: Validating the 19 refined values in four countries. *European Journal of Social Psychology, 47*(3), 241–258.

Sears, D. O., & Funk, C. L. (1991). The role of self-interest in social and political attitudes. *Advances in Experimental Social Psychology, 24*, 1–91.

Selman, R. L., & Byrne, D. F. (1974). A structural-developmental analysis of levels of role taking in middle childhood. *Child Development, 45*(3), 803–806.

Sharp, F. C. (1898). An objective study of some moral judgments. *American Journal of Psychology, 9*, 198–234.

Sharp, F. C. (1950). *Good will and ill will: A study of moral judgments.* Chicago: University of Chicago Press.

Shaub, M. K., Finn, D. W., & Munter, P. (1993). The effects of auditors' ethical orientation on commitment and ethical sensitivity. *Behavioral Research in Accounting, 5*(1), 145–169.

Shaw, M. E., & Sulzer, J. L. (1964). An empirical test of Heider's levels in attribution of responsibility. *The Journal of Abnormal and Social Psychology, 69*(1), 39–46.

Shiyong, X., Shu, W., & Junxia, L. (2011). The effect of moral consciousness of employees on their counter-productive work behavior. In *2011 international conference on management and service science* (pp. 1–4). Piscataway, NJ: Institute of Electrical and Electronic Engineers.

Sims, R. L., & Bingham, G. D. (2017). The moderating effect of religiosity on the relation between moral intensity and moral awareness. *Journal of Religion and Business Ethics, 4*(1), 1. Retrieved from https://via.library.depaul.edu/jrbe/vol4/iss1/1

Singelis, T. M., Triandis, H. C., Bhawuk, D. P., & Gelfand, M. J. (1995). Horizontal and vertical dimensions of individualism and collectivism: A theoretical and measurement refinement. *Cross-Cultural Research, 29*(3), 240–275.

Singh, B., & Forsyth, D. R. (1989). Sexual attitudes and moral values: The importance of idealism and relativism. *Bulletin of the Psychonomic Society, 27*(2), 160–162.

Singhapakdi, A., Marta, J. K. M., Rallapalli, K. C., & Rao, C. P. (2000). Toward an understanding of religiousness and marketing ethics: An empirical study. *Journal of Business Ethics, 27*(4), 305–319.

Singhapakdi, A., Marta, J. K. M., Rao, C. P., & Cicic, M. (2001). Is cross-cultural similarity an indicator of similar marketing ethics? *Journal of Business Ethics, 32*(1), 55–68.

Singhapakdi, A., Salyachivin, S., Virakul, B., & Veerayangkur, V. (2000). Some important factors underlying ethical decision making of managers in Thailand. *Journal of Business Ethics, 27*(3), 271–284.

Singhapakdi, A., Vitell, S. J., & Franke, G. R. (1999). Antecedents, consequences, and mediating effects of perceived moral intensity and personal moral philosophies. *Journal of the Academy of Marketing Science, 27*(1), 19–35.

Singhapakdi, A., Vitell, S. J., & Kraft, K. L. (1996). Moral intensity and ethical decision-making of marketing professionals. *Journal of Business Research, 36*(3), 245–255.

Singhapakdi, A., Vitell, S. J., & Leelakulthanit, O. (1994). A cross-cultural study of moral philosophies and ethical perceptions. *International Marketing Review, 11*, 65–78.

Sinnott-Armstrong, W. (2008). Framing moral intuitions. In W. Sinnott-Armstrong (Ed.), *Moral psychology: The cognitive science of morality* (Vol. 2, pp. 47–76). Cambridge, MA: MIT Press.

Skitka, L. J. (2010). The psychology of moral conviction. *Social and Personality Psychology Compass, 4*(4), 267–281.

Skowronski, J. J., & Carlston, D. E. (1989). Negativity and extremity biases in impression formation: A review of explanations. *Psychological Bulletin, 105*(1), 131–142.

Smith, A. (2016). *The theory of moral sentiments.* Los Angeles, CA: Enhanced Media Publishing. (Original work published 1759).

Smith, B. (2009). Ethical ideology and cultural orientation: Understanding the individualized ethical inclinations of marketing students. *American Journal of Business Education, 2*(8), 27–36.

Smith, B. (2011). Who shall lead us? How cultural values and ethical ideologies guide young marketers' evaluations of the transformational manager-leader. *Journal of Business Ethics, 100*(4), 633–645.

Smith, B., & Lord, J. B. (2018). Bracketed morality and ethical ideologies of sport fans. *Sport in Society, 21*(9), 1279–1301.

Smith, B., & Shen, F. (2013). We all think it's cheating, but we all won't report it: Insights into the ethics of marketing students. *Journal for Advancement of Marketing Education, 21*(1), 27–37.

Smith, D. L. (2011). *Less than human: Why we demean, enslave, and exterminate others.* New York: St. Martin's Press.

Spates, J. L. (1983). The sociology of values. *Annual Review of Sociology, 9*(1), 27–49.

Stearns, S. A. (2001). The student–instructor relationship's effect upon academic integrity. *Ethics and Behavior, 11*, 275–286.

Stefanidis, A., & Banai, M. (2014). Ethno-cultural considerations in negotiation: Pretense, deception and lies in the Greek workplace. *Business Ethics: A European Review, 23*(2), 197–217.

Stefanidis, A., Banai, M., & Richter, U. H. (2013). Employee attitudes toward questionable negotiation tactics: Empirical evidence from Peru. *The International Journal of Human Resource Management, 24*(4), 826–852.

Steiner, I. D. (1970). Perceived freedom. *Advances in Experimental Social Psychology, 5*, 187–248.

Strack, M., & Gennerich, C. (2007). Erfahrung mit Forsyth's Ethic Position Questionnaire? (EPQ): Bedeutungsunabhängigkeit von idealismus und realismus oder akquieszens und biplorarität? Reports from the working group Responsibility, Justice, and Morality (167). Retrieved from http://hdl.handle.net/20.500.11780/418

Strohminger, N., & Nichols, S. (2014). The essential moral self. *Cognition, 131*(1), 159–171.

Sunstein, C. (2005). Moral heuristics. *Brain and Behavioral Sciences, 28*(4), 531–573.

Swaidan, Z., Rawwas, M. Y., & Vitell, S. J. (2008). Culture and moral ideologies of African Americans. *Journal of Marketing Theory and Practice, 16*(2), 127–137.

Tan, B. L. B. (2002). Researching managerial values: A cross-cultural comparison. *Journal of Business Research, 55*, 815–821.

Tangney, J. P., Stuewig, J., & Mashek, D. J. (2007). Moral emotions and moral behavior. *Annual Review of Psychology, 58*, 345–372.

Tansey, R., Brown, G., Hyman, M. R., & Dawson, L. E., Jr. (1994). Personal moral philosophies and the moral judgments of salespeople. *Journal of Personal Selling & Sales Management, 14*(1), 59–75.

Thoma, S. J. (1986). Estimating gender differences in the comprehension and preference of moral issues. *Developmental Review, 6*, 165–180.

Thorndike, E. L. (1918). The nature, purposes, and general methods of measurement of educational products. In G. M. Whipple (Ed.), *Seventeenth yearbook of the National Society for the Study of Education* (Vol. 2, pp. 16–24). Bloomington, IL: Public School Publishing.

Tooke, W. S., & Ickes, W. (1988). A measure of adherence to conventional morality. *Journal of Social and Clinical Psychology, 6*(3–4), 310–334.

Treviño, L. K., Weaver, G. R., & Reynolds, S. J. (2006). Behavioral ethics in organizations: A review. *Journal of Management, 32*(6), 951–990.

Triandis, H. C., Leung, K., Villareal, M. J., & Clack, F. I. (1985). Allocentric versus idiocentric tendencies: Convergent and discriminant validation. *Journal of Research in Personality, 19*(4), 395–415.

Turiel, E. (2018). Reasoning at the root of morality. In K. Gray & J. Graham (Eds.), *Atlas of moral psychology* (pp. 9–19). New York: Guilford Press.

Turiel, E., Hildebrandt, C., Wainryb, C., & Saltzstein, H. D. (1991). Judging social issues: Difficulties, inconsistencies, and consistencies. *Monographs of the Society for Research in Child Development, 56*(2), 1–116. doi.org/10.2307/1166056

Ural, O., Gokturk, S., & Bozoglu, O. (2017). Assessment of the ethical orientations of Turkish teachers. *International Journal of Evaluation and Research in Education (IJERE), 6*(2), 183–188.

Uz, I. (2015). The index of cultural tightness and looseness among 68 countries. *Journal of Cross-Cultural Psychology, 46*(3), 319–335.

Valentine, S. R., & Bateman, C. R. (2011). The impact of ethical ideologies, moral intensity, and social context on sales-based ethical reasoning. *Journal of Business Ethics, 102*(1), 155–168.

van den Bos, K. (2018). On the possibility of intuitive and deliberative processes working in parallel in moral judgment. In K. Gray & J. Graham (Eds.), *Atlas of moral psychology* (pp. 31–39). New York: Guilford Press.

van Dijk, T. A. (1998). *Ideology*. Thousand Oaks, CA: Sage.

VanMeter, R. A., Grisaffe, D. B., Chonko, L. B., & Roberts, J. A. (2013). Generation Y's ethical ideology and its potential workplace implications. *Journal of Business Ethics, 117*(1), 93–109.

Vitell, S. J., Bakir, A., Paolillo, J. G., Hidalgo, E. R., Al-Khatib, J., & Rawwas, M. Y. (2003). Ethical judgments and intentions: A multinational study of marketing professionals. *Business Ethics: A European Review, 12*(2), 151–171.

Vitell, S. J., Lumpkin, J. R., & Rawwas, M. Y. (1991). Consumer ethics: An investigation of the ethical beliefs of elderly consumers. *Journal of Business Ethics, 10*(5), 365–375.

Vitell, S. J., & Muncy, J. (2005). The Muncy-Vitell consumer ethics scale: A modification and application. *Journal of Business Ethics, 62*(3), 267–275.

Vitell, S. J., & Paolillo, J. G. P. (2003). Consumer ethics: The role of religiosity. *Journal of Business Ethics, 46*, 151–171.

Vitell, S. J., Paolillo, J. G. P., & Thomas, J. L. (2003). The perceived role of ethics and social responsibility: A study of marketing professionals. *Business Ethics Quarterly, 13*, 63–75.

Vitell, S. J., & Patwardhan, A. (2008). The role of moral intensity and moral philosophy in ethical decision making: A cross-cultural comparison of China and the European Union. *Business Ethics: A European Review, 17*(2), 196–209.

Voegel, J. A., & Pearson, J. (2016). Religiosity and ethical ideologies as they pertain to business ethics: Through the lens of the theory of planned behavior. *Journal of Leadership, Accountability & Ethics, 13*(1), 30–48.

von Herder, J. G. (2002). *Philosophical writing* (M. N. Foster, Trans.). Cambridge, UK: Cambridge University Press. (Original work published 1887).

Wainryb, C., Brehl, B. A., & Matwin, S., with commentary by Sokol, B. W., & Hammond, S. (2005). Being hurt and hurting others: Children's narrative accounts and moral judgments of their own interpersonal conflicts. *Monographs of the Society for Research in Child Development, 70*(3), 1–122.

Waldman, D. A., Wang, D., Hannah, S. T., & Balthazard, P. A. (2017). A neurological and ideological perspective of ethical leadership. *Academy of Management Journal, 60*(4), 1285–1306.

Walker, L. J. (1984). Sex differences in the development of moral reasoning: A critical review. *Child Development, 55*(3), 677–691.

Walker, L. J. (1991). Sex differences in moral reasoning. In W. M. Kurtines & J. L. Gewirtz (Eds.), *Handbook of moral behavior and development* (pp. 333–364). New York: Psychology Press.

Waller, N. G., & Meehl, P. E. (1998). *Multivariate taxometric procedures: Distinguishing types from continu.* Thousand Oaks, CA: Sage.

Wang, L. C., & Calvano, L. (2015). Is business ethics education effective? An analysis of gender, personal ethical perspectives, and moral judgment. *Journal of Business Ethics, 126*(4), 591–602.

Waples, E. P., Antes, A. L., Murphy, S. T., Connelly, S., & Mumford, M. D. (2009). A meta-analytic investigation of business ethics instruction. *Journal of Business Ethics, 87*(1), 133–151.

Waterman, A. S. (1988). On the uses of psychological theory and research in the process of ethical inquiry. *Psychology Bulletin, 103*, 283–298.

White, J. H., Peirce, A. G., & Jacobowitz, W. (2018). The relationship amongst ethical position, religiosity and self-identified culture in student nurses. *Nursing Ethics*, 1–15. doi:0969733018792738

Whitley, B. E. (1998). Factors associated with cheating among college students: A review. *Research in Higher Education, 39*(3), 235–274.

Wienand, I. (2009). Discourses on happiness: A reading of Descartes and Nietzsche. *Ethical Perspectives, 16*, 103–128.

Wilkes, R. E., Burnett, J. J., & Howell, R. D. (1986). On the meaning and measurement of religiosity in consumer research. *Journal of the Academy of Marketing Science, 14*(1), 47–56.

Winter, S. J., Stylianou, A. C., & Giacalone, R. A. (2004). Individual differences in the acceptability of unethical information technology practices: The case of Machiavellianism and ethical ideology. *Journal of Business Ethics, 54*(3), 273–301.

Wolfgang, M. E., Figlio, R. M., Tracy, P. E., & Singer, S. I. (1985). *The national survey of crime severity.* U.S. Department of Justice, Bureau of Justice Statistics. Washington, DC: U.S. Government Printing Office.

Xing, F. (1995). The Chinese cultural systems: Implications for cross-cultural management. *SAM Advanced Management Journal, 60*, 14–20.

Yoder, K. J., & Decety, J. (2018). The neuroscience of morality and social decision-making. *Psychology, Crime & Law, 24*(3), 279–295.

Yuting, D. (2009). *A study of the relationships among personality traits, work value, ethical ideology, and ethical judgments of professionals.* Unpublished doctoral dissertation. Tamkang University, New Taipei City, Taiwan. doi:10.6846/TKU.2009.00734

Zakrisson, I. (2005). Construction of a short version of the Right-Wing Authoritarianism (RWA) scale. *Personality and Individual Differences, 39*(5), 863–872.

Zettler, I., & Hilbig, B. E. (2010). Honesty-humility and a person-situation interaction at work. *European Journal of Personality, 24*(7), 569–582.

Zhao, R., & Cao, L. (2010). Social change and anomie: A cross-national study. *Social Forces, 88*(3), 1209–1229.

NAME INDEX

SUBJECT INDEX

MAKING MORAL JUDGMENTS

Psychological Perspectives on Morality, Ethics, and Decision-Making

Donelson R. Forsyth

Routledge
Taylor & Francis Group
NEW YORK AND LONDON

First published 2020
by Routledge
52 Vanderbilt Avenue, New York, NY 10017

and by Routledge
2 Park Square, Milton Park, Abingdon, Oxon, OX14 4RN

Routledge is an imprint of the Taylor & Francis Group, an informa business

Library of Congress Cataloging-in-Publication Data
A catalog record for book title has been requested

ISBN: 978-0-367-35572-2 (hbk)
ISBN: 978-0-367-37083-1 (pbk)
ISBN: 978-0-429-35262-1 (ebk)

Typeset in Bembo
by Apex CoVantage, LLC